Tristan Jones is a Welshman born at sea aboard a British ship off the island of Tristan da Cunha. He left school aged 13 and has been at sea ever since. When World War II broke out, he joined the Royal Navy and was sunk three times before he was eighteen. He served on convoy duties to the USSR from Iceland, then later in Far Eastern waters. After the war he transferred to the Royal Hydrographic Service. His service ended in 1952 in Aden when an inshore survey vessel he was on was blown up by guerillas. He suffered a severe spinal injury that left him paralysed, was told he would never walk again and given a physical discharge.

Today Tristan Jones has sailed a record 345,000 miles in small boats under 40 feet in length. He sailed 180,000 miles of this single-handed. He has crossed the Atlantic eighteen times under sail, nine times alone. He is a Fellow of the Royal Geographical Society and a Fellow of the Explorers Club. His first book, *The Incredible Voyage*, was awarded the £500 Welsh Arts Council Literature Prize for 1978.

D1422357

By the same author

The Incredible Voyage
Ice!
Saga of a Wayward Sailor
Adrift
Hearts of Oak

Fiction

Dutch Treat

TRISTAN JONES

A Steady Trade

A Boyhood at Sea

TRIAD
PANTHER

Triad/Panther Books
Granada Publishing Ltd
8 Grafton Street, London W1X 3LA

Published by Triad/Panther Books 1984

Triad Paperbacks Ltd is an imprint of
Chatto, Bodley Head & Jonathan Cape Ltd and
Granada Publishing Ltd

First published in Great Britain by
The Bodley Head Ltd 1982
Copyright © Tristan Jones 1982
Dylan Thomas's poems 'The force that through the green
fuse drives the flower' and 'And Death Shall Have No
Dominion' from *Collected Poems* are reprinted by
permission of J. M. Dent & Sons, Ltd.

ISBN 0-586-06056-1

Printed and bound in Great Britain by
Collins, Glasgow

Set in Plantin

Dedicated to the Welsh and their descendants the world over, including the Falkland Islands, and to my good friends Wally and Marie Herbert, Allan Gill and Bernard Moitessier, explorers.

Acknowledgements to Joe Gribbins, Editor of *Nautical Quarterly*, in which this tale first appeared in a much shorter form, and to the Members of the Atlantis Society, who gave me peace while I wrote this book; also to my agent, Richard Curtis, for his enthusiastic activities on my behalf.

'Cas gŵr ni char y wlad a'im maco'
('*Cursed is the man who loves not the
land that raised him*')

Dafydd ap Gwilym, 14th Century Welsh poet

Contents

Foreword

During anyone's life there are many experiences, emotions, discoveries, which are the common lot of many other people; there are others which, by the very nature of one's birth, upbringing, times and circumstances, are shared with only a few others. Some events, occurrences, encounters, strung together in a certain order are one person's alone; they are what makes that person unique; they are what makes a *life*.

This book is, time-wise, the earliest in a series of five – soon to be eight – volumes about my life. Enjoy them all; if you can learn from them or laugh and cry with me, then my life shall have been made worth more. This added worth I shall accept gratefully.

Circumstances, too complex to go into here, drove me to write these books about my life out of their chronological order. The four volumes about the years from 1952 to 1977 were published between 1977 and 1981. They are about the deeds and misdeeds, the adventures and misadventures of my middle years. This book is about my boyhood and youth; about the forces that coiled my spring.

In offering these accounts of my life, I affirm my belief in everyone's own uniqueness. Without the recognition of each other's individuality there can be no dignity. Without dignity there can be neither honour nor justice and without honour and justice, mankind will surely descend into the abyss.

Note: Some of the names of people, places, and ships in this story have been changed, to avoid embarrassment to people who may still live, or to their relatives and friends.

New Orleans, St Louis, Santa Barbara,
San Francisco, London, Stratford-upon-Avon,
Llandudno, Abermo, Aberystwyth and New York—
August 1981–March 1982

PART ONE

Boyhood

The force that through the green fuse drives the flower
Drives my green age; that blasts the roots of trees
Is my destroyer.
And I am dumb to tell the crooked rose
My youth is bent by the same wintry fever.

The force that drives the water through the rocks
Drives my red blood; that dries the mouthing streams
Turns mine to wax.
And I am dumb to mouth unto my veins
How at the mountain spring the same mouth sucks.

The hand that whirls the water in the pool
Stirs the quicksand; that ropes the blowing wind
Hauls my shroud sail.
And I am dumb to tell the hanging man
How of my clay is made the hangman's lime.

The lips of time leech to the fountain head;
Love drips and gathers, but the fallen blood
Shall calm her sores.
And I am numb to tell a weather's wind
How time has ticked a heaven round the stars.
And I am dumb to tell the lover's tomb
How at my sheet goes the same crooked work.

DYLAN THOMAS
*'The force that through
the green fuse drives the flower'*

1

Llangareth

There's almost always a westerly wind over Merioneth. On winter days it's a wet west wind, driving clouds black and funereal, like a hundred hearses bringing home the ghosts of the drowned sailors of Wales to weep over their mountains. The west wind roars in from the Irish Sea, routing before it a billion charging white horses to send them smashing to their deaths on the shores of Gwynedd. The escaped seas scoot frothing, wildly subsiding along the long, long sands of Tywyn.

The west wind, insistent, tenacious, tendentious, scores the black and lonely peak of Cader Idris. Fat wool-sheep bleat under the shelter of low walls built before Rome, old when the Norsemen were beaten back from them, well-mossed when the Normans flung up their grim, grey castles on the shores of Wales.

In the patched sunlit summer though, with the wind tame and temperate, almost kind, then the tiny hamlet of Llangareth, a chapel, three cottages and our house, nestled, chimneys wisp-smoking, bread baking, hidden in a little valley so green that the yellow-golden rocky outcrops of the Ffestiniog mountains looked from the heights to us children like the claws of an eagle outsplayed on well-brushed green baize.

Three miles up and down this valley my sister Angharad and I rode our pony, Caradoc. He was now so old that he needed no guidance and frequent rest as he clambered down to and from the brew to the Barmouth–Harlech road, a narrow ribbon of sandy tar threading the ochre and emerald hollows along the coastal hinterland.

In 1935 I was almost eleven; Angharad was seven. She was attending the Elementary School a few miles away. One of my jobs, now that I was grown, was to see that she met and was met at the rickety little bus which took her to and from the school. In the mornings, with Angharad safely on board the bus, I waited for Rhys-the-Post, who, in his blue serge cape and double-peaked, flat-topped helmet with its great brass horn badge, rode his pony Powis on the rural delivery winter and summer. On joyful occasions there would be a letter from my Dad, far away in England, to where God directed the railway lines and telegraph poles from Dolgellau. There, it was said, the folk were strange and many and did not know each other's names. England, the homeland of *Mister* Jeffreys-Geography our thin, bald-headed, bespectacled teacher who spoke English so fastly lisped and funny that only Educated Evans, the fat boy from Aran Fawddwy, the son of Evans-Chemist and a Saxon mother, grandly dressed, could understand more than three words he said in any one sentence. England – *Lloegr*, 'The Land of the Moonrise' in our language, the tongue of the Cymry. 'A language ancient when Homer was a lad,' my Dad used to observe.

Dad was a Master Mariner, then a Trinity House Relief Pilot in the slump of the twenties. Then he guided great liners and cargo steamers into and out of the ports of Britain. Now he was the First Mate in a tug. He was the son, the grandson and the great and great-great grandson of Master Mariners, going back, so family legend had it, through Christopher Jones, Master of the *Mayflower* on her epic voyage from Plymouth, England, to Massachusetts in 1620. Certainly he could trace his line back to William Jones, born in 1749 at Beddgelert, and who was master of *Harlech Castle*, a brig of 85 tons, which was at St Petersburg, Russia, in 1795. The next year the *Harlech Castle* was captured by a

French frigate. Captain William and two of his crew were taken to France and lodged in Arras prison. They escaped the following year, 1797, and crossed the stormy English Channel in a rowing-boat. When they eventually landed at Hythe, Kent, to their delight and surprise they were greeted in Welsh by men of the Flintshire Militia, stationed there against an expected Napoleonic invasion.

William's son, Emrys, born in 1800, was lost off the coast of Madagascar in 1844, sunk by pirates it was said.

Emrys' son, Cadwaladr, born in 1843, went down off Brazil in a great storm in 1896. He was one of the few men ever to have a ship named after him while he was still alive. She was the 103 ton schooner *Cadwaladr Jones*, built in Borthygest in 1878. She sailed the hard North Atlantic passage to and from Newfoundland and the Mediterranean for more than four decades, then she was sold to Argentina, and was finally lost off the Scilly Isles in 1933 whilst under the command of a retired Royal Naval officer.

Cadwaladr's son, John Jones, my grandfather, was known as 'Johnny Star' and gained the reputation of being *the* cracker-jack skipper of the Western Ocean Yachts, as the Welsh Tops'l Schooners were known. He made the fastest run ever from Portmadoc to Harburg in Germany, where Welsh slates were unloaded. That was in five days. Almost seven hundred miles of what were some of the most difficult seas for a sailing craft, what with the shifting winds, strong tides and hidden hazards of the Irish Sea, the English Channel and the North Sea. That was around 1902.

'Johnny Star' went down in the schooner *Alpha* in the Irish Sea, bound from Dublin to Amlwch in 1906. Less known than 'Johnny Star', because perhaps he was a less colourful character, was his brother, my great uncle, Evan Lewis Jones of Barmouth, who was the master of one of the Lister vessels, *Cariad*, and who, in about 1896, made the fastest ever transatlantic passage for a small merchant sailing vessel in her. That was from Eurges, in Newfoundland, to Oporto in Portugal. The voyage lasted just under ten days. The cargo was salted codfish.

My Dad had been at sea since 1909 and, like most of the Welsh Master Mariners, he had worked his way up from cook/deckboy to master, under sail until 1916, in voyages as far as Seattle and Calcutta. Then, when the German U-boats found small, defenceless sailing craft to be easy pickings and sank one third of the British sail tonnage in the first eighteen months of World War I, he went into steam. From 1920 to 1924 my Mam accompanied him the world over in the 8,000 ton tramp steamer *Western Star*. The tramp ships were so called because they sailed no particular or regular route, but picked up their cargoes where and when they could.

It was on board the SS *Western Star*, on one of these tramping voyages, from Perth, Australia, originally to Halifax, Nova Scotia, that I was born on 8 May, 1924. The ship was approximately 150 miles north-east of the remote island of Tristan da Cunha, in the southern South Atlantic Ocean. The cargo was a strange one by any standards. It consisted of about a thousand tons of sheep bones and the first roller-skating rink exported from Australia, where that pastime was, I understand, invented.

My mother, in later years, often told me the story of my birth, although Dad was almost always silent, and shook his head and pursed his lips whenever the episode was mentioned. I was a breech birth; in other words I was upside-down in my mother. It was ten hours of pure hell for her, in a ship bucking crazily in a full storm, and her hanging on to the deckhead (ceiling) of the master's cabin, with one foot on Dad's desk and the other on the sofa which the mate, Ebenezar Roberts, had ripped away from the ship's side. The wireless operator, Owen Thomas of Nevin, tried to contact the Resident Doctor on the island of Tristan da

Cunha, but the weather conditions were such that very little of what that gentleman instructed could be understood. My Dad told me that it was at exact sunrise that he and the mate finally got my shoulders away from my poor Mam, then my head last. It was covered with a caul – a membrane. Ebenezar ripped it off and slapped me on the back. I squalled and Ebenezar said to Dad, 'By God, this one will always land on his feet! He may be a candidate for a hanging one day, but he'll never drown!' Dad grinned when he told me that.

Now, more than fifty years later, the Resident Doctor of Tristan da Cunha, Jones by name, has named his son, born in England, after me. So goes the wheel.

The ship was ostensibly bound for Halifax, Canada. In those days, when the British Empire was still far-flung, the law was that if a person was born on board a British registered vessel at sea, then he or she became a citizen of the country of the parents and of the first part of the British Empire where the ship next docked. If the ship had gone to Canada then I should have been a Canadian citizen as well as British. But a week after my birth a radio signal was received on board from the owners in Liverpool, changing the ship's destination to that port. Later, it turned out that the reason for this was that the proprietors of the New Brighton Palace, a dance-hall near Liverpool, had agreed to try out the roller-skating rink, with an option to buy it if it was a success. I am probably the only British subject ever made so by a telegram and a roller-skating rink. It was rather a pity in a way. If I'd been in the Royal Canadian Navy instead of the Royal Navy, my invalid pension would have been about ten times the amount it is today. But then, I might not have been propelled into sailing and writing, and my life in the past thirty years would most likely not have been anywhere near as rewarding, and surely not as much fun.

My mother never moaned about my birth, nor ever did

she resent it. She seemed to treat it as an exercise in affection
– and of that she had more than her share. She was a
Roberts, and her grandfather, Hugh, master of the 216 ton
brig *Evelyn*, son of Hugh, master of 142 ton *Constance*, was
one of the most renowned Welsh seafarers of the nineteenth
century. In *Evelyn*, great-grandpa Hugh Roberts made
voyages to every port on the east coast of South America,
and he took many hundreds of emigrants from Wales to
Puerto Madryn, in Patagonia. After sailing *Evelyn* for thirty-
six years, without ever once having a serious illness or
accident on board, Hugh Roberts finally lost her in a
tremendous mid-Atlantic hurricane in May 1914. He and
the crew of three were saved by a steamer minutes before the
Evelyn surrendered to the ocean. Hugh said afterwards that
they would have died anyway, as they had fresh water left
for only one more day. For thirty-six years *Evelyn* plied the
oceans, from St Petersburg to the Horn, and carried
hundreds of thousands of tons of freight – fertilizer, slates,
phosphate, fish, salt, coal – all over the Atlantic. Bear in
mind that *Evelyn* was only 109 feet long, had no engine, was
manned by only three men and a boy, and she paid for
herself hundreds of times over, and did it *gracefully*.

After we reached Liverpool Mam took me to Llangareth
while Dad continued plying his craft on the oceans. That
lasted until 1926, when hundreds of cargo ships were laid up
because of a shipping slump. Dad went to work as an
assistant supervisor on Liverpool docks for two years, then
he landed the Relief Pilot's post. That meant that he
travelled from port to port in the British Isles, filling in the
shoes of men sick and dead, and the Pilots on vacation –
which in those days meant about the same thing. Then, in
1931, he was laid off and was lucky to find the job on the
tugs. He came home for a few days every six months or so to
Llangareth and an excited family, in his bowler hat, pea-
jacket, corduroy trousers and black boots, and always with

some money, toys, books and wonderful tales told in gusts of laughter.

The only clear memories I have of between 1924 and 1930 are of being chased by a hen, gigantic to me at three, of course, across a farmyard, and, on rainy days, of staring through the front window through the drizzle in the valley, at the sea, blue or grey and beckoning, a half mile away, and of warmth, love, and affection in between, and, later, of cold and wet and slow rides on the pony, Caradoc, to the one-roomed Church school two miles away. There, Jeffreys-Geography, the teacher, tried to ram into us what was, as he put it, 'entirely for your own benefit'.

Another early memory is of being in Chapel. I must have been six or seven at the time. My parents were Liberals in the old British tradition of self-sufficiency and hard work. Mam packed us off to Chapel every Sunday, my sister Angharad and I. Angharad was three years younger than I and a lot more romantic, so she took much more notice of the preacher, while I tended to day-dream and itch to get out into the fresh air even in winter. I don't recall who the preacher was on this particular occasion. I vaguely remember the fire and brimstone bit coming out, and I clearly recollect suddenly asking myself 'Who gave him the right to tell us what we should do or not do?' I've been asking myself that question ever since, every time I encounter anyone who exercises, or tries to exercise, power over anyone else. But then I kept my thoughts to myself. I was, with my family, on to far too good a thing. There was no point in upsetting the status quo. I became a secret rebel. With my mother and sister, and Dad too when he was home, there was very little imposition from them. More it was a case of their helping me to grow from the inside out, not of pushing their thoughts and beliefs on to me. 'He will be what he will be,' as Mam used to say. Whether it would be right for other parents to hold that attitude is not for me to say. I know that for me it was exactly right. I was never pushed toward classical music or literature, for example. Hints were given, examples were made, but I was never led by the nose, and for that I have always been grateful to my family. If I had been forced into those things I am sure I would have rebelled and lost interest in them, and my life would have been much the poorer for having missed a great deal of the wonderful human heritage which has been passed on to us. Forcing culture on to a child is, to my mind, like trying to make him *eat* Everest instead of encouraging him to climb it. The poor little wretch would never again even look at the mountain without flinching, much less ever try to climb it.

The world which I first knew as a child was vastly different from the one we know now, fifty years later. West Wales, and particularly the rural areas, was, apart from the odd bus, steam engine and motor car, still, in effect, in the mid-nineteenth century. It had been very little touched by the Industrial Revolution. For the majority of people, communications, apart from the infrequent buses, were difficult. For example, our post was delivered by a pony-rider. He had collected it from a horse-drawn coach which, complete with horn blower perched atop, had delivered it from a steam-engined train in Dolgellau. I do not recall seeing any airplanes. The first man-made thing I ever saw in the sky was, I think, the German Graf Zeppelin with its great Nazi swastikas on its rudders. That must have been in 1937.

Practically everything we had in Llangareth had been made in the area, by hand. The furniture was highly polished, gracefully carved chairs for the drawing room; sturdy, solid ones for the kitchen, where we lived usually. The drawing room was used only when there were special guests visiting us. There were also a sofa and intricately carved china dressers, too, in the drawing room. The only things in that room, and probably in the whole house, that had not been made in Merioneth were the carpet, brought back from India by Grandfather 'Johnny Star', the grandfather clock, brought from France by Grandfather Roberts, and the piano (every Welsh dwelling, in those days, had a piano – and people who could play it and accompany it superbly well). The piano had been brought from Germany also by Grandfather Hugh Roberts. The tale was that as his ship *Evelyn* bounced and bucketed her way through a full gale in the North Sea the piano was heard playing itself down in the hold. '*Guide me, O Thou Great Jehovah*' was the tune it played, according to some accounts. Grandpa Roberts is supposed to have told the scared helmsman, Hugh Parry of Talsarnau, 'That's all very well, but I'd rather get a sight of the North Foreland Light!' For a deeply religious man he had a great sense of humour.

Even the wooden handled knives and forks, the china plates and tea service (they are great tea-drinkers in West Wales), even the brass-bound wooden water buckets hanging on their iron hook on the whitewashed kitchen wall, everything had been made locally. The materials we lived with were wood of all kinds, some brought from as far away as California and Burma, brass, iron – beautifully worked by Velog Hammer, the local blacksmith – steel, copper, bronze, tin, and stone, lace and linen, wool and cotton.

Next to the drawing room, which was a holy of holies, the most important room in our cottage was the kitchen. The inside of the two-foot thick outside walls of the cottage was whitewashed in the kitchen. The outside door was of massive oak and divided into two parts, so that the upper part could be opened while the lower part was kept closed to keep cold draughts, animals and poultry out of the house, and to keep small children in.

On one side of the flag-stoned kitchen was a massive fireplace, so big that two adults could sit inside it close to the fire in wintertime. Chains and hooks hung down the

chimney, for hanging hams to smoke, and for suspending a
stew-pot over the fire. Since the patent stove had been
brought into the house, back in the 1860s, the fireplace was
not much used for cooking or water-heating. The patent
stove was of black iron, with brass and steel trimmings kept
brightly burnished. One of my chores was to blacken the
stove every Saturday morning, and burnish the brass and
steel. The stove had an oven either side of the grate which
burned coal, coke or wood, and on either side of the ovens
were hot-water heating tanks which contained about five
gallons of water each. The water was brought into the house
by a hand pump from a spring only a few feet away from the
outside wall. It was then pumped into a bucket and poured
into the heaters through a lid-opening in the top of each
heater. There were brass taps in front of both heaters. The
stove stood on ornate iron legs about two feet off the hearth,
so the ashes fell into a sort of iron box. I never remember the
stove fire ever being allowed to die out, even in summer.

In the corner of the kitchen was a large pot-boiler. This
was a triangular brick furnace with, set inside it, a large
hemispherical iron water pot, which held about ten gallons
of water. This was used for doing the laundry and for
heating up bath water. It was drained through another brass
tap. Baths were taken in a zinc hip bath which, when not in
use, hung on the outside wall of the kitchen. The only time
we children ever were alone in the holy drawing room was
on Friday and Monday nights for an hour, when Mam took
her bath.

By the pot-boiler was the mangle. This was a contraption
set in an iron frame, standing about four feet tall, and three
feet wide, in which two wooden rollers could be turned by
means of a handled wheel. Wet clothes from the pot-boiler
were inserted into rollers, the handle was turned (usually by
me) and the water was squeezed out of the clothes. The
ironing board and three different sized irons, heated on the

stove, the outside clothes-line, and a drying rack on the kitchen ceiling, which could be raised and lowered by means of a rope reeved through pulleys, completed the laundry arrangements. The inside clothes-rack was used in wintertime, of course. The kitchen was almost always busy. It was someone's bathnight every night (except Sundays), and Mam baked all her own bread and made all the cakes and biscuits we ever saw as children. Afternoons were pastry making time, and the large, heavy wooden kitchen table was rarely not in use for something or other. Mam made all her own jam and bottled all her own fruit. There was no refrigeration of course, but there was, at one end of the kitchen under the stairs, a deep, stone-built larder, and there anything that might 'go off' was kept in cool darkness; cheeses, hams, milk, cream, preserves.

Practically all the victuals we ate and drank in Llangareth were homegrown, with the exception of such things as tea, sugar, salt, pepper and the like. Our garden was about an acre and a half, and much of my childhood which was not spent in school or in bed, or reading, was spent there, working. This had to be so as my Dad was rarely home. We grew all our own potatoes, beans, cabbages, broccoli, sprouts, peas, strawberries, gooseberries, onions, lettuce, and a score of other things, and we had about two dozen hens which gave a regular supply of eggs. There were half a dozen pigs. Lamb could be obtained very cheaply from the neighbouring farmers. Even though there was very little money àt any time in the house, we never went short of food, and there was always roast lamb every Sunday. It was hard work looking after the garden and the stock, and from the age of six onwards all my days were fully occupied from the time the family rose at sunrise until about nine o'clock, when everyone turned in.

There was no electricity in Llangareth in those days and so most of my reading was done in bed in the light of a small oil lamp. I started reading very early, and I recall clearly ploughing through Macaulay's *Lays of Ancient Rome* when I was about eight or nine. Of course there were *Treasure Island*, *Tom Sawyer* and *Black Beauty* among many others of that kind, but my favourites were a vast heap of old *Illustrated London News* magazines from the 1800s onwards, right through the Boer War and the Great War, as we called World War I. Now, fifty years later, I often wonder what those old magazines would be worth. Most of the books I read were fetched by Mam from the Public Library in Dolgellau, and gradually I discovered the Welsh writers of the thirties, who were creating some exciting new forms in literature – Glyn Jones, John Pritchard, Nigel Heseltine, Idris Davies, and, later on, Dylan Thomas and Vernon Watkins. It was necessary for a boy to know the works of those writers, in order to be able to understand what some of the people who visited Mam and Dad (when he was home) were talking about.

It wasn't all work though. There were rides among the hills on Caradoc with Angharad perched in front of me hanging on but ladylike, and there were fishing trips out into Tremadoc Bay in the summer with local fishermen, as we shall see.

There was only one kind of plastic in existence in those days, and that was called 'Bakelite' and it came in only one colour – brown. I think I saw my first piece of it in 1935, when I was eleven. It was when Dad proudly brought home to us our first radio set, only it was called a 'wireless' then. It was an ungainly box shaped like a Non-Conformist chapel with its embroidered, silken round speaker looking like a Bethel window. It was powered by two glass batteries filled with acid and distilled water. One of my jobs was to take the spare battery into town to get it recharged with electricity at Evans the Garage. That was a chore, because over rough country I could not ride Caradoc. His jogging caused the batteries to jerk and the acid to spill, so I was forced to walk about half the distance – six miles or so. Then I found that by blocking up the ventilation holes in the Bakelite battery compartment stoppers with plasticine I could stop the spillage and so could ride all the way to Dolgellau and back with the batteries slung on to Caradoc's saddle. There was no other plastic about in those days, as far as I recall. The look of absolute astonishment and delight on the faces of Angharad and me, when Dad first switched on the wireless and we heard the voice of a singer far away in London must have been something to behold. Time had been miraculously compressed. Two or three days had been cut down to a split second. That is how the Communications Age, and with it an inkling of the twentieth century, first came to Llangareth. That sudden leap is taking place still, all over the world. I have seen it happen from New Guinea to Greenland, for good or ill.

Our neighbours were simple folk. There was the widow Carregen, who was rumoured to be a witch, but a kindly one, and who could cure any ailment with the herbs and berries she collected in her meanderings along the walls and hedgerows of the fields. She must have been in her eighties, with a face like a relief map of Gwynedd. Her English was non-existent, but her Welsh was pure music and she made lace which would have been the envy of any Belgian lass. She was the widow of a Mate who had gone down off Para, Brazil, in the brig *Wild Rose*, lost with all hands in 1889. She was tiny, frail, and always dressed completely in black, from her straw bonnet to her button-up calf boots. She had two cows and about six sheep and she did all her own gardening. Her income was mainly from midwifing and fortune-telling. She invited Angharad and me into her cottage on rare occasions, and told us tales of her girlhood in Pwllheli across Tremadoc Bay, where she was born in the 1840s. Her cottage was, apart from about a hundred fading photographs in silver and brass frames, and lace cloths everywhere, even on the mantelpiece, sparsely furnished but spotlessly clean. I sometimes saw her on her hands and knees scrubbing the stone kitchen floor with a pumice stone. Once, when I was about seven, and very ill with bronchial pneumonia, she cured me with goose-grease and vinegar. It made me sweat like a Caerphilly cheese on a hot July day.

The third cottage in the hamlet was the home of the Powell family. There was Davy, the father, a farm labourer, dark and morose, his wife Catrin, a big woman with wide hips, red hair, and beauty enough for the whole of Wales, and their four children, two lads and two lasses. Catrin was a literary woman, well-read in both English and Welsh, and she named her children well: Cei, the eldest boy, named after Sir Kay, the senior of King Arthur's knights; Gwrtheyrn (Vortigern), after the British king who first invited the Saxons over to England to fight his enemies, the Picts and the Scots; Branwen, the oldest daughter, after the princess in the Mabinogion, the tale of whose burial on the cliffs of Gwynedd is one of the most moving passages in any literature anywhere, and Lisbeth, named after Queen Elizabeth I of England, 'a Welsh-woman through and through if there ever was one,' as Catrin explained, with no sign of a blush on the fair, milky skin of her face.

The other building in the hamlet, apart from two barns and a few hen-houses, was the chapel. This brought people in from the remoter farms and cottages every Sunday. There the news and gossip from all the six miles around was exchanged. There business was initiated and concluded, there marriages were arranged, and there the Celtic longing to touch and see the dark Secret of the Universe was partly fulfilled, for some at least. The singing was . . . angelic. I suspect that for many of the congregation the singing was their main reason for attendance. I cannot envisage a Welsh congregation in a church or a chapel where there was no singing. The hills all around seemed to shake when the choral '*Oh hear my plea*' was raised. The hills shook and the light over the sea trembled and the Archangel Gabriel must have wished that he was himself in the chapel at Llangareth, horn and all. They sang in four parts – the men, the women, the lads and the lasses, and the parts went so well, each with the others, that it was as if they had been mitred together by Johann Sebastian Bach in person.

We were simple. We believed, for example, if money was washed in rainwater it would never be stolen, and if a newborn child was washed in rainwater it would speak perfect Welsh by the age of two. We were not well off. To one side of us we had the frowning dark mountains, and to the other side the fickle sea. We knew full well that in the South, in Dyfed, the coal pits were closed and the miners hungry for bread and work, and in the rest of Wales stark poverty stalked through the land and near-despair was the order of the day, but in Llangareth we were safe. No one had ever done anything for us in the past, and it was natural for us to shift for ourselves. But we had the singing, and as long as we had that we were safe and strong; we were ourselves and Wales was our land.

2
Blind Sioni

Angharad only cried twice on her seventh birthday. In West Wales that was all right; if she had cried three times bad luck would have been hers for the rest of the year, so it was said.

As a birthday treat, and because it was a June Saturday afternoon, Mam allowed her to go with me – I should say that I had been persuaded to take her – on Caradoc to the penny cinema in Barmouth, the seaport eight miles from Llangareth. Visits to the cinema were very rare events for us. Mam gave us threepence apiece – a penny for the show and twopence to spend on sweets or chocolate. It was a beautiful summer day, with hardly any rain about at all, and we set off for Barmouth in high spirits. The film sound-track was always in English, and usually in the very strange-sounding English of America. It was a bit difficult for a ten-year-old Welsh lad like me to follow everything perfectly, but on that occasion I managed to interpret most of what was said for Angharad. At that time her English was practically nil, as she had been at school for only a month or so.

The road traffic in Merioneth in 1934 was sparse, mainly horsedrawn farm carts and pony-traps. Most of the country people, though, walked. Now and again the local doctor drove past in his new, open-backed motor-car which seemed to us children like the chariot of the heralding angel of birth and death. On the Saturdays of summer, though, the road saw quite a few charabancs. These were gaudily coloured tourist buses, which plied mainly between the railway station at Barmouth and the rural coastal boarding houses, with the few English people who could afford to take holidays then.

On this occasion, on our way back home, after four or five of the charabancs had noisily roared past Caradoc, he was becoming nervous and distraught. Sensing his distress, I steered him off the highway on to a narrow path which led up on to the ridge of hills that bordered the coast. The path, which I had never before travelled, led up over the short grass of the open sheep meadows, then through low brush and gorse. Soon it was closed in between high blackberry and bramble bushes over which it was difficult, and often impossible, for me to see. After a while the path reached the crest of the ridge. There we found that the way ahead along the ridge was so thickly overgrown that it was impossible for Caradoc to go on that way. Instead of sensibly returning to the highway, I decided to push on along the narrow trail down the far slope of the ridge. I didn't want to look like a fool either before the pony or Angharad.

Down he went, over the stony, broken ground, weaving this way and that between the thorny bushes, until we were down in a narrow, deep valley, more like a gully; an arroyo, I suppose the Americans would call it. There, in a dense copse of thickets and brambles, not knowing whether to go forward or back, I lost my sense of direction. The sky was overcast with dark clouds and dusk was falling. That was when Angharad started to cry, and no wonder; by that time we were both badly scratched on our bare arms and legs by the thorns, which seemed to reach out for us malignantly as Caradoc scrunched and painfully pushed his way through an almost solid wall of spiky vegetation ahead of and all around us.

As Caradoc struggled bravely along through the dense brambles, I saw in my head Mam's strong dark features as they would be when we arrived home two or three hours late – perhaps even more. I hoped that she might have visitors – perhaps Cadell Rum, an old sailor-friend of Dad's. Mam was always good tempered when Cadell was around. He made her laugh. I imagined his angelic-devil face, dark, sharp-featured, with his black eyes gleaming in the firelight; but that brought to me visions of shadowy things and demons of the night, or the *Tylwyth Teg*, the little folk, who might be lurking down there in that death-quiet, thorny, tangled grove. We might even be at the entrance to *Annwfn*, the Other World, the Welsh Hades; we might be held there for a hundred years by Arawn the Mighty King, and return home to find everyone we knew dead and gone.

Anxiously now, I drove Caradoc on with my heels, kicking his belly and the grasping branches that impeded us, and shouting at him, not so much to press the pony on as to somehow cast away from us the sombre, demoniacal forces which I thought I could see all around.

Caradoc pushed on, his head jerking this way and that to avoid the clutching thorns. Then, with my insisting that he follow as straight a line as possible, he had scrambled his way right through the miniature jungle. By that time he was bleeding from a score of deep scratches. Both Angharad's and my clothes were torn in a dozen places, and our arms and legs were a mass of cuts and nicks. Dusk was upon us and I was completely lost.

We came across the road just as complete darkness fell. It was a narrow, tarmac track only twelve feet or so wide, which wound its way along the bottom of the valley. When we reached it, I hesitated for a few moments, puzzling out which way to head along the road. I decided to turn left along the road, calculating that would be in a northerly direction, towards the neighbourhood of Llangareth.

Angharad, even though she had many scratches from the thorns, was very brave until we followed the lane around a bend and saw in the deepening gloom yet another bend ahead, and the night was upon us. Then, even though I gave her my last toffee, she sniffled quietly; she sobbed, and finally she gave way to tears. I, too, felt like crying, but I couldn't do that in front of Caradoc and my sister. I was the man of the house while Dad was away from home, and men didn't cry. I decided to push on into the darkness.

Now we were in wooded country and on both sides of the lane the elm and ash trees rustled in the light breeze overhead. Behind the high roadside hedge things whispered and stirred in the undergrowth, but now the sky was clearing and the moon shone fitfully between the high branches. Angharad and I kept silent, afraid to attract the attention of the *Tylwyth Teg*, who must surely be busy planning the night's mischief in the darkness under the trees, or perhaps watching us with little brown eyes from behind the hedgerow, waiting for Caradoc to stop so they could overcome us and take us to the Other World, there to make us tend the magic cauldron for ever and a day, as they were said to have done with other children who had disappeared.

Then, as we passed from under the shadows of the trees, we saw a figure ahead of us under the moon. I urged Caradoc on. He, too, had seen the dark shape along the road, and loped off at an easy trot towards it. As we drew near to the figure, it stopped and turned to face us. As we drew closer, I saw that it was the form of a big, upright man. His hair was grey under a flat peaked cap, and he had about a week's growth of whiskers. He was smoking a short clay pipe, upside-down, and above it his eyes smiled as he stood and waited for us to pass him. He wore a red neckerchief and his jacket was grubby grey in the moonlight. Below the jacket he wore black moleskin trousers tied with thick string below the knees, and we knew he was either a farm labourer or a roadman, for that was their habit. On his feet were big dusty boots. As we approached closer to him Angharad sobbed even louder as she clung on to my back.

'*Syr!*' I hailed him. Welsh is usually an informal language among the country folk and normally I would have called '*cyfaill!*' – 'friend', but this was something of an urgent occasion. For all I knew we could have strayed into some strange country, even China or England, or where there were black-armoured giants and dragons.

The man smiled broadly at me as Caradoc stopped a yard from him. Then he said in a high-pitched voice, yet strong, in Welsh, 'Is that a little wench I can hear crying?'

'It is.' I tried to deepen my voice. Then, despite my wish to appear manly before the man I blurted out, 'We're lost! We've been to the pictures in Abermo. Our way has taken its own road, and it won't let us know it!'

'Where do you live, bach?' He almost coughed the end of the word, so I knew he was from Gwynedd. Angharad still sniffled as the man addressed me.

'Llangareth, sir.'

The man leaned closer to me. He had a strange way of looking slightly to one side of me, as though he were avoiding my eyes, yet his eyes were open and clear, and he stared straight ahead, unblinking. 'Llangareth, is it? Well, come on, lass,' he was speaking to Angharad. She was straightening her auburn hair silently now. 'Llangareth isn't far – it's on my way home. Come, I'll take you.'

As the man took hold of Caradoc's bridle, Angharad burst out, 'Our Mam will be angry with us and send us to bed early every night for a week!'

The man leaned towards Angharad. 'Hush now, *cariad bach*,' – 'little sweetheart' – 'Llangareth's only two miles away over the next hill. I'll tell you what I'll do; as we brave the road it's a story you will hear from me; one told to me when I was your age . . .' The man stroked Caradoc's nose, then took his bridle, and led him and us along the road between the shadows of the scudding clouds under the moon.

We reached home well after our bed-time, but by the time our guide knocked on the cottage door I cared little how late it was, and so, I think, did Angharad. The story that the old man told us, as he steadily plodded on leading Caradoc, all of us tired and torn, along the lane, on to the highway and so to Llangareth, had enchanted and delighted us. He had brought to our minds picture after picture of a world full of magic and wonder, mystery and brave doings. The story he told us, I found later, was a tale from the *Mabinogion*, the ancient collection of Welsh legends. It was about a Roman Emperor, Magnus Maximus, who had a dream that he was to rule Britain first, with a British wife, and then to rule Rome. In the *Mabinogion* the tale is called *Macsen*. The way that the man described the Emperor's dream – the castles, the meadows, the rivers, the ships, 'all silver and gold and precious stones,' – was spellbinding to us children, so that we completely forgot the film we had seen that afternoon, it seemed such a tawdry thing.

Mam greeted the tall man; she obviously knew him. She was somewhat short with him because she was both angry at me yet relieved by our return, late as it was. The tall man went off into the night. Mam walloped me on the ear and sent me straight to bed with no supper.

Later, Angharad brought me some buttered bread and jam, so I didn't suffer too much. Then we whispered in the night, as the druid moon cast silver beams through the open windows and a soft breeze fluttered the lace curtains. We whispered of the story that the old man had recounted to us, and I retold to Angharad what I could remember of it, until she closed her eyes and fell asleep. Then I told the rest of what I could remember to myself.

Our Mam depended upon me too much to be angry with me for long, so next day, when I woke her with a mug of tea to make up for what I'd done the previous day, she was affable enough.

'How was Sioni last night when he brought you home?' she asked me. I told her how we had met him in the dark,

Boyhood

frightening lane, and of the marvellous tale he had told us as he led Caradoc by the bridle in the darkness and moonlight.

'Aye,' said Mam, 'he is a good storyteller, that's for sure. The old people still call him round for birthdays and burials and such, to tell his tales.'

I stood for a moment at Mam's bedside. I stared at the blue ribbon on her nightgown, where it was tied at the neck. It was forever strange for me to see Mam with her hair down. She was always more tender towards me then. I asked her, 'What does he do? I mean where do the stories come from? Does he read them and learn them off by heart?'

Mam smiled at me, then she took a sip of tea and replied, 'Bless you lad, no. Sioni ap Rhisiart has been as blind as a bat since he was six years old. His brother Dilwyn shot him with an arrow. It was accidental, of course. They were shooting quail up on the marshes below Dolgellau. That's all of seventy years ago. Sioni's never read a word in his life! He breaks up the stones for the roadmending gangs. Well, after all, *bach*, it's better than being a charge on the parish, isn't it?'

I met Sioni many times after that, in the next four years. Now that I knew him I could go and find him, where he sat at the roadside breaking stones with his hammer. Summer and winter, on days when I had time off, I looked for Sioni, and listened to him as he cracked away at the stones and told me his tales. Some of them, like the legends of Peredur, and Gereint and Math were so long that they took several days in the telling.

Forty-seven years after I first met Sioni I wrote down an English translation of all the *Mabinogion* tales as he recounted them to me in Welsh, only to find that publishers thought the public would not be interested. They thought that readers preferred the translations by Lady Charlotte Guest, an English aristocrat; George Borrow, English; A. P.

Graves, Irish; T. M. Chotzen, Dutch; or the Anglo-Welsh brothers, Gwyn and Thomas Jones, with all their 'thees' and 'thous' and 'forsooths', or works by Italians and Germans . . . anything but the real thing: anything but the direct translation from the old Welsh verbal legends, pure, raw, and uninhibited.

But Sioni ap Rhisiart taught me the best lesson of my life; to appreciate our inheritance of the past. That drew me even more to literature, then, in turn to music, painting, sculpture, and architecture, and in those arts I retained my interest all through an otherwise hard existence at sea. Life would have been much tougher without those interests, those solaces.

Mam was a strong willed woman, with a deep belief in independence and self-reliance. As far back as I remember, I was left to fend for myself in practically everything except clothes and food. If I had a problem of any kind she told me to try to sort it out for myself. If I failed, and went back to her for advice, only then would she give it, and she was usually right about whatever it was. Her days were always full; she was at the household chores from dawn to dusk, but I don't recall her ever resenting it, not to us children, at any rate; nor do I recall her treating any man as more than an equal. She wasn't 'liberated' in the modern, specious, sense of the word as regards women. There was no electricity, nor washing machine, nor spin dryer, nor unending hours of inane television soap-operas to impel her into dissatisfaction with her lot as a woman and a mother. She was certainly not unschooled, nor was she ignorant of what was going on outside the cottage door in the world outside. That she loved Dad, Angharad, and me there was never any doubt, but for us children at least, it was a practical love, with little sentimentality. In the middle thirties, every day that went by with food on the table and a fire in the hearth, to her was a victory. She was rarely idle. She knitted all our underwear, our jerseys, socks, scarves, and she made most of her own clothes, too. She had little patience with gossip, which made her an exception in that part of Wales, and yet she seemed to know everything that was happening, and to whom, for miles around. She had a good sense of humour, she was a brilliant mimic, yet she could be acerbic in the extreme if she wanted to be.

She missed Dad while he was away, and after four or five months of his absence she became edgy and morose, but all that changed as soon as Dad showed up; then she blossomed. Both she and Dad had been born in the last decade of the nineteenth century, but in retrospect they were both surprisingly 'modern' in their outlooks and beliefs.

I doubt if there is very much in the general discourse now which Mam and Dad would not sympathize with, except probably, for the loosening of sexual morality. In that matter they were truly Victorian.

I never once heard sex discussed at home, and rarely outside, apart from a few jokes heard at school, which these days would be thought of as innocuous. If an unmarried girl became pregnant she was 'in trouble' and it was *always* the man's fault. Mam said 'Only good girls get into trouble, the really bad ones know how to avoid it.' Later, if the girl's family could afford it she went 'on holiday' to Dublin. Years later I discovered that before abortion became legal in Great Britain, Dublin provided that service, as there was a surplus of doctors there, and the job could be done much cheaper. If the girl's family could not afford an abortion, the offspring was usually put in a Home or farmed out to a foster parent, until it was of age to go into the Navy, the Army, into 'service', or on the dole.

Sexual 'morality' was foreign to the Celtic nature. It had been imposed only since the seventeenth century or so.

Behind the lace curtains, behind the politeness at the shop
counters, under the piety of chapel-bound faces, there was a
seething mass of dark, repressed libido, a lurking lust,
forever there, just below the surface. The chapel singing, the
bright conversation, the poetical turns of phrase, flanged it
all down like the lid of a pressure cooker, so no stranger
would ever know. Most of the Anglo-Welsh writers, and
many other writers about Wales, were hypocritical about
this matter. It only started to come slightly to light with the
poets of the thirties, but that fizzled out with the coming of
war; after that the sexual drive was channelled by many into
a nationalism which is little more than a group 'morality'
instead of being the old-fashioned Victorian personal
'morality'. The Celt seems to be drawn to snares. If it's not
religion, it's politics. Will they never learn that these are
traps, set to subvert their real natures, to destroy the love of
life?

Wales was not all hills and valleys and violets and sweet
innocence as some crawlers-to-Hollywood would have had
us believe. Nor was it all doom and despair. It was arduous
work making something out of nothing each and every day
and I had to force myself, at times, to love the bleak land. At
other times, as I watched the clouds fly over the hills, and
the changing greens and purples of the heights, the majesty
of it all came home to me. Then the love in me for our
perplexing land gushed forth so strongly that it was a
physical thing, almost beyond my restraining. It was as if my
heart flew with the clouds over the mountains, as if my
blood ran down the streams into the cynical sea.

On my eleventh birthday I was to have received the first
significant material gift I ever had. Mam hid it with the
Powell family just down the valley, but I knew it was there
days before the great day. My best friend Cei, the oldest of

the Powell boys, had told me, and he took me to their tool-shed to see it. It wasn't new; Mam could never have afforded that, but to me it was magnificent.

Dusk was approaching when Cei took me to the shed. He opened the door quietly, so as not to be heard by Cei's parents, and there it was, a bicycle leaning against the work-bench. It was one of the old-fashioned sit-up-and-beg models and in its new black paint it looked stately indeed. Silently, I felt the bike's frame and the pneumatic tyres. There was even a pump to blow up the tyres, and an acetylene lamp on the handle-bars, just like Williams the Police had on his bicycle.

'Look,' whispered Cei, 'even a tool-bag, there is, hanging on the back of the saddle.' He opened the small leather bag. 'Spanners and all inside it . . .'

'It's a beauty, Cei, but it's a shame I can't ride it until my birthday. It's only the fifth – three days to go.'

There was silence in the shed for a moment or two, as Cei knit his brows in thought. He was already eleven, and so wiser than I. Then he said, 'Well, if we're quiet there'd be no harm in having a little go on the bike now, would there? As long as you don't make any noise getting out of the gate. Once you're out there my Mam and Dad won't hear you . . .'

I started. 'Do you think I could?' I asked.

In reply Cei grasped hold of the bike handle-bars and quietly, slowly, started to wheel it out of the open shed door, into the deepening gloaming. We wheeled the bike, me holding on to the saddle, along the grass verge by the path, so as not to make a noise scrunching the gravel. Soon we were at the gate and out on to the rough trail which served as a roadway down to the pond at the bottom of the valley.

'Come on, hop on,' whispered Cei. 'I'll hold the bike for you.'

I perched my leg over the frame and hunched myself up

on to the saddle. The distance from the saddle to the pedals was a bit too much for my legs. 'It's too bloody big, Cei,' I said in English.

'Perch your bottom over the cross-bar,' he whispered, 'you'll be able to manage then.'

I did as I was bid. Cei was right. I could reach the pedals. 'What about lighting the lamp? It's a bit dark in the hollow,' I said to Cei.

'Don't be daft, man. If Dad comes out and sees the light he'll know what's up and flay me alive,' replied Cei. 'Go on, you don't need to go far. Just try it out. You've to be home shortly, anyway.'

'Right, here we go,' I murmured, and started to pedal down the rocky hill. As the bike gathered speed I stopped pedalling. It was as much as I could do to avoid the big rocks that burst out of the trail. The night wind was on my face and I was afraid but determined not to be so in front of Cei. On down the hill the bike flew, with the bushes and sheep on each side flashing by faster and faster. I remembered the brakes. I grabbed at them and slowly squeezed them . . . neither of them worked. There was evidently no rubber in the brake-pads. Headlong down the steep hill I clattered, sparks flying from both wheels. I was only yards from the pond. To either side of the path were big boulders. If I crashed into one of them I would surely break something. In a flash of fear and terror I decided and . . . went splash into the pond.

There was black, cold water all around me. The bike had disappeared. I was struggling on the surface of the pond, spluttering green slime and reaching for the overgrowing plants on the edge of the pool. Then I had a willow branch in my hand and dragged myself, dripping wet and freezing, on to the grass. Then Cei was at my side. 'That's done it,' he said.

I climbed to my feet, struggling to hold back tears and

shivering violently. 'Wha . . . wha . . . what about the bike, Cei?'

'It's too deep. We'll never get it out tonight. We'll have to get a hook and a line and drag for it. We'll have to make a raft . . . Thank Jesus it's Saturday tomorrow.'

'What about Mam?' I asked him. 'She'll kill me for this.'

'Don't tell her about the bike. Tell her you fell into the pond walking by it,' he replied.

'What about your Dad, Cei?'

'Oh, he won't go into the shed tonight, and he's off very early tomorrow, repairing a wall up in Ty-Glyn. His day-tools are in his bag in the kitchen, see.' Cei took my arm. 'You'd better get home and out of those wet clothes, Tristan. You'll catch pneumonia.'

Silently, with me quaking like a leaf in a gale, we walked back up the treacherous rock trail. Cei, with a whispered '*Nos dda*' disappeared into his cottage. I carried on home, trembling with cold and trepidation.

As I neared our house, I had a bright idea. The front door was never locked unless Mam went out. I crept around to the front of the cottage, opened the door quietly and gingerly made my way up the stairs. They were old stairs, centuries old, but I knew every squeak and creak in them. Once in my room I quickly changed into dry trousers and a jersey and slippers. Then I silently made my way out again through the front door and so round to the kitchen door. I took some wood logs in with me, so as to appear more casual.

Mam looked up from her sewing. 'When did you change your clothes, *bach*?' she asked me quietly.

'Er . . . just now . . . I went through the front . . . didn't want to disturb you, Mam . . .'

'You're late, *bach*.'

'Yes, I was out repairing the fence over by the pig-sty and tore my shirt on the wire . . .'

'Well, your supper's in the oven. Wash up when you've

done, and let me have your shirt in the morning so I can mend it.'

I was able to dry my clothes by hanging them out of the bedroom window. I stayed awake most of the night, watching that it didn't rain. Making a tear in the shirt was simple. I ripped it on a nail before I took it down to the kitchen.

After doing my chores and eating breakfast, I was just about to set off down the valley to the Powells' cottage when Branwen Powell, Cei's oldest sister, about nine, appeared at our door, her face as gloomy as her Dad's. 'Mrs Jones,' said she sorrowfully to Mam, 'it's gone!'

'What's gone, *bachgen*?' said Mam.

'The thing that you put in our shed . . . you know . . .' Branwen had seen me glaring at her. Her face was almost as red as her hair.

Mam bustled out of the door, out into the yard. There they talked in low tones for a few minutes. Mam came steaming back into the kitchen. She stared at me sternly for a moment or two, then she said, 'Tristan, *bach*, what happened last night?'

My eyes dropped from Mam's, I shuffled my feet, and I kept silent.

'Were you riding a bike last night by any chance?' Mam asked.

As I looked up at her I could feel the tears welling in my eyes, despite my trying manfully to hold them back. Suddenly there was a big dollop on one of my cheeks, then another, and another. I burst out crying. Then, in fitful sobs, I told Mam what had happened as she stood, her arms folded across her apron bib in front of me. When I'd finished the tale, I started to inform Mam how Cei and I were going to salvage the bike that very day. She grabbed me by my ear and twisted it as she dragged me towards the door.

She flung me through the door. I went skittering out into the yard, still sobbing pitifully. 'Now,' she cried, 'you go down to the pond and you get that bicycle out yourself. If I see anyone else with you it's early bed for you for a whole year! You put the thing in – now you get it out, and don't come back here until you've done it. You get that thing out of where you put it or you're no son of mine!'

When I'd recovered my wits I started off down the valley. Cei and his brother Gwrtheyrn were both out in their garden when I passed by. They did not appear to look at me as I shambled down the hill. Branwen must have told them what Mam had said. She had witnessed the anger and humiliation.

Nearing the pond I had a bright idea. I flew all the way down the valley, right to the shore to the shed where Goodness Gracious Jenkins kept his fishing tackle. When I got back to the beach he was just about to shove off in his dinghy out to his lugger. I hailed him at the top of my voice. He stopped pushing his boat down the beach and turned to me.

'Are you coming out with me?' asked Goodness Gracious.

'I can't. I'm in trouble . . .' I told Jenkins the story of what had occurred. 'I want to borrow a bit of line and one of your shark-hooks, Mister Jenkins,' I pleaded.

'What about a grapnel?' he suggested.

'Even better.'

Jenkins disappeared into his shed and came out after a moment with a four-pronged grapnel-iron and a length of rope. 'This should do the trick, *bach*. Now, it's off I must go, for I'm late already.'

I ran back up the hill to the pond as fast as I could, and was soon casting the grappling iron into the water. It took a half hour for me to finally get a grip on the bike, but finally it surfaced and I dragged it on to the bank. There I found that the front wheel was buckled, so I had to wheel it back home on its back wheel only, but I managed it. I leaned the bike on the outside wall and quietly entered the kitchen. Mam was sewing my shirt. She looked up at me seriously. 'Well?'

'I've got it, Mam . . . but the front wheel is bent.'

She looked down at her sewing. 'Then go and straighten it,' she said, almost inaudibly.

Cei and I straightened the wheel as best we could, using the simple tools in the Powells' tool-shed. It never was perfectly straight, but I managed to ride the bike a few times before Dad came home and did the job properly. I never did ride the bike much, though; I was too fond of Caradoc for that.

Of course Mam was right. She taught me self-reliance, and I honour her memory all the more for that.

3

Goodness Gracious

My closest friend, Cei Powell, was three months or so older than I and slightly taller. Like his Mam, he had red hair and light hazel eyes but his face was a mass of freckles. He was always on the go (what the Americans nowadays call 'hyper-active'), in complete contrast to his brother, Gwrtheyrn, who was two years younger. Gwrtheyrn was dark, quiet and slow-moving, like his father, and preferred the company of his two sisters to that of Cei and me. Despite that, Cei was always protective towards his brother, and bore no word spoken against him. Cei hated school lessons and was never happier than when he was out fishing with Goodness Gracious, bird's-nesting or making something in his Dad's toolshed. Once or twice I tried to get him interested in reading, but it was no use; his eyes glazed over and he looked around for something to do with his hands.

At school Cei kept as quiet as could be in the classroom. He sat on the next desk to me, and practically every examination paper or composition he wrote was either copied from mine or followed my scribbled suggestions surreptitiously handed to him while Jeffreys-Geography gazed through the school-room window, dreaming of England, tea, and crumpets.

Outside, in the school-yard, Cei became a dynamo, a whirling dervish of devilment. At soccer he was almost always centre-forward. While he scored the goals, I tagged along at his side wondering about the logistics of the game – what was coming from where, when, why and from whom. Naturally, in a tiny school like ours the teams were a very mixed bag, ranging in age from strapping lads of thirteen down to sprogs of eight or so. Cei was the hero of them all, but it was to me that they came for advice. Many an excuse, many a white lie, I invented for them when they in some way transgressed the school rules. No harm in that, they were Jeffreys-Geography's rules, not ours.

At home, Cei was generally in one kind of trouble or another. It was rare to see him without a bruise or two where his Dad had belted him. That was not too unusual in those days. Most Dads had the Bible in one hand and the belt in the other. 'Spare the rod and spoil the child,' they piously quoted the Old Testament at home, and the New Testament: 'Suffer the little children to come unto me,' they reserved for best-dressed Sundays at Chapel. In that respect I was most fortunate; never once did my father lay his hand to me. He didn't need to; a mere dark glance, a quiet word of warning or chastisement, was enough to curb the most mischievous spirit. With Mam it was different. She cuffed my ear or spanked me a few times, but that was only when I really deserved it, when I had driven her beyond her tether.

When Cei and I were not at school, or working in our gardens, or tending livestock, there was always something else to do. We went on the cliffs collecting sea-gulls' eggs, or up on the hills gathering mushrooms or dandelion leaves, burdock and sorrel for greens, or wild watercress in the brooks nearby. We also set rabbit snares where there were no sheep. In the summer we collected tens of pounds of blackberries and wild strawberries, which our mothers used to make into jam. If there was a surplus of jam it was bartered in Barmouth for other provisions such as tea or sugar. In the winter-time we caught blackbirds. This was done using a net frame propped up with a stick at one end. On the stick was tied a long string which led through a crack in the kitchen window, and under the frame was set bread and other tid-bits. In went the bird, jerk went the string, down went the frame, and there we had another bit of meat for the pie.

The only time Cei and I ever went hunting for anything except rabbits, that I can recall, was for a wildcat which had gone on a rampage, and was coming down from the mountains, killing our hens. It took us three nights of silent stalking, but eventually Cei got the cat with a steel arrow, and finished it off with a blow from a sawn-off broomstick. The wildcat was huge by domestic standards, and as black as a preacher's hat. Dead, he had a sneer like the devil himself. Cei skinned the cat, intending to present the pelt to his mother for a rug. He nailed it to the tool-shed door, but after two or three days it stank so much that he had to throw it away into the cess-pit at the end of the Powells' garden.

Generally, the girls of Llangareth helped their mothers indoors. They started this at an early age, and by the time they were nine or ten, as our Angharad and Branwen Powell were, they had become quite expert at housewifery and cooking, and adept at sewing and knitting. This tended to make them lady-like at a tender age, compared to modern little girls, but I don't think that the girls I knew when I was a boy were any less happy than the ones I know now. I think those I knew in my childhood were more content somehow. Despite their being in the house much of the time, they also did many things we boys did. They went riding and walking the hills, fishing and swimming. I think the only reason they were not quite as active is that it was not usually considered in the female nature to be so. They did not try to ape the boys, as so many young females seem to do these days. I don't think the sharper difference between the sexes was imposed all that much. To a great extent I think it's always been there. There were 'tomboys' in the neighbourhood, but they were not frowned upon; rather, they were thought to be amusing, and to some extent, admired. Nowadays we hear so much about the repression of females in the past, but try as I may, I cannot bring to mind any instances where this was any more evident than it is today. There have always been the odd wife-beaters, more's the pity, but then there have always been nags, scolds and shrews, so it probably balances out evenly in the long run.

Rock-climbing was a venture in which only boys took part. I don't recall hearing of it causing any deaths, although I expect it did, considering some of the hazardous climbs made with none of the usual mountaineering paraphernalia. It must have been in 1936 when the story got around that Germany, in connection with the Olympic Games, had sent a rock-climbing team to climb the highest in Britain, somewhere in North Wales, but I can't remember where exactly. The cliff was over a thousand feet high and overhung the sea. The Germans climbed it, using pitons and ropes and other fancy foreign impedimenta, and when they were close to the top of the cliff, after many hours of climbing, they planted a big Nazi flag in the cliff face. They then retired to the local inn to swig beer and eat their fill, thinking, naturally, that they had well earned it. The local lads, seeing the flag hanging there, determined to remove it. They set out to climb the cliff using nothing but their hands and feet, and on the way up they removed every piton that the Germans had set into the face, as well as the flag, which they carried back triumphantly to the inn and returned to the Nazis just before pub closing time.

Cei, a few other local boys, and I used to go climbing in the foothills a few miles off when the weather was fine. Even now, I shudder when I think of some of the risks we took, our toes clinging to an inch-wide ledge in the rock, our numb fingers gripping another tiny nub or crack in the face of the rock. I did not dare tell Mam I was going rock-climbing. I used to lie that I was going fishing or walking. The elation I felt when we had made it to the top of an almost sheer hundred-foot cliff still stays with me whenever

I think of it. Then we used to throw ourselves on to the top of the rock and lay there, panting at the sky, grinning at the blue above and the green below, then at each other, until it was time to make our way back down again, and tramp the long weary trudge back home as the light faded. We took very little with us; perhaps a jam or dripping sandwich and a bottle of water. If Educated Evans from Aran Fawddwy came along, though, he always had some sweets, his uncle being well off. That was the only reason we let him come. He was too fat to climb, and used to wait for us at the bottom of the rock.

I think that rock-climbing was the only activity for us boys, apart from our schooling, that did not produce something towards the family larder. That was the way it was in West Wales in those days, for everyone except the few lucky rich people.

There were several longshoremen on the coast near to Llangareth. They were the local fishermen. Most of them did their work in small, open boats close in shore, but a few others, like Goodness Gracious Jenkins, worked Tenby luggers, which they kept moored off the beach when they were not in use. The longshore fishermen were in general the peasants of the West Wales seafaring community. While they could claim some kind of independence, being self-employed, they were also usually at the mercy of the middle-men in the towns, who bought their catch, and they prospered according to the whims of the weather and the sea which beat against their abodes. They were a very close-knit lot, as it was the custom for a longshoreman to marry another longshoreman's daughter. How else could it be? What other woman would know how to braid nets, bait long lines, make lobster and crab pots, or search for bait along the mud-flats and rocks, or how to smoke fish?

Goodness Gracious was fortunate. He had a contract with

a couple of small hotels and boarding houses on the coast to supply them with fresh fish. Now and again he found an English gentleman who hired his boat and him to go out mackerel spinning. Sometimes he picked up a group of tourists from the hotels or boarding houses and took them out for a sail on Tremadoc Bay for a few shillings. But that was only in the summer-time, in the high tourist season. In the middle thirties that season was nowhere near high enough. Tourists were rare creatures. Goodness Gracious (who was so called because that was the only expletive he had ever been heard to use) mostly scrabbled a living on his vegetable plot or doing casual work, when that was needed, on a local farm.

Goodness Gracious was a thin, wiry man of medium height, about as old as the century, I guessed. He had jet black hair and startling light blue eyes, the colour of Festiniog slate when it's dry. Unlike many of the longshore-men, he was clean-shaven, at least when he was ashore. He had a small, sparrow-like wife who, despite appearance, was as tough as a gravestone and about as loquacious. He also had two sons, Tomas, nineteen in 1936, and Pedr, eighteen. They were, of course, part of the immediate post-World War I 'baby boom' – Goodness Gracious had spent the war in Royal Navy armed trawlers. Now Tomas was in the Royal Naval Reserve, and for a week in the summer he went off to Plymouth for bugle calls, shouted commands and incessant drill, on what he thought was, compared to working with his Dad, a good relaxing holiday. Tomas, being an enterprising lad, also sometimes went crewing on yachts for fine English gentry down off the Isle of Wight. He had arranged this through his naval friends, and he thought that several days and nights of continuous labour, hauling sails up and down, repairing them, scrubbing decks, sleeping in a crabbed yacht fo'c's'le, was a bit like heaven after a winter of hauling nets and long-lines onboard *Gwenhyfar*, his father's Tenby

lugger fishing boat. While Tomas was away, it was a chance
for us local lads to accompany Goodness Gracious and Pedr
to sea. There was no pay, of course, except for perhaps a few
fish at the end of the trip, but it was interesting and
adventurous, at least to Cei Powell and me. Pedr was a
thickset lad who said very little.

Gwenhyfar was a typical Tenby lugger, launched at that
small port on the western end of Carmarthen Bay. She was
comfortably built, of massive timbers for her size, and about
22 feet overall. She was clinker-built; that is her planks
overlapped one another. The hull was decked from the bow
to the mainmast, and below the deck forward there was a
small triangular cuddy about seven feet long. That was the
only shelter in the boat. She had three rowing thwarts (seats)
along the hull, and another thwart aft for the helmsman, who
steered with a tiller. Stone ballast was carried in the bottom
of the boat, under a floor supported by massive beams. The
heavy wooden keel was about eighteen inches deep. The
mainmast was stepped about one-third of the way back from
the stem post. The mizzen was stepped on the transom
(sternpiece) and followed its sharp rake. Forward, a
bowsprit, about seven feet long, was carried through a
gammon iron, while an outrigger for the mizzen was stepped
through a hole in the transom. The mainsail was a dipping
lug, with three rows of reef-points, but in winter this was
replaced by a trysail which was secured to the mast by
parrels (hoops). *Gwenhyfar* had three jibs of different sizes,
which were set according to the strength of the wind.
Gwenhyfar sailed surprisingly well on the wind, although to
us youngsters it was at first a mite frightening, to be in an
almost open boat with a tremendous spread of sail for her
size, heeled over so that on the lee side there was no more
than three or four inches of freeboard (the amount of hull
above water level).

Goodness Gracious mainly fished offshore from the

Merioneth coast, but now and again, if the weather signs looked fair (a licked thumb stuck up into the breeze) he took off for Pencilan Head, thirty miles away across Tremadoc Bay. He made the crossing overnight and arrived off the Head just as dawn was breaking. So, I made my first ever night sail, in 1936. It was unforgettable, the sea gleaming in the moonlight, the soft breeze and a field of stars overhead. I was yet a mere twelve years old, but I felt, as I drank in the scene and my heart quickened, as if I had been alive, and would always be alive, forever.

An hour before dawn, as we approached the Head about five miles off, the wind dropped and the sea flattened, so we lads, Cei and I, and Pedr, set to pulling the oars. By the time *Gwenhyfar* lay off Pencilan we were, at least Cei and I, exhausted. We grabbed the jam sandwiches and cold cocoa which Goodness Gracious handed us for breakfast. We were just about to wolf down the repast when Goodness Gracious held up his calloused hand. There was a flat silence, except for the creaking of the boat's gear. 'Boys,' said Jenkins in a sepulchral tone, '*Gwenhyfar* is a Christian vessel.' A seagull cried in the distance.

We knew what that meant, so we bent our heads whilst Goodness Gracious intoned the breakfast grace: 'Lord, accept your servants' thanks for this day, for the work of the day, and for the food you have given us. Amen.'

After that, Cei and I scoffed down the sandwiches and cold cocoa, after which we helped Pedr set the nets. Then we set to rowing up and down off the headland. We pulled all morning, but caught only a dozen fish. I think they were bream. Lunch was the same – grace, jam sandwiches, and cold cocoa, but it was welcomed. Then followed eight more hours of back-breaking oar pulling, until dusk, when we hauled our nets again. This time there were about three dozen fish, which were all thrown into wooden barrels. That done, Goodness Gracious grinned at us, when everything had been squared away. 'A special treat for you tonight, lads,' he cried. He delved into the cuddy and brought out a clay pot and four pint-sized tea-mugs. From the pot he ladled out a cold lamb and potato stew then he said grace. To us the stew was delicious. In the years since, decades later, I have eaten in some of the world's finest restaurants, but that cold lamb and potato stew at dusk in an open boat reeking of fish, rocking away off the coast of Caernarvon, was one of the most memorable meals I have ever partaken. There were no spoons in the boat. Goodness Gracious and Pedr merely lifted the pint-mug to their lips and let the stew slide down, then they refilled their mugs. Seeing this, Cei and I did the same. With the stew finished and everything washed in salt water, we set off to row back the thirty miles to Merioneth, each of the four of us with half-hour spells on the tiller as a relief.

It was well into the morning when *Gwenhyfar* finally was pulled slowly up to her mooring. There had been not a capful of wind all the night. Even Goodness Gracious said that 'It's as if God was resting.'

Both Cei and I got three good-sized fish each for our labours. My Mam's face, when I turned up at the cottage with my prizes was a study in relief, surprise and delight. One of the bream we had that night for supper, and the other two she smoke-dried in the chimney for use later on.

On a later trip in *Gwenhyfar* that summer of '36, there was a good breeze and the lugger was dancing along bravely with Pedr at the helm while his Dad and I (Cei was not with us) got the nets ready for shooting. We were heading up the coast off Harlech, when there appeared a sight which any lad of twelve would recall until his dying day. It was a fine day, blue sky and sunshine in between fluffy white clouds, and we could clearly see all the coasts of Merioneth and Caernarvon to our north. The wind was in a rare quarter, north-east. Suddenly, from behind the headland at the mouth of the River Glaslyn we saw emerge a fully rigged Welsh Topsail Schooner, one of the last of the 'Western Ocean Yachts' as they used to be called. As she headed south, past us, we could clearly make out her squaresail under her foreyard and a stun-sail and boom hoisted to the upper yard-arm. She carried three jibs, two squaresails, a staysail, a fisherman's staysail, a foresail, quite small, a main and a main-spritsail as well. As the breeze freshened the stun-sail and boom were taken in even as she approached our beam. She had a figurehead on her stem-post, but she was too far away for me to see it clearly. The lines of her hull were fine and graceful, and she had a rounded stern. She was painted black with white trimming and was about ninety feet long overall, at a guess. Goodness Gracious said that he thought she was the *M. A. James*, but we had no way of knowing for sure as she was too far away for us to read her name on her stern. If she was the *M. A. James*, then she was the very same ship in which my grandfather, 'Johnny Star', made the fastest run ever from Portmadoc to Harburg in Germany – and that had been about 34 years before I saw her. Whatever craft she was, she was beautiful, a proud cloud of shining canvas over an elegant, powerful hull, creaming over a sparkling sea.

'They had to be good and fast,' remarked Goodness Gracious. 'They were in the fish and fruit trade, see boys. Fish from Newfoundland to the Mediterranean and fruit from Italy and Greece to Britain. You had to know your stuff and have a good fast ship when most of what you carried was going to rot in the hold if you didn't get a move on, see?'

The next year, in the autumn of 1937, Cei and I were again invited to go out fishing in *Gwenhyfar*. Tomas, Goodness Gracious' oldest son, had gone to join the

Merchant Navy and Pedr had cut his thumb rather deeply with a fish-gutting knife and so was only able to manage the tiller. It was to be another all night trip and Goodness Gracious said we should be back at Llangareth by noon the next day. That was a school day, but by this time Cei and I were both thirteen and Jeffreys-Geography had long given up trying to make little Englishmen of us, and so he willingly gave himself the day off from us.

As we gathered on the beach in the evening, Cei, Pedr, Goodness Gracious, and I, to push the Jenkins' battered old dinghy into the water, the sea was all crinkled silver. *Gwenhyfar* rode to her rusty old mooring chain like a swan. The breeze was from the south-west, not very strong, but steady. Goodness Gracious, standing in his oilskin jacket, heavy woollen jersey, moleskin trousers and knee-length sea-boots, sniffed the air and looked around him. Under his dark-blue, woollen bobble cap his blue eyes sparkled. 'Fine night, tonight, boys,' he crowed, as we all four piled into the dinghy. Cei and I had no sea-boots. We had to take our boots and socks off and roll our trousers up to the knees in order to board the bobbing boat. The water was freezing, so it seemed. Once on board *Gwenhyfar* we dried our legs and feet with the outside of our jackets as there was nothing else, then we donned our boots and socks again.

Soon we had let go of *Gwenhyfar*'s mooring chain, after securing the dinghy to it. Cei and I set to on the oars, pulling her out to sea, while Goodness Gracious hauled up the jib, main and mizzen. *Gwenhyfar* felt the wind in her sails, raised her fine bows to a swell, lowered her fat little stern in a trough, and we were off. She was only a scruffy little fishing boat with discoloured red sails, but to me she was a galliass bound with embassy to the golden halls of the Emperor of China.

The night-breeze remained surprisingly steady for the

Irish Sea. All the night *Gwenhyfar* slowly shoved the sea out
of her path with a chubby sort of joy, until at false dawn we
could discern Pencilan Head and Bardsey Island out to the
west under the descending moon. We set the trawl over the
stern just as the wind dropped. Cei, Jenkins, and I set to
pulling the oars, while Pedr managed the tiller. Apart from
the squeak of the oars in the rowlocks, there was only the
thin, plaintive cry of the dry main-halyard block jerking to
and fro above us to pierce the quietness of the dawn. The sky
had clouded over and overhead of us was a grey, sloppy sky,
all around us a grey, sloppy sea. The air was heavy with
moisture and the slight breeze had a faint iodine, kelp-like
smell. Goodness Gracious stopped rowing, sniffed the air
and said, 'Boys, we're in for a bit of fog.' Then he lowered
his head and gazed along the tops of the slight swells, like a
pool-player sighting a shot. He glanced up at Bardsey Island
from under his brows the while, then he murmured, 'Just
so's I'll know which way to go home if it gets too thick, see?'
There was no compass in the boat. Goodness Gracious stood
up in the boat and gazed around the horizon. 'No other craft
nearby – just a couple of row boats way up to the north.
They must be out from Criccieth.' He doled out breakfast,
jam sandwiches and cold tea, said grace, and we boys had the
lot scoffed down almost as fast as the fog came down around
us like cold cotton-wool. It was uncanny, not to be able to
see anything in a fog so white, so full of light in itself. It was
so thick that I soon could barely make out the dark shape of
Cei, only three feet away from me on the next thwart.

   The only sound we heard, apart from the squeaking block
overhead, was after two or three minutes of sitting there, still
as statues, except for the boat's slight rocking, in absolute
silence. Then we heard the plaintive sound of Jenkins' voice.
'Goodness gracious,' he said, quietly. I thought I heard Cei
giggle ahead of me, but I wasn't sure; it could have been a

wavelet lapping *Gwenhyfar*'s side. Many of the other local
fishermen would have made God's ears ring with their
cursing.

There was almost dead silence for a minute or so, broken
now and again by the far-away, deep moan of the Bardsey
lighthouse fog-horn, then Jenkins repeated, 'Goodness
gracious!' We heard him cluck his tongue in annoyance,
then sigh and say, 'Well, boys, we'd better get the net up.
This is going to last for hours. Be very slow and careful.'

We slowly and carefully made our way aft to help with the
net. Goodness Gracious changed places with Jenkins Junior
and took the tiller. Cei and I started rowing through the
thick fog. It was eerie, a bit, I imagine, like sleep-walking
through a space one imagines to be devoid of shape, form or
proportion. We kept pulling at the oars for six or seven
hours, a steady stroke, stopping only now and then to listen
in trepidation for other craft. When the fog lifted, towards
one P.M., I saw to my amazement that *Gwenhyfar* was only a
mile or so from her mooring off Llangareth.

How Jenkins did it, how he found his way without a
compass or another type of navigational aid, I can only
guess, but I'll never know for sure. All he said when Cei
blurted out his surprise was, 'Well, goodness gracious, you
wouldn't want me to go to Barmouth now, would you?'

There was no fish for Mam, of course, but she was happy
enough to see me back that it didn't seem to matter to her.

Another fisherman I went out with a couple of times was
Morgan Whistle. He, too, had a Tenby lugger, *Lovely Lass*,
but he was a difficult man to work with. In the Great War
he'd been a deckhand in a trawler which was shelled and
sunk by a German surface raider. The explosion had blown
off Morgan's lower jaw. The German surface raider's crew
picked up some of the trawler crew from the water and had

taken them back to Germany as prisoners. The German doctors did what they could for Morgan, but it still left his face quite a mess. They replaced his lower jaw with a stainless steel one, which was covered with a pink material of some kind. Morgan could eat in a fashion, by opening and closing the jaw by hand. Otherwise the jaw was kept closed by a strap which passed over his bald head. However, he couldn't speak. Instead, he used a police-type whistle, with which he blew signals, high pitched and low. Despite his handicap, he was a lively man, and he could be very funny with his eyes rolling and the whistle playing. It was said that there was hardly a barmaid in any pub on the coast of North Wales who was not enamoured of Morgan Whistle, though he must have been well into his late thirties and was as bald as an egg. It might have been because, apart from being cheerful and funny ashore, he was also reputed to be the best fisherman in West or North Wales. He used to teach us lads the Morse code, blowing on his whistle in dots and dashes and at the same time writing down what he was signalling. He wasn't married, which was just as well, as legend had it he had a 'girl in every port'. He was so successful with women and fish that jealous competitors said his catch were becharmed by the music of his whistle. He always carried a mouth-organ, too, which he somehow could play quite well. With the whistle and the harmonica, Morgan was the life and soul of any gathering and soon had everyone dancing and jigging or singing to his pipe.

At sea in his lugger, though, Morgan was a different man, always edgy and nervous, frowning to himself and cursing in quiet hoots, as if he hated the sea, which is not surprising. But I never saw any fisherman, anywhere in the world, braid a net faster or neater than Morgan Whistle, though. His fingers flashed quickly as his shuttle flew, and the net he was making seemed to grow on its own, as if by magic.

Morgan slept in his boat-shed, among all the fishing gear, but he had started to build a cottage a few hundred yards up from the beach, and there, if he wasn't out trawling, we would find him quietly whistling to himself as he lugged the heavy stones up his ladder to the top of the wall.

The cottage was never finished. Morgan was wrecked on Bardsey Island in early '38, and was drowned trying to get ashore on the steep rocks.

4
Cadell Rum

My father was not a big man physically, but nor were most of the sailing captains and mates that I met as a child. They were more wiry but very tough. If they survived the hard life at sea over decades, the tropical diseases and other misadventures common to sea-rovers, they generally lived to a decent old age. Most of them were religious; Welsh ships were renowned the world over for the hymn singing when they held Sunday services on board. They were also famous, back in the days before David Lloyd George, in 1906, introduced his Parliamentary Bill to ease the lot of deep-sea sailors, for the humane conduct of the skippers and the good, if plain, food doled out daily in the clean, if spartan, crew's quarters. Pay, before the demise of sail in the mid-twenties, had not been over-generous, ranging from about five pounds a month for a master, to fifteen shillings a month for a deck-boy.

Most of the very old captains and mates I knew had started their sea careers at a very early age, some of them as young as ten and eleven. A few of them, by the time they were ready to retire, could make their way with ease in a half-dozen languages, and corresponded with old friends all over the world.

Three kinds of men were truly respected in West Wales; a learned man, a man who could tell a story well, and a master of his trade. My Dad was all three, and so when he was at home in Llangareth we were visited by many of the leading maritime lights from all of Merioneth, Caernarvon and Cardigan, and on rarer occasions from as far afield as Pembroke, Carmarthen and Glamorgan, too. Then, with the

fire blazing in the hearth and the Aladdin oil-lamp at full
blast, our kitchen was warm and crowded and full of the
tales of the old Sail-in-Trade.

There might be Morgan Lewis, a robust man of saturnine
appearance with a huge walrus moustache and possessed of a
sharp memory despite his seventy-odd years. He was from
the now-deserted harbour of Barmouth, but he was still a
Power-to-be-Reckoned-With. He could reel off the names
of all the three-hundred-odd sailing ships known on the
coast of Wales during the past sixty years: *Hope, Isallt, Jenny
Jones, Linus, Maid of Meiron, Palestine, Oleander, Six
Brothers, Wave of Life, Twelve Apostles, Summer Cloud,
Pride of Wales* (what names they had!), *My Lady, Morning
Star, New Blessing, Fleetwing, Excelsior, Confidence,* and
Cariad – Captain Morgan Lewis described them in all the
shifting glory of canvas, sea and sky. He could also name
practically every man-jack who had ever shipped on board
each craft on every trip of note that she had made. They
were all gone now, at the bottom of the sea, or skulking in
some far-away backwater as hulks, where their inheritors,
the upstart steamers, loaded coal over their shattered decks
from their battered guts. Now Morgan Lewis was a lay-
preacher at his local chapel. When he rendered his account
of, for example, how starving rats in the hold of *Palestine*,
bound from Manchester to Capetown with coal, in 1892,
had gnawed holes through the ship's side and sank her in the
South Atlantic, and how her captain, Owen Parry of
Criccieth, navigated all his crew in safety to the African
shore in an eighteen foot open boat; when Morgan Lewis
told the tale it was as if he had learned it from Saint Paul's
epistle to the Corinthians. His words rolled and thundered
like a telling of the *Odyssey*.

There might also be Mereddyd Phillips, a short, rotund
man with hair and beard as white as sea-foam, a large, red
nose, and a wooden leg. Mereddyd talked little. He was in

his late sixties and had rounded the Horn under sail fifteen times. He carried a big red-star tattoo on his forehead to show it. There was, it was said, no waterfront pub in Hamburg or Liverpool that would charge Mereddyd for a drink in the past thirty years, nor in Bristol, Harburg, Copenhagen, or Amsterdam, either. As Dad commented out of Mereddyd's hearing, 'By God, his nose shows it, too. Why, two foxes could hide in it!'

Angharad and I liked Mereddyd a deal; he always brought some toffees for us, which he dredged from the depths of his blue serge watch-coat before he perched Angharad on his knee above the wooden leg. He was the only square-rig sailorman I ever saw with more than one ring on his fingers, and one of those was mounted with a huge onyx. On his one foot he wore a red leather boot with beautiful chasing worked into it.

Two other memorable men were Rhodri Griffiths and his brother Iago, ancients from Neath in the South, but still merry for all that. They had sailed, always together, on Norwegian and American whalers in the mid and late 1800s. Their hands bore masses of deep scars from the fletching knives and freezing lines, their eyes were green and bright shining, and they held themselves as upright as expectant lighthouses. Their whaling had been by hand-hurled harpoons from open boats and many a tale of capsizing in the freezing waters of the Southern Ocean, many stories of dories and the Azores they had to tell in voices strong and quiet, like the hum of forebraces in a stiff breeze. Under all their gentle words, as they told their tales was suspense and a threat of impending calamity. 'Rhodri's ninety-three next month,' I remember Mam whispering in an awed voice as he and his brother sprang down from the pony-trap and rolled their wide shoulders up to the cottage door. Rhodri carried a walking stick, but that was, as he delighted in showing us wondering children, only to contain a two-foot-long glass phial of a sparkling golden liquid. 'Hebridean sunshine' Rhodri called it, his eyes twinkling. Iago had only one eye. The other he had lost when a harpoon-line snapped as a right whale had sounded, and the broken end had cracked Iago in the eye. He wore no patch, and the blinded eye stared, forever open and innocent, at the middle ground between him and the far horizon. The two brothers always wore bowler hats, pilot jackets, Rhodri's with brass buttons, and corduroy trousers, and their black boots shone like sea-slugs. Iago was the religious one of the two, and always carried a Bible with him wherever he went. Both had been widowers for some years, and now lived with their sister, who was older than either of them, although her I never saw. She was, they said, 'too busy looking after the house to go gallivanting around the countryside.' They were strong people in Neath; still winter in summer there. The two brothers, when they spoke Welsh, did so in the funny accent of South Wales. Compared to the bubbling tones of Gwynedd, they sounded a bit, to us children at any rate, like the outlet of the kitchen pump at full gush.

Besides Morgan and Mereddyd, Rhodri, and Iago, there were quite a few other old captains and mates who visited us when Dad was home. Ordinary sailors, too, but most of those were well over forty. Very few local boys had gone into sail after 1916. A great part of the Welsh slate trade had been with Germany. When the First World War broke out it had been a cataclysmic disaster for North Wales, but the friendly ties with German mariners had been so strong that when the Kaiser started his war the tug-masters of Bremen, Hamburg, and Harburg actually towed many Welsh sailing ships out to sea after the British declaration. The few ships and crews remaining in Germany had been interned, but the German sailors made sure that the Welsh seamen in internment camps were fed and looked after right through the four years of purgatory. Apart from sustaining the close bonds forged through the previous decades between Welsh and German mariners, though, it did little good. Sail was finished by 1918, shelled, torpedoed, sold into neutral countries, stranded, and abandoned. Early in the war the U-boat captains had been professional sailors, many of them trained in sail. They had allowed the ship's crews fair warning, and even let them take with them into the lifeboats personal effects and mementoes of the ship, but as the war ground on, younger, more ruthless, men were promoted in the German Imperial Navy, and there were many tales of utter callousness and barbarity, especially towards the end of the war. The collapse of Wales' slate industry and the loss of most of her great sailing fleet during the First World War was the start of an economic decline which was to continue for the next two and a half decades. As I recall, the consensus of opinion in Llangareth was that although the Allies had defeated Germany, it had done Wales no good at all, even that we might have been better off had Germany won the war (which God forbid, said everyone but Fychan Evans, who had married a German woman from Nordenham and so was silent on the matter). Ports such as Portmadoc and Barmouth, which before the war had been full of sailing ships mustered for their passages, were now deserted, except for a few small coastal schooners and bobbing fishing boats. The mountain brooks which once had filled the water-barrels for voyages to Aruba and Newfoundland now cried directly into the sea. Now the great blue slate mountain of Blaenau Ffestiniog was still and dead where half a thousand men had wrested fortune in the rain. But as Mereddyd Phillips pointed out, the quays in Portmadoc bore eternal testimony to the old hard passages. They were constructed of Welsh granite and filled with ballast from Chile, Newfoundland, Greece and Germany, all mixed with the soil of Wales. On the roofs of Valdivia and Buenos Aires, San Francisco and Baltimore, can still be seen the slate of

Blaenau Ffestiniog, as grey and blue as the rains of Eryri, as unmistakably recognizable as the lines of the Borth-y-gest schooner.

In the late afternoon, when there were visitors, Mam set out high tea: a cold leg of lamb, a great china tureen of boiled potatoes, ham and beef sandwiches, a pudding and custard, tea-cakes, and the biggest teapot we had, which held about half a gallon. Then the grand captains sat meekly around the table, Morgan Lewis with his napkin tucked up under his chin under his walrus moustache. Angharad and I were placed at the far end of the table from Dad, staring at Morgan, waiting for him to sip his tea, wondering how he managed it with a half pound of hair sprouting from his upper lip and never a drop of tea spilled on his napkin. When Iago was there, Dad always asked him to say the grace. When he wasn't, Dad usually said 'God save all here' and left it at that. When Dad wasn't there Mam said 'Eat your greens, *bach*.'

Once or twice a year Mam's sister, Lowri, who had married an Englishman, a railway guard from Manchester, came to visit us on holiday, bringing her husband John with her. He was a mild little man with sandy hair, fishes' eyes and a pension due in fifteen years. On arrival Aunt Lowri handed to us children a largesse of lollipops, sweets and comics (the only ones we ever saw), Sexton Blake and the like. She wore powder and scent so it took time for Angharad and me to get used to her. By the time we'd done that it was time for her to go back to England. So many rings and bracelets had she that it was like being visited by the Empress of China, and there was only Uncle John to spoil the illusion. Uncle John rarely talked of anything but his work. Listening to him was like having a London, Midland & Scottish Railway time-table read to us. He used to go down to the shore, roll his trousers up to the knee and wade in the sea along the sand so that some people thought he was an escaped lunatic. He did not drink at all, but he smoked a foul-smelling tobacco in a huge curved pipe and wore suspenders as well as a belt. He had been gassed on the Somme battlefield in the War, and had asthma, and he snored so loudly that we were always glad to see the back of Uncle John when the time came for him to leave. He was a very short man and Dad said he had duck's disease, 'His rear-end is too near the deck.'

But the most memorable of all our visitors, as his voice rose and fell, with the firelight leaping on the whitewashed kitchen wall, was Cadell Rum, a tall, lanky, gaunt sailing-skipper of a man of around sixty. His hair, eyes, and beard were gypsy-dark. He had the face of a weather-worn devil when it was worked up, and a benign sea-sprite when in repose. He was a magical man who brought to Llangareth the emerald palms of silver coral islands waving in the Trade Wind breeze. He brought them to moving life; he made them weave in the wind, like shaggy mountain bulls at the challenge.

As Mam poured the tea from the great cosied pot, her dark head bent, her eyes forever glancing, smiling, at Dad, Cadell's voice sang and chanted as he took us to where the bergs calve off the glaciers, or up some dark alley-way rife with skullduggery in Bombay or Madagascar, or to some storm-swept open anchorage on the bleak coast of Chile. When Cadell told a tale everyone, even Mr Jeffreys-Geography (although he understood little Welsh) stared entranced at his gestures and expressions, enchanted, as Cadell's voice, full of the rolling seas and the calls of the petrel, nailed us all to his eyes, lashed us to his memories and had us riding with him on his laughter. In those moments Cadell held Llangareth in his warm, gentle, calloused hands.

I don't recall Cadell's real family name, if I ever knew it. It was probably Jones, Roberts, Williams, Hughes, Jenkins,

Lewis, Evans, Griffiths, Lloyd, Morris, Powell, Parry,
Pugh, Howard, Rhys, or Thomas. Family names in West
Wales are few, mainly due to the want of imagination on the
part of the English censors who first imposed 'surnames' on
the Welsh, a person was and is known by his calling, the
locality of his home, or some personal idiosyncrasy. The
nature of Cadell's tendency was quite clear. If rum and
bottles had not been invented, they would have needed to
have been for Cadell, yet I never once saw him falter or
stagger, nor did I ever hear him swear or slur a word.

Once a discussion was taking place between Dad, Morgan
Lewis and Cadell on the differences between sailing in the
far north and the far south. 'The Arctic,' expounded Cadell,
'and the sky a hummingbird's wing, all the rainbows that
had ever been lighting the ice with the gleams of Paradise;
the sea slate blue and the hump of Cape Farewell away to the
north, the only welcome farewell that ever a sailor had in a
lively wind and a rising sea.' Cadell hesitated, took a swig of
strong tea, frowned and went on, 'The Antarctic, and the sky
a lake of blood painting the ripples of the sea with snakes'
forked tongues, and scorpions' stings and the sea green-deep
over the skulls of the green navies shimmering below and
above the light leaping. Our ship a poor intruder in the halls
of the Mighty and the words of mere men nibbling at the
moon's face under the Aurora Australis and the frosted
Cross over the edge of a frozen universe, and shadows of
priest-like clouds traipsing over the rimed beaches like
mammoths tramping over stones, and a scavenger's wind,
cold and vengeful over the world. In those seas' dark-
coming it is all a man can do, to remember the presence of
Jehovah . . . and the penguins (Welsh word that is, *bach*)
debating over bleached bones of deep-diving right whales,
like landlords arguing a rent-increase on the day before the
crack of doom . . .'

'Hard winds in the north, hard men in the south,' concluded Morgan Lewis.

Dad was at home for Christmas only once between 1934 and 1937. That, of course, was a more joyful Christmas than the others, although Mam always did her best for us. We took no trees to the houses in West Wales, but we did hang holly and mistletoe around the house. No one wore their best clothes at Christmas or Easter; it was supposed to be an affront to God. There was a droll contrast between the drawing room, with a sparkling white tablecloth and the best china service out for Christmas dinner, and our family, the widow Carregen and Blind Sioni, all in our oldest clothes. I don't know if this was the custom in the rest of Wales, but in the west it was. The widow and Blind Sioni were not only invited because they were friends and poorer than we; Carregen played the piano well, and Sioni had a very good bass voice. In those days, when the wireless reception left much to be desired, that was important. The presents for Angharad and me were put before the fireplace on the day *after* Christmas. The ones from Santa Claus were unwrapped, so that Angharad knew what he had brought, and what Mam and Dad had given her. They were not much, for we were not well off, but as we had no comparisons to make we were content enough.

Presents to outsiders were mainly in food from the garden – eggs for the postman, a sack of potatoes for Carregen, and only Blind Sioni had a bought present – a half pound of Dutch tobacco.

The winters were hard outside the cottage. The rain drove in almost continually from the Irish Sea and the wind scrambled over the roof and howled up on the heights, but inside the house we were warm and cosy enough, and so was Caradoc in his stable. We had three big wooden barrels of fresh water inside the house by the end of October, in case the spring supply froze. When the hay was taken in during late autumn, some of it was carried up into the house attic, to act as extra insulation under the slate roof. This worked, and it gave refuge to a host of mice, so our two cats were both well fed all winter, until the last of the hay was taken outside in the springtime.

Cesar, our dog, was a Welsh Collie. He slept in a kennel outside the kitchen door, winter and summer, guarding everything around. He was so jealous of Llangareth that he would never leave the place willingly, and instead of running on the uplands, like the other dogs around, he ran barking and whoofing round and round the house. That was except when the widow Carregen's Bulldog bitch was on heat; then Cesar haunted her gate, but he never, I believe, got anywhere with her, as she was a fierce bitch and proud of her lineage. In some ways that was a pity; it would have been interesting to see the outcome of that union.

Throughout my schooling, most days were long and wearisome for much of the time. Although Mam was always up before me, I rose at dawn and was out of the house to feed Caradoc, the pigs and chickens. Then I got the day's coal into the kitchen, pumped water into the pot-boiler while Mam got the breakfast ready. It was usually oatmeal. By seven o'clock Angharad and I had eaten, and I had saddled Caradoc. By seven-thirty we were off to school, at Penybont, four miles away, where we arrived about eight-thirty. We always took our lunches with us, usually bread and dripping in the winter, bread and jam in the summer. We stayed in the one classroom all day, except for the hour lunch break, when we were forced out into the playground, regardless of the weather, to play and fight with the other children. I don't recall learning much at school: simple sums and that a lot of the map of the world was coloured red, and that we had a new King in London (the old one had died after his Jubilee mugs had been passed out to us in 1935). The new King was the old Prince of Wales, and we were told that now he was monarch he was going to usher in a new world of hope and joy for the Principality of Wales.

Our teacher, Jeffreys-Geography, was a tall, ascetic Englishman with gingery hair sparse above his ears and nothing on the crown of his head but the light that shone through the classroom window. He always wore a jersey, a tweed jacket, and grey-flannel slacks and he pursed his lips as if he was sucking on a gooseberry. When he spoke at all fast, which was about eighty per cent of the time, he immediately lost the attention of twenty-nine out of thirty pupils, who were mainly Welsh-speaking. The one exception was Iolo (Educated Evans), the fat boy from Aran Fawddwy, away up over the uplands. He was staying with his uncle a mile or two from Llangareth, his English mother having gone to London with her fancy man.

At school I enjoyed history, geography, art (which meant drawing on a slate in one chalk colour – white), and composition. It was only in composition that we children of the singing land were ever allowed to let our imagination roam freely – as long as it was not too freely. The lessons I disliked the most were religious instruction, which bored me to silent tears, arithmetic and algebra.

History generally commenced with an account of how the Greeks and Romans were the only fount of our culture, and how the rest of humanity (the Celts especially) had been savage barbarians. History generally stopped somewhere in the 1880s, with the English having civilized practically all the world. Very little was ever taught of the American Revolution and the loss of the first British Empire, but Jeffreys-Geography went into minute detail about how the heathen Indian mutineers had imprisoned English women and children in the Black Hole of Calcutta, or how General Gordon had quelled whole armies of fanatical enemy in the Chinese wars. The greatest heroes were Wolfe of Quebec, Clive of India, and David Livingstone. The heroines were Queen Elizabeth I, Florence Nightingale, Grace Darling, and Queen Victoria. I never knew, until I was much older, that, for example, the men who won the battle of Agincourt were Welsh archers. To Jeffreys-Geography, Wales seemed to be a sort of appendix to England. In what little he taught us of literature, there was Chaucer and Shakespeare, of course, Milton, Byron, Keats, and Tennyson, but I never recall him mentioning once any of the Welsh poets or writers. No Dafydd ap Gwilym, no Taliesin, no Caradoc Evans, no Rhys Davies, no Arthur Machen, no W. H. Davies; it was if the mountains of Wales had always been deathly silent, and as if the echoing valleys and the chanting uplands had been the home of faceless, dumb, illiterates, as cloddy as the bogs of Saxonia, as dim and silent as the fog-bound marshes of East Anglia.

But you can't make an Englishman out of a Welshman any more than you can a cat out of a canary, and so it was that towards the end of my school days Jeffreys-Geography was beginning to show signs of discouragement over us. He even, in unthinking moments of frustration, descended into making mocking mimicry of the English-speaking Welsh, of such worthies as the local tobacconists and post-office proprietors, with their 'indeed to goodness' and 'look you man' and all that false balderdash even now copied by a fascistic minded bourgeoisie from the ravings of the nationalistic Little-Wales crowd of 'Anglo-Welsh' writers; that shoal of tweedy gentlemen peering through their bifocals over the valleys of Wales and wanting to make of it a reservation for ruddy-faced peasants shuttling away at weaving looms, a sort of medieval Disneyland at the dead-end of the motorways.

Caradoc was left tied to a tree while we were in school. The ride to and from school in the spring and summer was always a pleasure, but in wintertime it could be a misery. One good thing; so near to the sea we rarely got more than a foot of snow at a time. Llangareth was only snow-bound once. I think that was in the winter of '36. Along the road there was very little traffic. Perhaps a horse-pulled hay-wain and one or two motor cars, or a lorry, but most of the time the road was deserted except for a few foot travellers, tramping gentlemen of the road and some gypsies, whom we avoided as they were (falsely) supposed to steal children. In the summer I took short cuts on Caradoc across the uplands, among the gorse and heather in the patches of sunlight between the rolling shadows of the clouds.

In the evening, after tea, there was, except in the depths of winter, always an hour or two's stint for me in the garden or in the small greenhouse where we grew young plants for spring sowing. There was always something to do. Then it was supper at eight o'clock and bed at nine, but I was allowed to read with my little oil-lamp until ten o'clock. So the days went, except for Sundays. No one worked then, of course, except for Mam, and my feeding the livestock.

Mine was not an easy childhood, but it had its compensations, and it was good training for the many harder years to follow. It was not an unusual childhood for that part of Wales. The land was harsh and not easily worked. Money was in short supply, and I doubt if, between 1934 and 1938, I ever saw more cash at any one time than a half-crown piece. I doubt if anyone in the neighbourhood did. The average pay of a farm labourer then was rarely more than twenty-eight shillings a week. Throughout the land hundreds of thousands of unemployed men and their families were subsisting on a dole of only about seventeen shillings a week.

Sometimes, in the early autumn, at harvest time, we saw men, shabbily dressed and gaunt, who had tramped the eighty miles or so from the idle coal-fields of the Rhondda Valley in South Wales, looking for casual work. They were a piteous sight, with patched up clothes and broken boots, but they were generally given food and drink and some kind of shelter by the country folk. Some of them were so poor that they split up wooden matches with a razor blade, in four slivers, to save spending a farthing on a box of matches. But towards the time I left home, in the late spring of 1938, the situation had eased up a little and there were less men on the road. We didn't know why this was, of course. We didn't know that the country had started slowly, very slowly, and perhaps without knowing it, to gear itself for another war.

5

Something for Wales

During the winter of 1937–38 Dad came home for about three weeks. The tug on which he worked was in dock for an engine replacement. I got to know him, and his ideas, more during that period than in any other. Although he was proud of being Welsh he was far from being a Nationalist. His attitude was that the Welsh are the ancient British race, and we are, therefore, more British than anyone else. If any nation in the British Isles wanted to separate themselves, then it was from *us* they should separate, and not us from them.

We had a radio by then, and on the night of the Tommy Farr–Joe Louis boxing match in New York, all the neighbours from miles around crowded into our kitchen to hear the fight, which, I believe, was the first direct transatlantic public broadcast ever made. After a hard, punch-for-punch match, Joe Louis was declared the winner on points. When the result was declared, as millions listened in all over the English-speaking world, the American commentator shoved his microphone under Tommy Farr's nose and asked him how he felt. Tommy, an ex-miner from South Wales, replied breathlessly, 'Well, as you can see, I've got plenty of guts. That's old Tommy Farr, you know . . .' Then, as if it explained everything that made him stay the whole course, hammering away at and being hammered by 'The Brown Bomber', he said quietly, 'I'm a Welshman, you know.'

'There's a real Welshman for you!' cried Educated Evans the fat boy from Aran Fawddwy, him with an English mother. All over the little, tight land of Wales two million people had been waiting for many years, for someone to say that to the world.

Dad said, 'If Tommy Farr had been Irish everyone in America would have known he was, long ago. The Irish make such a noise over there, what with songs and films, and here we are, the Irish the closest race to us physically and mentally (except for our religion) and no one, or hardly anyone, even knows the Welsh exist. They look upon us as some kind of semi-English, and the land as a sort of English county. God knows we've been here twice as long as the English, probably twice as long as that too.'

'Arr, you're just jealous of the Irish,' retorted Cadell Rum, 'the Irish who've almost completely lost the Gaelic tongue and are so busy beating down the English with their own language; so busy proving that they are capable of doing anything the English can do, and do it better, so busy aping the English – especially in America. Why, I never met an Irish-American yet that wasn't so busy trying to clamber up the ladder of social success that he'd never had the time to even think about his own true culture. There's damned few of them I ever met that knew anything further back than the potato famine, and none at all who ever knew that before the American Revolution a good third of emigrants to America were Welsh folk, starved out of their own land . . . but practically every one in the States knows about how hard the Irish have had it, and the Irish, with their damned sentimentality, and penchant for self-pity, play on the tune to the hilt. Let's face it, we Welsh are just plain jealous of the Irish. We're jealous of the English, too, the Germans, the Russians, the Italians, even the Americans, God help us! But most of all we're jealous of the Irish in America. We can't see why everyone in America knows all about Ireland, takes Irish names – except most of the negroes; they have

Welsh names they got from the white plantation settlers in the South (there's shame on us!) during their slavery. Why, the Americans like to sing Irish songs – what there are of them, for compared to our many songs, Irish songs are like palm trees in Wales, few, far between and ragged. We can't understand why the Americans like to crack Irish jokes and visit Irish beauty spots. We think that the English and the Americans should do all these things with us, for we're far more richly endowed with them, Lord knows.'

'So we are, so we are,' murmured Dad in agreement, then he added, 'Wales is one of the smallest countries in the world, right enough, but there's no earthly reason why it should be, and it certainly is, one of the least efficiently publicised. Although we have, by every reasonable criterion, far better claims to be labelled as a "nation"' (when Dad said this we could hear the quotation marks) 'than either Scotland or Ireland, it is, as you well know, practically impossible to find anyone in all of Europe, away from the docks, who even knows that Wales exists.'

'True,' said Cadell, 'and most of those that do know it exists think that our land is part of England.'

Dad warmed to his subject, 'Right! *You* try to tell them about Wales. I've tried it, God knows I've tried it! Tell them about our language, one of the oldest in Europe, and probably the most beautiful and musical. Talk to them in Welsh. They listen dubiously, sceptically, not knowing what they are hearing, but they nod knowingly and say – and this is the ultimate insult – "No doubt it is an English dialect". This they say of a language as different from English as is Greek, which has ten different words for one English word, which boasts art-forms and poetic rhythms unknown in any other language, and which, God save us, has attracted scholars from all over Europe for centuries.' Dad paused for a moment to let all this sink in.

'Right you are, Sion,' agreed Catrin Powell who, besides Dad and Cadell, was probably the best read person in the room.

Dad was warming up even more now. He stood up and placed his thumb inside his jacket armpit, just like Morgan Morbid Preacher, who visited Llangareth Chapel from time to time, whenever the congregation was off-guard. Dad went on, 'We Welsh are not a popular race. That, we know, is true. The English don't like us much, but we don't allow that to worry us. The English have verbs – "to Scotch", "to Jew", "to Welsh". There are subtle distinctions. "To Scotch" is to get the better of someone, vigorously, even ruthlessly, but not exactly unfairly. "To Jew" is to swindle, right enough, but there is the suggestion that the victim got all he deserved. "To Welsh", however, means to be just sheer mean, "caddish" as the English say. It's like if you took money out of a blind man's collection tin. When a bookie tries to clear off without settling his debts on winnings due, that's "Welshing". That meaning of the word, that obscenity, is used all over the English-speaking world.'

Everyone was silent as Dad thought for a moment, then he said quietly, 'Perhaps it's us who've been *Englished*?'

There was muffled laughter in the kitchen for a moment, until Cadell raised his hand for silence. 'The English, in their wisdom,' he said, 'are convinced that we are a dishonest race of people. A lot of Welsh lasses work as servants in London; the English, who don't at all mind having them because they work hard without grumbling, say they tell lies and steal silk stockings. The English, poetic souls that they are, have a rhyme – "Taffy was a Welshman, Taffy was a thief, Taffy came to my house and stole a side of beef . . ." Of course, they don't know that they are referring to the frequent invasions of England in the Middle Ages by Welsh cattle-rustlers – if you can call stealing stock on land which by rights should be yours "rustling" – but we have our own subtle and secret notions about property and abstract truths, because we are odd, tortuous people. George Meredith, who was of Welsh descent, said: "There are two natures – Human Nature and Welsh Nature!" Then again, my son in America sent me a cutting from a magazine which is published over there. In it, the biologist J. B. S. Haldane wrote about the English for the Americans. He referred to the unpopularity of the Welsh among the English and said that for himself he found us quick-witted, emotional, and, if you please, delightful company. This is probably the first time that an Englishman has ever called the Welsh delightful, and no doubt it will be the last, and I think it is a good job that the article was not printed in Wales. We've *hauled* a few *Danes* before, usually six feet off the ground with a rope.'

Almost everyone in the room, with the exception of the youngest children, caught Cadell's pun, and laughed uproariously. When the merriment ceased, Dad rejoined, 'The English find us cock-sure and offensive. This is curious, because we ourselves by this time, after four hundred and two years of English domination, are rather proud of boasting of our racial sense of inferiority. The national pastime in Wales is using this as an alibi for failure to make money or become famous. Our sense of racial inferiority is the handiest crutch most of us have at this time, and without it we'd be limping along vacuously. There are a lot of Welsh folk in England today, right enough – about one hundred thousand in Liverpool alone, and probably a quarter of a million in Patagonia, God only knows how many in Australia and New Zealand, and three million or so in America, if you count the ones with parents born in Wales – and if we have not the commercial insidiousness of the Armenian in Istanbul, or the blatant acquisitiveness of the Corsican in Marseilles, at any rate, we are not doing too badly.'

Dad paused for another moment, to let all this sink in, and
to take a swig from the mug of hot tea which Mam had set
before him. He went back to his declamation: 'Welsh
politicians are shrewd, flexible, telepathic fellows, who once
they abjure principle, become extremely useful instruments
of the vested interests. David Lloyd George, J. H. Thomas,
Frank Hodges, and others, are Welshmen who have gained
considerable rewards for their services to England, to John
Bull Limited, from time to time. Wales has specialized in
helping the British Empire to turn nasty corners. A Welsh
family, the Tudors, took over after the bloody gang-warfare
of the Wars of the Roses, Oliver and Richard Cromwell were
Welshmen; their real name was Williams; Lloyd George
took over as Prime Minister in 1917, when the War was
going at its worst for the Allies. That was a job no Scot or
Saxon was keen on at all.'

Dad took another sip of tea and stared for a moment
through the kitchen window. Outside, rain was falling,
veiling the early evening hills in a blue mist.

'Today,' Dad's voice filled the room, 'in this year of grace
1938, Welsh politics are . . . complex. Our tradition is
Liberalism, which was Wales' way of showing she wasn't too
enthusiastic about British jingoism and the Empire, but
today the South is solidly Socialist with strong Communist
leanings, and no wonder, with an unemployment rate of
twenty-eight per cent, and even more among the miners!
The tradition in recent English politics suggests that if ever
there is a revolution in Great Britain it will come about
through a general strike. This strike will be forced on the
miners by the South Wales Miners Federation, the most
militant organization of its kind in Western Europe. That
Federation is in the charge of a man that very few people in
Britain know anything about, and of whom practically
nobody in Europe or America has heard. He is Arthur
Horner, known to every industrial worker in South Wales as

the President of the SWMF. He is a tiny, bespectacled Marxist who really means business, and his business is a Soviet Britain. The problem is that Horner is respected by even his bitterest opponents. That makes him the most important man in Wales in 1938. If Socialism ever comes about in Britain, it will be through people whom Horner has sponsored, or at least sanctioned – men like Nye Bevan of Ebbw Vale.'

Heads were nodding in agreement as Cei stuck his head out of the door and announced that the rain had stopped. Soon, one by one, our guests bade us goodnight, and soon Angharad and I crept up to bed, and left Mam and Dad alone in the kitchen, in the firelight and their own warmth for each other.

We were proud, after all, that Tommy Farr, a Welshman, one of a nation of only two millions, had stayed the course with the best boxer in a nation of one hundred and seventy million souls. It wasn't a great deal, except for Tommy Farr, but it was something that someone, at long, long last, had done for Wales.

6

To England and to Sea

The widow Carregen died early in April, 1938. Mam had
visited the old woman two or three times a day for weeks,
taking gruel and clean clothes down to her cottage and trying
to find out if Carregen had any relatives. Finally, just before
she died, the widow gave Mam the address of a grandson of
hers in Monmouth, Davy Harris. Mam wrote to Davy right
away, but by the time he arrived, chubby and prosperous
looking in his Melton overcoat, brown shoes, and motor-car,
Carregen was already in her coffin. That had been made by
Goodness Gracious Jenkins, who also served Llangareth as
undertaker and grave-digger. Davy stayed for the wake,
which was a lively affair. People came from miles around,
because Carregen had delivered practically every child in the
area for thirty-five years and more, and she'd cured just
about anyone who either couldn't afford or did not trust the
doctors.

Davy's car was a tiny Austin Seven with a dicky seat. It
wasn't practical to carry the coffin on it, so the local men,
Goodness Gracious and Pedr and Blind Sioni among them,
all in their best Sunday suits, lugged it up the hill from
Bwthyn Carregen to Llangareth Chapel. The choir and
other folk had a fine time roaring out 'Nearer My God to
Thee' and other hymns. After the service they set to on the
wake high-tea which Mam and Mrs Powell had worked to
put together all the previous night in the Cottage Carregen.
It was quite a spread. Beef and lamb sandwiches, biscuits
and pastry, and a half dozen bottles of ale each for the men,
which Davy had brought over in his Austin Seven. Every-

one seemed to have a good time, even Angharad, who had loved Carregen more than anyone else had. The wake ended about dusk, and then Davy was left alone in his grandmother's cottage, and in the next day or so returned to his job as a travelling salesman, saying that he would look for a new tenant for the cottage on his rounds.

By this time I was almost fourteen. Both Cei and I were missing school now more and more. Jeffreys-Geography didn't seem to mind. He knew that we were working casually wherever we could find the opportunity to earn a few pennies or shillings for our families; planting potatoes, digging ditches, repairing stone walls – whatever odd jobs we could find on the local farms. It was not unusual in those days for boys still at school to do that. We also were going out fishing more, and on a few occasions Goodness Gracious' catch was good enough for him to give us both a shilling or two, to take importantly home.

As we were now earning a little money, Cei and I both were now allowed to go into one of the nearby towns on Saturdays, to the cinema or rugby matches. There we made many pals among the local lads. Some of them were only interested in what was before their noses – films, girls, football, rugby and playing illegal pitch-and-toss with pennies in the alleyways, always with a couple of youths on the look-out for the bobbies. Others seemed to be much brighter, and we talked about what was going on in the world, about the Spanish Civil War and the Italian invasion of Abyssinia. So far as I remember, I don't think there was any one of the lads who did not believe that another war for us was inevitable. They accepted the prospect just as we accept the coming of winter. Many of the older single men who hung around had been in the First World War, in the trenches, and the gory stories they told us did little to cheer us up. They said that the chances of 'going over the top' to charge an enemy trench and surviving alive or unwounded were about one in four. I hear a lot these days, a half century later, about the British desire to appease the dictators. As far as West Wales went, all I remember hearing the ordinary folk talk about was getting over there and clobbering them. It was probably different among the upper classes. It usually is.

'What will you do if they call you up?' Cei asked me as we rode home one Saturday evening.

'Join the Navy. You won't catch me in a muddy trench with a bullying sergeant and one chance in four of getting through it alive,' I replied. 'What about you?'

'Air Force, ground-crew,' replied Cei, 'that's what I'll go for. Learn a lot and no fighting, see? You won't find me getting gassed like your Uncle John or poor old Nye Philips. Anyway, there's plenty of time to make up our minds. There won't be a war for several years yet. It'll take those silly old buggers in London that long to wake up . . .'

A few days later I rode Caradoc up the valley to the road to meet Rhys-the-Post. Now he no longer wore the old flat-topped, double peaked helmet as he used to, with its big brass badge. Now he wore an ordinary-looking peaked cap, like a bus driver or a cinema attendant, and he rode a bicycle instead of a pony. But it was still the same old Rhys, whistling away as he pedalled along the road. 'Something for you, *bach*!' he hollered as he drew up to me in the thin rain. He handed me a brown envelope. I grabbed it. Dad's handwriting!

I shoved the envelope into my belt under my oilskin cape, turned Caradoc, and egged him on back down to our cottage. The pony sensed my excitement and trotted as fast as he could at his age down the rocky track into the valley.

'Letter from Dad, Mam!' I hollered as Caradoc picked his way through the broken-toothed rocks on the lee side of the house. The smell of baking bread wafted through the window where Mam stood, her hair pinned back, her strong features relaxed in the smile she kept especially for me. I jumped off Caradoc, who wandered off into his lean-to stable warm with hay.

'Wipe your feet, *bach*! Mam called as the half-door creaked open.

'He's still in Liverpool, Mam; see the postmark . . .'

Mam took the letter, damp and brown and folded. She brushed the flour off her hands and sat down at the kitchen table to read it. Outside Cesar bumped his tail against the door even though I'd been too hurried to pat him, as I usually did.

'What does he say, Mam?' Dad had promised to try to find me a job on the tugs in Liverpool. I doffed my dripping oilskin cape and threw it over the clothes-horse.

'Wait a minute, *bach*,' she said, off-handedly as she concentrated on the letter.

I waited, impatiently. There were several pages, and Mam read each one carefully, her brows knitted at first, then smiling to herself as she read the last page. Finally she looked up at me and said, 'Dad's found you a job, *bach* . . . look.' She read out part of the letter '. . . and Mr Albert Edward Lee, the captain, I've known for years. He's a good man in a steady trade. The experience will be good for Tristan and will stand him in good stead when we later get him into the Conway Training Ship . . .'

I butted in, 'What's the ship, Mam? Is she ocean-going? What's her name?' Despite my excitement, I tried to keep my voice low.

Mam gazed at me over her reading spectacles. 'Mm . . . let me see now . . .' She turned back the page. 'Here it is: "*Second Apprentice*, out of Harwich" . . . well, that's a good respectable port, plenty of chapel-folk there, as I recall . . .'

'When can I go, Mam? Can I go tomorrow?'

For a moment Mam gazed at me silently, showing no

expression. Then she said, 'Your Dad says next week. He's going to send your fare then. He says it's not legal in England for you to work until you're fourteen anyway, and that's not until the eighth of next month. You'll be off at the end of April. Dad says the boat will be in . . . let's see now . . .' She gazed at the letter, frowning the while until she found it . . . 'Rye.' (Mam pronounced it 'Reeya'. It was not a deepwater port, so she'd never been there, and she was speaking Welsh.)

'Reeya, where's that, Mam?'

'Somewhere near London, your Dad says.' She looked up at the clock on the mantelpiece above the big old iron stove. 'Time for you to be off and meet Angharad. School's out now, and the bus will be half-way here.'

I grabbed my oilskin cape off the clothes-horse and flung it over my shoulders. Mam came to my side and put her arm around my shoulders, 'I'll make you a cup of tea before you go, *bach*,' she murmured.

On the way up to the road, perched atop Caradoc, I reflected that it would be some time before I could attend the Conway Training Ship, up in the Menai Strait off Anglesey. I would need to be sixteen before I could go there to study until I went to sea in a merchant ship as an apprentice. Then there would be a further three or four years before I could expect to sit for my Fourth Mate's certificate. As was the custom in those days, I must support myself until I was old enough to go to Conway. What little money my family possessed had been put by for that very purpose. Now Dad had kept his promise and, after months of asking and writing to many friends, he had found me a ship.

Angharad was at first pleased and excited at my coming fortune, but then she fell into a pique as Caradoc jogged his way down the valley towards the cottage. She didn't like

the thought that I would be going through London and I
would see the new king and queen, while she wouldn't; so I
promised to send her a doll from America when the ship
arrived there, and so she forgot about my coming visit to
London, the great, grand capital of the mighty world-
embracing Empire on which the sun never set.

The new king was not now the old Prince of Wales, who
had promised to perform such miracles for his Principality.
The new king was his brother, George. There had been a
scandal of some kind, but we children had been kept in the
dark about it. It was not 'fit for children's ears'. From what
little we knew an American woman was involved, but her
name was never mentioned in adult conversations.
Mysteriously, she was always referred to as 'That Woman'.
Now that the old Prince of Wales had gone off and left us
to our own devices, 'That Woman' was *never* mentioned at
all. It was as if she had never existed. Soon it was as if the
Prince himself had never been; he too was never mentioned
after the new king was crowned. It was as if a favourite son
had gone to the bad and was disowned.

That night, after Angharad had become accustomed to
the idea of my leaving home, we lay awake for hours, while
I told her of the wonders of London, the Crown Princes
and their gowned Princesses and Indian subahdars wearing
diamonds in their turbans and riding Arabian horses, their
eyes and medals and scimitars flashing in the sunlight as
they trotted down the wide avenues lined with tall
buildings, just as we had seen, our eyes wide with wonder,
at Coronation time in the three-penny picture-house in
Dolgellau.

'Then you won't want Caradoc any more!' Angharad
pouted, her eyes brimming with tears. 'You'll say he's too
old and scruffy. You won't want to ride him; you'll leave
him until the day he dies.'

'Not I, Angharad *bach*,' I promised her as a tear left her

cheek and dolloped on to her counterpane. 'I'll never forget
Caradoc, nor you, nor Mam, nor Dad; not anything nor
anyone in Llangareth. That way, you see *chwaergen* (little
sister), none of you will ever die . . .'

Angharad looked at me, her hazel eyes shimmering. 'And
we won't forget you, Tristan *bach*,' she whispered, half
asleep. Her auburn hair had fallen over her elfin face palely
lit by the *derwydd* moon casting silver dream-drifts from
over the shadowy, magical hills. Then a cloud-curtain was
drawn by the west wind-breeze, but gently, over
Llangareth, and Angharad slept, *plentyn yng Nghymru*, a
child in Wales.

It's a long time ago. Since that night, the first night I
ever found it impossible to sleep, the earth has voyaged
round the sun forty-three times, and she has spun on her
axis almost sixteen thousand times, and an extra ten spins
for the leap years – and for luck.

The week that followed was one of excitement mounting
and diminishing in turns. Both Mam and Angharad made
extra fuss over me, with larger helpings than usual of
puddings, and going through my shirts and socks again and
again, to make sure no darning was needed. It was arranged
that when I went away Cei would look after my chores and
take a share of the garden and stock produce for his
trouble. That would help both Mam and the Powell family
out a great deal.

Each afternoon I was up at the top of the valley, waiting
on the road for Rhys-the-Post to bring the letter from Dad.
Each day Rhys stopped to chat and tell me all about the
wonders of London, which he'd visited for a rugby match
ten or eleven years before. Each evening friends called at
the cottage to visit and converse with Mam and me. The
news had spread around the neighbourhood with amazing
speed and inaccuracy, which we were only anxious to put

right and set the record straight. No, I had not been left a fortune by a rich uncle in New Zealand; no, I was not going into service as a stable boy; no, I was not going to work for the Post Office or the railway (almost every lad's parents' dream at the time).

Finally, after waiting for one of the longest weeks of my life, Dad's letter, together with the fare to Rye, arrived. I was quietly wild with excitement and could not understand why Mam and Angharad seemed to be so sad.

'A sea-going vessel trading to the Continent,' wrote Dad in his letter, 'to France, Belgium, Holland, and Germany, so you will see something of the world and foreign customs. *Second Apprentice* is a good, sound, sea-worthy vessel, a ketch-rigged topsail "boomie", and Captain Lee is a most respectable, very able gentleman who will teach you a good steady trade and who will look after you as if you were his own son instead of being the well-loved son of your affectionate, Dad.'

'PS. The pay is not much, but it will keep you well until you can go to Conway.'

On the same day that Dad's letter arrived, so did Davy Harris, the dead widow Carregen's grandson. He had been on a selling trip through North Wales. Now he had called in at his grandmother's cottage to check that all was well, and to have a word with Mam, who was taking care of the place for him until Davy could find a tenant. So far he had not been successful.

Upon hearing that I was bound for London, he offered to take me in his car as far as Newport in Monmouthshire; then I would catch the train from there to London. It would save a few shillings in fare. Mam jumped at Davy's offer, and arrangements were set for me to be on my way the next day. I was pleased. I liked Davy, who was plump and jolly, even though it was difficult for me to understand either his strange Welsh or his rapidly slurred South

Walian English. He was about in his late twenties, I guessed, and had a wife and eight-year-old daughter at home.

The next day, the day of my departure, was fine and sunny. Angharad silently burst out crying over breakfast and Mam was quieter than usual. I went into the stable to wish Caradoc a fond goodbye. Cei turned up early to see me off, and was strangely terse and more manly than had been the case until then. That was not only because I was going out into the wide world, but also because he was assuming my responsibilities. He carried my new seabag, which had been sewn up from sail-canvas by Llewellyn Griffith, the half-daft lad from Caernon. Mam fussed over me and made me promise to spend my few shillings saved-fare on a meat pie and sandwiches for the train from Monmouth, and to pick a corridor coach on the train so I could go to the lavatory, to make sure to follow Dad's written instructions on how to get across London, and to be sure not to lose the ten shilling note which she had secured inside my coat inner-pocket with two big safety-pins.

I told Mam not to fret and that I would be home at Christmas and would she like a green and red parrot in a cage? She laughed at that and hugged me tight. Then she let me go, and I followed Davy Harris into his car and we were off, up the rocky track that led from Llangareth and my childhood, up to the main road and an unforeseeable future. I waved my hand cursorily as the car engine spluttered to life, and then I was off, to England and to sea.

As the little motor car trundled along the road to Barmouth in the early morning, I could see all the familiar places along the seashore and the beautiful, sad, shapes of the mountains back from the coast. Now that I was really on my way to a ship and a job I was not sure that I was so keen on it after all. Now that the dream had become real, or would be in a day or two's time, my mind kept going back over things that were trivial and yet somehow important, and the prospect of going to England became less and less attractive.

But I knew that I would have to go to sea sooner or later, and Dad had made a great effort to get me the berth on board *Second Apprentice*. I would have to persist.

The car passed into the streets of Dolgellau. Davy Harris stopped outside a chemist's shop, took a folder from out of the glove-compartment, and disappeared into the shop. I sat in the car, waiting, watching people, some of whom I knew, pass by. I lowered myself in the seat; I didn't want them to see me. I felt as if I were in some way betraying them. Then I thought to myself that perhaps my feelings had nothing to do with going to England and the sea. Perhaps I was just growing up. Perhaps it was both together, going to England making me know so suddenly and clearly that my childhood was over.

As I sat there in the car, and later, as Davy drove at a steady rate through the valleys of Montgomeryshire, Radnor, and Breconshire, all greens and blues and little white-washed cottages just like ours, I remembered many things, like the way I had been always drawing faces in books and filling in newspaper pictures from my cheap tin box of water-colours. I'd spent hours like that, in the rainy winter nights, with Mam knitting in her wooden chair by the fire, smiling at me now and then. In chapel on Sundays I had drawn the ministers and the people sitting in the same pew had looked at my Mam and laughed quietly.

My mother used to say that I took mostly after her father-in-law 'Johnny Star'. Many people have asked me why I first went to sea. Almost always I've told them jokingly that it was because my grandfather was a sailor, and I thought I had been funny. But perhaps what I said was true enough.

As we meandered through the mid-counties of Wales –

the furthest inland I had ever been, although we were never, I think, more than thirty-five miles from the sea – I remembered the fuss that Mam had made over me that morning, how she had fried some eggs for sandwiches, and wrapped the sandwiches in paper napkins, which we normally saw only at Christmas and Easter; and how she had filled her one thermos flask with tea and pressed it upon Davy Harris, pretending it was for the two of us, and her sorrowful dark eyes all the while upon me, and her hand straying to my arm.

We drove on and on, from village to village through the green-gold valleys, with knots of countrymen, threadbare but healthy-looking and ruddy, standing around at the crossroads or before the rises to the tiny hump-backed bridges. It was tiresome, waiting for Davy. He'd collect his papers and catalogues from the cubby hole and say he wouldn't be long, but he was rarely in the chemist's shop for less than half an hour. He wouldn't allow me to leave the car in case he was delayed getting away, waiting for me, and I had to sit there, watching people passing now and then in the quiet village street, wherever we were.

Then we passed over the heights of South Brecon and in an instant the land changed. Suddenly there were grey slag heaps all around, and the sky above was grey, and the pouring rain wrote bleakness on the side of a mountain below which flowed a river, black and poisoned from pollution. All the green freshness of Wales, which I had accepted as eternal through all my life was here choked and all around were grey stones, wooden huts, grey stones.

We followed the long, meandering street of black-grey little terraced houses down the valley. Around us were a dozen pit-wheels, only one of them moving 'Rhondda' muttered Davy, as he alighted from the car and disappeared into a tiny, miserable-looking little shop with no display in the grimy windows.

'Is this still Wales?' I called after him as he stepped over the broken-stoned pavement. He didn't hear me and went inside.

The rain fell heavily and the street was empty except for a tattered scattering of figures barely recognizable to me as human across the road, young to the fore, the aged and crippled to the rear. They had sacks across their shoulders and under their arms and they shuffled along in the rain towards the slag heap, down from which rumbled tip-wagons. The thin line of coal scavengers – that is what Davy called them – moved towards the slag heap with the rain falling like dust upon their bent shoulders. Steadily, as they turned the corner off the main street and moved towards the mountain of mine-spew, they moved from greyness to black. Men and women, old men, children, babes, dragging after them all kinds of vehicles; battered old prams, bicycles, crude carts, two planks of wood and a bent wheel, they all moved slowly or quickly, the seven ages of mankind, loud and boisterous, silent and morose, crying children, feeble old men, the human debris of a hell that we in West Wales could hardly have imagined, flanked on either side by an amorphous mass of rust and filthy litter, South Wales' legacy from the 'Industrial Age'.

'They're allowed on the tip, to scrounge for good coal,' said Davy, quietly, as I watched the thin string of humanity ascend the dirty, wet mound. They were all bending now, those who had reached the slopes, scratching in the muck for a few moments of warmth. So they went on, stumbling and falling, scratching at the wet muck and on their way back treading over the richness of the Welsh earth, barred to them forever. The only right they had was to pick and scratch and curse and cry through all their days, wet or fine, that curious pathetic army that now, as

their sack or battered pram was filled, moved slowly away
and began the tortuous journey back down from the hill of
hell.

All the while I stared. I stared at the slag-tip, I stared at
the people, I stared at humanity brought down to a
shambling collection of wrecks, and I hated, with all my
heart and soul, whoever had caused this to happen in our
land of Wales.

A siren blew. As he started up the car, Davy murmured
to me, 'Look, they're coming out from a shift.' I turned my
head and looked down the grey, woe-begone street. The
street was suddenly full of black grimed miners, some of
them, with no jackets, walking in their shirts in the
thinning cold rain. They went past the stopped car on
either side of us, old men and young boys, staring at us
with their white eyes. Their faces were thickly grimed and
their lips, pale pink, seemed made-up, like the girl's who
worked in the café at Barmouth. The miners all stared hard
at us as they passed, and I think both Davy and I got a bit
uncomfortable, in the presence of these stern lords of the
underworld. There was a kind of pride, a challenge, in their
eyes. It seemed to me, as I watched them go by, that they
were making things very awkward for Davy in his Melton
coat and motor-car. The miners looked at us as if there was
something they could not quite understand, but once they
were past us they did not look back. It occurred to me that
they were thinking about us as they hurried silently back to
their tiny homes straggled up the hillside street. They had
looked at both Davy and me as if we had come from
another planet. I felt a distinct relief, as the car started and
took off down the street, gathered speed and left the town
behind.

But even as the rain finally stopped and we emerged
once more out into a green valley, I glanced at Davy, and
felt that I understood the miners even more than I

understood him, and I felt a strange sort of pride for Wales and for myself because of them.

Later, as the car pulled up outside Davy Harris' semi-detached house in Newport, and we were greeted by his even chubbier wife and girl-child, I forgot all about the Rhondda Valley and remembered only how London seemed to be such a hell of a long way from Llangareth. To go there seemed such a big thing for a lad like me to do.

I never did find out what Davy sold. He wouldn't talk about it to me, but it must have been a medical item of some kind because on the way to Newport we stopped at every chemist's shop we came across, and, despite the depression, there seemed to be one of those in every sizeable town we passed through.

I recall Newport and the train ride to England that night from Monmouth only vaguely, as if it were a long-lost dream. The Great Western Railway train was pulled by a steam engine that to me was a great panting wonder. I stared through the window as we wound out of Wales (Wales!) and through the seven-mile-long Severn River tunnel, then through the dark, moonlit fields of rich-looking England in 1938. Then, in the early morning light the station masters all seemed to wear walrus moustaches and gold watch fobs over their waistcoats and there were fishmongers' carts on high wheels waiting at the station yards, the fine horses jibbing at the impatient engine; and the English folk I overheard in the train, those that I could understand, even this early talked of 'peace in our time'.

PART TWO
Tricks of the Trade

Daeth dirwnod i ffarwelio
Ag annwyl wlad y Cymro,
Gan sefyll am hen dir y Werddon fras;
Fe gododd y gwynt yn nerthol,
Y môr a'i donnau'n rhuthro,
Gan olchi dros ein llestr annwyl las,

Chorus: Dewch Gymry glan, i wrando ar fy nghân,
Fel bu y fordaith rownd yr Horn, rownd yr Horn!
Sef y trydydd dydd o'r whythnos,
Ychydig cyn y cyfnos,
Gan basio ger glân greigio glannau Môn.

(The day of sailing came around,
We were bound to leave our land of Wales,
We were heading out towards green Ireland's
    shore,
The wind was blowing out the sails,
The seas were running high, boys,
Tumbling o'er the rail with thunderous roar.

Chorus: Come, Welshmen all,
And listen to my tale,
How we sailed our schooner round the Horn,
    round the Horn!
Third day of the week it was, boys,

When dawn was just a-breaking,
We passed the rocky shores of Anglesey!)

First verse and chorus of 'Round the Horn'.

This is a capstan shanty sung on board Welsh Schooners, and on board South Georgia whalers, which often took on Welsh crews. In the whalers the second 'Rownd yr Horn' was usually bellowed in English –'Round the Horn!' The above is my translation. I have never heard it sung completely in English.

7
Ships of the Trade

In the late nineteen-thirties the number of working-sail craft on the coasts of the British Isles and Ireland was around five hundred. Their variety was great. Some were employed only in fishing; others purely in cargo-work, some in a combination of both.

Now that they are all gone it is easy to be sentimental about the working-sail craft. Many of them were beautiful things, whether at rest or under sail, and with their passing has disappeared, too, a whole way of life. It was a way of life dogged with hazards and dangers, poorly paid and leaving small profit. Very few working sailors led much better than a poverty-stricken existence. Yet the life demanded a skill, agility and toughness which few, if any, other livelihoods have called for, with the exception, perhaps, of a circus acrobat or a mountain Sherpa.

The men and youths that I was to meet during my two years in working-sail still command my utmost respect for their abilities, their competence, their honesty and their hardiness. They were probably the hardiest, and hardest-labouring, workers in the whole of the British Islands.

The variety, the build and rigs of the craft were of an astonishing individuality. I doubt if anyone ever saw two working-sail craft which were exactly the same as each other, and each craft, each skipper, each crew, had their own idiosyncrasies. Each harbour, each creek, each beach around the British and Irish coasts developed, over the centuries, its own particular type of hull; its rigging, its spars, its sails and fishing gear. The craft were rarely fancy;

there was little money to spare from meagre profits for decorations, but their honest fitness for their particular job was the core of their appeal, and bestowed on them the very spirit of their beauty. No honest sailor, looking over them, could deny that. None of the working craft ever looked 'quaint' to a sailor. For every line, every form, every curious shaped hull, spar or sail, there was a good solid reason, grounded in centuries of experience in the often tempestuous seas around the British Islands.

There were and are two kinds of construction employed in the building of wooden sailing vessels. One method, rooted in the tradition of the Vikings, is known as clinker construction. This was only used where plenty of timber was available. The other method is known as carvel construction, and stems from an ancient Mediterranean practice.

In clinker-building a 'V' shaped groove is cut into a massive wooden keel on either side, and also in the stem (bow) and stern posts, already joined to the keel. Into these grooves, to port and starboard, the first two, lowest planks of the hull (the 'garboard strakes'), are fitted. Then the other planks are added on each side, one after the other, each plank overlapping the one below it. The amount of overlap is known as the 'lands' and is proportionate to the width of the plank. When a craft ages, and gaps develop in the lands it is possible to patch these with quarter-round fillets of wood nailed along the underside of the lands.

Clinker-building, as we might expect from the Vikings, demands little calculation but a fair amount of craftsmanship, to get the shape of the hull right.

Each plank is fastened to its neighbour with copper, iron, or galvanized nails, clenched or riveted on the inboard side of the hull over washers known as roves. This job requires two men, one outboard with a hammer and the other inboard supporting the rivet-head. To hold the planks in position while they are riveted, iron clamps are used. In the old days, wooden pegs, like enormous clothes-pegs, were used.

As the shape of the boat takes form, so wooden 'floors', or beams, crossing the keel at right angles, are added. These are through-bolted to the keel with either long copper bolts or 'trenails'. Trenails were common in all types of wooden vessels in the old days. First a deep hole was made through the floor and into the keel with an auger. Then hardwood pegs, like dowels, usually of oak, were driven very close fitting into the holes. When the trenails had been driven home another hardwood wedge was driven into its top, so forcing outwards the trenail's fibres. Then, when immersed in water, the trenail expanded. A good one would stay in place for the life of the ship – sometimes as much as a hundred years, but others, with the quality of the wood or the wedge omitted by some fraudulent shipwright (they were very few), would often leave widows and orphans ashore before a year or two were out.

Slightly aft or forward of the floors, the ship's main frames are fitted. These are bent into shape in a steam-chest. Apart from tools and a winch or two, that was about the only 'capital equipment' in most of the old ship-yards.

Between the tops of the frames, athwartships, beams are added, and on to these the deck and any superstructure are fixed.

Clinker-built sailing vessels were found everywhere in Britain, except for West Devon and Cornwall. They had a lot going for them; they were simple to build and easy to repair and could stand a great deal of very rough handling both by men and the sea. The clinkered planks tended to bend before they busted.

Carvel construction demands considerably more draughtsmanship and design than clinker-building. First the keel is set up, then a series of carefully cut and shaped frames is fixed vertically on the keel. Over this rigid scaffolding a skin of planks is fixed, and then that shell is reinforced inboard by another skin of planks called a 'ceiling'. Each frame is made up of a number of pieces, and a deal of skill is required to set them up properly. Each plank butts on to the top of its neighbour, then the joint between the planks is caulked with hemp made from old rope. In the old days, after caulking the hull was completed, iron straps were added over the hull, on which to anchor the standing rigging, decks were laid, and all the other fittings, such as windlass bitts and hatch-coamings, added.

Whichever method was used, the old-time coastal ship-builders rarely made much money at construction. They made more on repairs to hulls which they had already built. In the old days, before the turn of the century, the reasons for wood-rot were not well understood and ventilation in the hulls was usually bad. The resulting repair and replacement of rotting timbers kept many an honest ship-yard going up to the Second World War, and some even

Taking a quick trip around the coasts of the British Isles in 1938, starting just north of London, and seeking only the offshore 'coastal' craft, we would have seen:

Essex Smacks, rarely more than thirty feet in length, but very beamy, and with a deep straight keel. They were all cutter rigged with a gaff main and longish bowsprit. When they were not working the oyster beds off Jersey or Holland, they were either poaching oysters from the beds on the coasts of Wales or Scotland, or hauling potatoes from France or lobsters from Norway. Of the Essex Smackmen it was said that they would steal a cargo of brimstone from the devil as long as there were two shillings to be made.

From a little further north, on the coast of Norfolk, hailed the *Lowestoft Sailing Drifters*. These were handsome vessels, with a straight stem which seemed to disdain the rough waters they pushed through and drifted over. They were about sixty feet long, and were yawl rigged, with a boomless gaff mainsail. This was so that no one, while working the fishing gear on deck, would be clouted suddenly by the boom. A peculiar thing about them was that once the fishing nets had gone over the side, the mainmast was lowered until its masthead was touching the mizzen masthead. The mainmast was then secured to the mizzen masthead, and the mizzen was reefed down as a weathercock to keep the boat's head to the wind while the vessel drifted with her nets strung out from her bow. I saw only one of these, and I think she was being used as a yacht. Modern yachts could well take their example in getting rid of top hamper in a blow.

The *Grimsby Sailing Trawlers*, again handsome craft, were about eighty feet long with a beam around twenty feet. They were ketch-rigged with a straight stem and a long, deep keel. In the hull the cod trawlers had both holds for salted fish and wet-wells for live fish. When the cod were caught their swim-bladders were punctured and they were sent down a pipe into the wet-well. In this way, if the market was down, cod could be kept alive in floating pens in harbour, to await a rise in the price of fish.

All around the south-east coast of England worked the *Billy Boys*, which were said to be the largest clinker-built craft in Europe. They were ketches, and the larger ones were rigged with a square topsail and t'gallants. They were equipped with lee boards for windward work. Their hulls were almost square in section, which allowed them to sit on a beach at low tide to discharge coal into horse-drawn carts, or load bricks, clay, manure, or whatever the cargo was.

Having so much sail and spars, they could not sail with an empty hold, and they often loaded gravel on the beaches for ballast.

The *Scottish Zulus* were lug-rigged ketches around sixty to seventy-five feet overall. Over their carvel hull they had fixed along their sides three massive iron rubbing strakes. Woe betide any other small vessel that got in the way of a Zulu! They and the Fifies were the only vessels I ever saw with horizontal steering wheels, which were set way aft in the sternsheets. When they were fishing they lowered the mainmast into a large crutch alongside the mizzenmast (again an example to modern sailors). Their massive bowsprits were set through a gammon iron and the heel of the sprit was housed close to the mainmast. Neither main nor mizzen had a boom, and both were lugsails. In 1938 there were very few Zulus about, but those that were sailed as far afield from northern Scotland as Iceland, Norway, the southern North Sea, and the English Channel. They were simply rigged, strong, seaworthy and magnificent sailors.

The *Scottish Fifies* were double-ended (that is sharp at both ends). Both the stem and stern posts were vertical when the boat was at rest in calm water – which for the Fifies was a rare occasion. The rig was a high, dipping (lowerable) lug-mainsail forward, something like an American catboat, and a smaller standing lugsail aft. Like most Scottish deep-sea fishing craft, their mainsails had six rows of reefing points, which silently told the tale of the rough seas they voyaged. Neither sail had a boom. They carried about twenty tons of stone ballast beneath the fish-holds. The frames of the hull were left about eighteen inches above deck level, and planked over. This made a bulwark (low wall) around the deck about seventeen inches high, and that was the only thing between the crew and the freezing seas. Now, in 1938, very few Fifies were fishing, those that remained of a formerly numerous fleet were engaged either in coastal cargo hauling or as yachts. The bowsprit was set to port of the stem post, as they were in all Scottish vessels and English West Country craft. English east coast vessels always carried their bowsprit to starboard of the stem. There probably was no reason for this except tradition.

On the west coast of Scotland there were still one or two *Gabberts*. These were true sailing barges, built so that their hulls conformed to the dimensions of the locks on the Clyde and Forth Canal. They were seventy feet long with a beam of twenty feet and a draught of no more than six feet. They were round-sterned and on inland waters carried a gaff sloop rig. When they ventured out to sea in the summer months (the Scottish west coast is no playground) they set a bowsprit and jib. As they were flat-bottomed and shallow draughted, they were the very devil to work to windward, and it was said that half the oaths ever heard at sea were invented on board the Gabberts.

Around Liverpool had been the haunt of the *Weaver Flats*, but by 1938 there were only two of these left. One was named *Keskadale*, but I cannot recall the name of the other. The Flats were massively built of great oak timbers. The lowest planks of the hull were of *four inch thick* rock elm. They were always carvel-built and it was said that they were so long lived (*Keskadale* was well over a hundred years old) because of the salt cargoes they hauled which preserved the timber. The biggest of the Flats were about ninety feet long, drew nine feet and loaded one hundred and seventy-five tons. They had a high peaked gaff sloop rig, with no bowsprit. The owner's colours were painted rings on the mast above the houndsbands. There were also, working from Liverpool, a couple of *Jigger Flats*, gaff-ketch rigged vessels of about ninety feet length, but by the late thirties these had been fitted with auxiliary engines, and used their sails less and less.

Mention must be made of the *Liverpool Pilot Schooner*. Although there were none left in service as Pilot boats, there were a couple still remaining as yachts. With the Bristol Channel Pilot Cutter they were probably the most efficient small sailing vessels ever devised anywhere in their time (the 1850s to the 1920s). The Liverpool Schooners, with their yellow upperworks and black trim, could hold their own with any rich man's yacht for looks, just as well as they could hold their stations at sea in any weather while waiting for ships to arrive in Liverpool Bay.

The *Morecambe Bay Prawner* was one of the most graceful fishing craft ever built. They were required to work well to windward, and yet at the same time be able to lie off quietly while their two-man crew worked the prawn nets, and they also had to be able to turn completely in their own length, which was about thirty-five feet. Their beam was nine feet and they drew about five feet aft. They were cutter rigged, with a high-peaked gaff main, a tops'l on a long yard, and a long bowsprit with no bobstay, so the fishing gear would not be fouled. The accommodation on board was so simple as to be primitive. Below, there was not even headroom enough for sitting in an upright position. Some of the prawners had a boiler on deck, and the catch was made ready for sale even as the vessel sailed home from the prawning grounds. The profile of the hull was yacht-like, with a rounded forefoot flowing into a shaped keel, ending at a steeply raking sternpost. All this made the prawners very quick indeed on the helm. They ranged as far as South Wales and Ireland. One Morecambe

Bay prawner, *Mink*, however, converted to reasonable acommodations, has made at least two circumnavigations of the world in the years since the Second World War, and I believe she was later to set out on her third. I was to see her in the Seychelles in 1970, and she would then be eighty-five years of age.

Another craft frequently sighted on the Irish Sea were the *Isle of Man Nobbys*. These were luggers with a cutter rig and were about thirty-five feet in length, not counting the longish bowsprit. They had a rounded forefoot, long, straight keel, and a lifting rudder for beaching. The Manxmen, practically all of Viking descent, were daring seamen and in their Nobbys ranged as far afield as the Shetlands in the north, the East coast of England and the West coast of Ireland, and they landed their catches and sold them wherever they could.

The *Welsh Topsail Schooners* we already know about, but a word or two on their construction. The schooners were built with a full bilge (a 'fat sectioned' hull) so that they could sit upright in dry harbours when the tide went out, and so that they could load as much cargo as possible. They usually had a wheelhouse and a small galley iron-strapped to the deck. Roller-reefing was commonly fitted on both the main and foresail booms. In 1938 three fully-rigged Welsh Topsail Schooners were still working on the British and Northern Continental coasts, while many more, with auxiliary engines and reduced sail, were also in service. They were between seventy and ninety feet long and drew about nine-and-a-half feet. Their lines and their rig, and the long voyages they made, as far afield as Newfoundland, Greece, and Argentina, and the reputation for fair treatment of the crews by their skippers, and of sobriety and cleanliness of the crews, made them the cream of Britain's smaller merchant sailing craft during the nineteenth and early twentieth centuries. Those were the good reasons that they were generally referred to as 'The Western Ocean Yachts'. Later, it would never cease to amaze me that the majority of Welsh and Welsh-descended people, to say nothing of folk of other nationalities, would have little or no idea of the great maritime exploits of Welsh sailors in the past. But in the ranks of the great mariners will be found many and many a Welsh name, as in the names of headlands, bays and straits the world around, while the entry and departure logs of practically every port in the world, large and small, bear testimony to the old Welsh sea-traffic. Wales was, is and always will be, a maritime country. How could it be otherwise, surrounded by the sea on three sides, and not one acre of the country more than forty or so miles from salt water?

From far away on the West coast of Ireland came the *Galway Hookers.* These were to last until well into the 1960s. They were smack rigged, with a high-peaked gaff main and a dumpy-looking staysail. The bowsprit was carried to starboard of the stem post. They had a rounded forefoot and long straight keel. They were generally larch planking on sawn oak frames and the crews were usually two men, or one man and a boy. As the western Irish harbours all dry out, the sides of the hookers had a 'tumble-home' (they curved inwards at the top) so that the vessel could conveniently lean against the dock when the tide went out. The mast was heavy and short, and supported by one shroud (wire) either side. The mainsail was loosely laced to the mast. They were no more than forty feet long and drew about six feet. The word hooker is derived from the ancient Mediterranean lingua-franca word 'urca', and means a small, far-ranging, fore-and-aft-rigged maid-of-all-work vessel of jaunty appearance, (which might also explain the common usage of the word 'hooker' in the United States).

In the west of England, off the mouth of the River Severn, worked the *Severn Trows*. In 1938 there were only a couple of these vessels, the direct descendants of a medieval type, remaining. They were ketches and carried a long bowsprit which was cocked up at an angle of about twenty degrees from the horizontal. They were gaff-rigged ketches and carried a tops'l in fair weather. Their cargo holds were never, for some reason which to me is unfathomable, covered. They were about seventy feet long with a beam of seventeen feet and a draught of six feet. Some of the Trows, to improve their sailing qualities, had a removable keel about two feet deep, which was fixed into position by means of chains. In 1938, the oldest Trow afloat and working was *William of Gloucester*. She was built in 1808!

From the Severn Sea hailed a type of vessel which, for sea-keeping ability and ease of working, is known and has been acclaimed the world over. This was the *Bristol Channel Pilot Cutter*. They were reputedly the first sailing vessels ever to have roller reefing and self-draining cockpits. Those two amenities, along with self-steering gear, have been probably the greatest advances of safety and ease in sail-voyaging since the first hull was ever launched. Although, by 1938, there were no Pilot Cutters still at work waiting to transfer pilots to arriving ships, there were quite a few of them which had been converted to cargo carrying, and they worked all the coasts of Britain, the Channel Islands and Northern Europe. The largest of them were sixty feet long. Their size had been limited by the size of their crew. When the pilot had boarded his ship there were only two men, or one man and a boy, to sail the craft home to port. The main features of their hulls were the high bows and freeboard. They had a rounded forefoot and a long straight keel, and their ballast was shipped inside the hull, amidships, usually, although some of the later-built vessels had ballast built into their keels. The great quality of the Bristol Channel Pilot Schooners was their more than excellent sea-keeping abilities. They could ride winter storms for days hove-to (stopped), head against the sea, with an easy motion that made an otherwise burdensome life a little more tolerable for their crews. As the Pilot Cutters were usually sailed by one man on deck at a time, the sailing rig had to be simple. The topmast was short and so could stay aloft in the hardest blows.

The last of the working Bristol Channel Pilot Cutters was to be still hauling cargo around the English Channel into the 1960s. She had been built in 1904. It was fitting that her name, *Cariad*, should be Welsh for 'Sweetheart', and that she should be seeing out her days in the Exeter Maritime Museum.

Another English west coast bred craft was the *Falmouth Quay Punt*, whose lines were copied, and still are, to some extent, by designers of modern, ocean-going sailing yachts. The punts originated as ferry craft to the big square-riggers lying off Falmouth harbour. For this reason their masts were short, so that they would not foul the gear of the bigger ships when the punt lay alongside. With the coming of steamships, competition for the ferry-work became so brisk that the punts, now built up to thirty feet long, had to go out far to sea to seek incoming ships. The hulls, as in many Cornish craft, had a greater beam aft of amidships and a sharp bow. The keels were rockered (that is it sloped down from the bow to the middle of the keel, and then horizontal from there to the stern). The ballast was all carried in the outside keel, as it is in modern yachts. The punts had a low-aspect gaff-yawl rig and the mizzen mast was set just forward of the transom. The tiller had a 'U' bend in it so it could work around the mizzen. Normally the mizzen was of 'leg-o'-mutton' (or 'Bermuda') shape, but sometimes a large standing lugsail was carried. In the late thirties there were still many punts in use as fishing craft and for taking out tourists, and quite a number of them had been built as yachts.

Also from Cornwall came another type of craft which was seen all around the coasts of Britain. This was the *East Cornish Lugger*. They were built with very sharp bows, so that they could poke their way into the tiny, crowded harbours of east Cornwall more easily. For this reason they also had massive wooden rubbing strakes along their sides. The hulls had to be very strongly built for the boats pounded on the harbour ground every time the tide went out and came in. They were the only sailing craft that, as the weather deteriorated, substituted the mainsail with the mizzensail simply by lowering the main, stowing it, and shifting the mizzensail to the mainmast. Then a smaller mizzensail was hoisted aft. Often in fair weather, they hoisted a mizzen topsail. The ballast that the East Cornish Luggers carried was inboard and loose. When they went to windward the three-man crew shifted the ballast to the windward side of the hull, so that they could keep as much sail clapped on as possible. They also carried a jolly-boat, and when they were headed home on a fast passage they filled this with seawater and rigged that also on the windward side as additional ballast. The Cornishmen were renowned for their seamanship and fast passages. One occasion in 1910 three Luggers made the voyage, in ballast, from Mount's Bay, Cornwall, to the fishing grounds off Scarborough Head, Yorkshire, six hundred miles, in seventy hours. That was an average speed of about seven knots; not at all bad for vessels only thirty feet in length, and especially in those seas.

In 1938 there were about twenty-five *Brixham Trawlers* working around the Northern European waters. Many of these gaff ketches were still fishing, but a few had been converted to cargo-carrying. They were about seventy-five feet in length, eighteen feet beam, and drew eleven feet, and they were built with a sweeping sheer (a lovely convex curve of the deck from the bow aft). The stern post was raked and the transom was elliptical. The masts had a forward rake, which made them appear at first sight a bit drunken, but this was to make the luff (forward edge) of the sails 'bite' better into the wind. One of these fine vessels, *Provident*, was to be still trading into the mid-sixties, and later was to be restored to her fishing condition by the Maritime Trust.

Also from Devon and Cornwall came the *West Country Barges*, though the few that remained in the late thirties were mostly fitted with auxiliary engines, but they still carried a decent spread of sail. They were gaff-rigged cutters which often hoisted a topsail. Their length was fifty feet, and their beam about sixteen feet, while they drew no more than seven feet. They had sharp bows and a good run aft to a shallow (low) transom. The stem raked forward, the stern post raked aft, and the forefoot was rounded, while the keel was straight.

There were more than twenty *West Country Trading Ketches* working in the late thirties. These were built all over south-west England and in South Wales, too. They were often to be seen, in my early youth on the open beaches of North and Mid-Wales, and in the harbour at Barmouth between tides, off-loading coal or loading hay or sacks of grain. They were gaff-rigged ketches, which carried both main and mizzen topsails and three jibs as well as a staysail. Some of them regularly crossed the Atlantic Ocean on the Newfoundland fish trade, and others made occasional voyages to the continent of Europe, but most of them coasted the British Isles. All the sails were small enough to be har¹led by a master and mate, or two men and a boy. Most of them had roller reefing on the main, and some on the mizzen, too. The gaff topsails were set from the deck on a jackstay and they were fitted at the head with a long yard. They were not comfortable vessels for their crews; the cooking was done in the poky fo'c's'le and there was no shelter on deck of any kind from the elements.

From the waters north of the Isle of Wight came the *Itchen Ferry Boats*. These were gaff-rigged cutters, which hoisted a topsail in good weather. They were about thirty feet long and very beamy for their length. They had deep keels as they could lay to moorings in sheltered waters. Their fishermen–owners worked in the summer seasons as yacht skippers, so that the Ferries had to be small enough to lay up for the summer and be easily prepared again for the winter fishing season. Competitiveness is the very heart and soul of yacht racing, and this rubbed off on the Itchen Ferry fishermen. The hulls were carvel-built, of red pine planking, copper-fastened in oak frames and all the wood in the ship was soaked in linseed oil before it was painted. Many of the Ferries were converted to yachts in the years between the wars, and one of them, *Fanny*, built in 1872, was still to be cruising as a yacht in the early 1980s. Some of the Solent area fishing smacks were the first British working vessels to be fitted with centre-boards, for working their way to windward more efficiently.

Also in the Solent area was the range of the *Cowes Ketches*, although by the late thirties most of them had been fitted with auxiliary engines. They were carvel-built and double ended. Their draught was shallow, to enable them to ascend the tiny creeks of the Isle of Wight and the mainland opposite, to pick up and discharge cargoes. Both the main and the mizzen were long in proportion to their height. This was to maintain a low sail profile in consideration of the shallow draught (to lessen the risk of a capsize in high wind). One of them, *Bee*, still working in 1938, was built in 1801!

Around the River Thames and the Thames Estuary worked the *Spritsail Barges*. These were to be the very last of all the sea-going commercial sailing craft of Northern Europe. (There were still to be some afloat in 1982.) They are solidly built between forty and ninety feet long, and (most important of all) they can be worked by a crew of two. This is made possible by the spritsail rig. The large mainsail practically always remains hoisted aloft and it is furled by means of brails, which draw the sail up the mast, like drawing a curtain. The sprit boom also allows the topsail to remain set when the main is furled, thus enabling the vessel to be manoeuvred under a minimum of sail. Both main and mizzensails are sheeted to a horse (a rail across the deck) which allows the sails to go about (shift from one tack to the other) without needing to be handled by the crew. The heel of the bowsprit is set in a tabernacle (a frame with a hinge in it) so that it may be steeved (raised) up vertically when the vessel is entering a crowded dock. Both main and mizzenmasts are set in tabernacles so that they may be lowered when passing under bridges. A century ago the Spritties could be counted in their thousands. In the late thirties their number was around fifty or so. Their main trade was farm supplies, to the farms up the creeks of East Anglia, bricks up into London, and stone from Portland in Dorset, to towns and cities all over south-eastern England. They were able to carry up to two hundred tons of cargo. All the Spritties were fitted with lee-boards (that is outside keels on hinges, which could be raised and lowered over the side), and iron winches on the quarters to handle the lee-boards. Spritties were built in a simple, box-like section, with a few grown oak frames or 'crooks'. They were all flat-bottomed and the biggest ones drew around eight feet loaded, four feet unloaded. When they set off on a coastal trip the Spritties winched on board a box-galley (kitchen) which was lashed down on deck. The food on board was none too special as they escaped the Board of Trade regulations for sea-going craft. Most of their skippers had no certificate of any kind at all. But in the estuarial craft these two disadvantages were not grave. Their sailing range was short and usually bicycles were taken along so that the skipper and mate could go back home in the evening for a good supper and a couple of pints with their pals in their own 'local'. On the coastal barges, however, the disadvantages were telling. There was no escaping bad food and a bad skipper once beyond the North Foreland or the Naze and out into the rough open waters. For many a young lad before me, especially those from poor families, or families with no connections, or no family at all, a berth on a Sprittie was the usual second step in advancement in a life at sea. The first step was, by rights, either a Stumpie, a Bawley or a Mulie.

The least glamorous cargoes in the Thames Estuary, the garbage and muck from a metropolis of eight million souls, was carried out to sea by the *Stumpie Barges*. They also hauled the dull, dirty bulk freight such as timber or cement from the ocean-steamers to the building sites around the Thames tide-waters and explosives from and to the munitions factories up the River Lee and at Woolwich. They were the 'maids of all work'. The crew of two were nearly always Cockneys and they could be recognized by their corduroy trousers tied with string at the knee and red neckerchiefs.

The Stumpies were so-called because they had no top-mast. Practically every trip for them was above river bridges, which meant lowering the mast; awkward with a topmast and all its tackle. The Stumpies always worked within tidal range, so they moved to the tide's orders and thus the lack of the tops'l was not too great a loss. The Stumpies carried a peculiar diminutive mizzen, the mast being stepped on the rudder-head. They were, however, despite the mundane cargoes, fancy craft in which their owners took a great deal of pride, much of which came from the fact that a Stumpie's sprit was proportionately longer than the Sprittie's. The hulls were always brightly painted and the transom decorated, sometimes even in gold-leaf. The average length was thirty-five feet, with a beam of around fifteen feet, and they all carried lee-boards.

There were the fishing craft; the *Medway Dobles* and the *Thames Bawleys* whose name came from the boiler they used to carry on deck to cook the catches of shrimp so it would keep its savour until they reached the mooring and market. Hard craft and hard, smelly work.

Last, but not least by any means, there were the *Mulies* and the *Boomies*. Both were ketch-rigged barges. The Mulie, which coast-traded between the Humber and the Isle of Wight, say two hundred miles in either direction from the Thames Estuary, was a bastard rig born of combining a spritsail barge and a ketch. Thus the sprit-main enabled two men and a boy to handle the rig. The main difference between the Mulie and the Boomie ketch, however, was that the Boomie had its mainmast stepped on the keelson in the manner of a sea-faring ship, and this made all the difference in the world, both to the Boomie ketch's crew's attitude to their ship and to the Board of Trade's attitude to the Boomie.

Whereas the Spritties and the Mulies were confined to

the coastal trade, the Boomies were granted certificates to trade 'foreign'. Their skippers were examined for certificates (by 1935) and the conditions of work and welfare were beginning to be regulated by the Government; but only just beginning.

The ketch-barge *Second Apprentice* was a Dandy, as the Boomies were alternatively, and more commonly, called. I was lucky; instead of having to work my way up from the Bawleys or the Stumpies, through the Spritties I was going directly on to a foreign-going Dandy ketch. Dad had found me a berth in one of the aristocrats of British working sail!

These, though I knew little about it at the time – only a few scraps of information picked up from some of Dad's sailor-visitors – were the main material components of the peculiar world that I was entering. These were the ships of the Trade.

8
Second Apprentice

The night train from South Wales to London stopped at only one or two places – they must have been Swindon and Reading, middling sized towns, but to me, a small boy with his face pressed to the steamy carriage window, staring at the lamp glow and at all the bustle on the platforms, they seemed to be sprawling and enormous, with more people about than I had ever seen in one place before.

Various people alighted at the first stop, and a lady – she seemed very rich and beautiful – came into my compartment with her two children, a boy and a girl, both better dressed than me, of course, but a little younger. In the English fashion, they sat in silence for a while; then the boy asked me if I was going to London. He spoke refined English, like the BBC announcers on the wireless, so it was not too difficult for me to understand him.

'Ssh,' said his mother, flustered and embarrassed. There were a couple of other people in the compartment, silent, hugging their Englishness.

'No, it's to Reeya I'm going,' said I, and showed the boy my ticket, which I'd stowed in the pencil pocket of my jacket. The boy looked at me nonplussed for a moment, trying to make out what I had said, then he turned and looked up at the beautiful lady and said 'Oh, mother, I think he's a foreigner.'

His mother smiled at me. There was silence for a few minutes except for the noises of the train, then she delved into her bag and brought out three red shiny apples. She gave one each to her children, then reached across with her gloved hand and offered one to me. I took it, surprised by her generosity and awed by her beauty, but I was so astonished that I thanked her in Welsh – '*diolch*' – at which her smile broadened wider. '*Il n'y a pas de tout*,' she replied softly. As I'd eaten all the food Mam had given me, I took the apple along the corridor, and ate it outside the toilet, but by the time I returned to my compartment the lady and her brood had left the train at Reading station.

In the morning-light the train seemed to take forever to pass through the western suburbs of London and it was all I could manage to notice each house, each building, each bridge, and street as we flashed by.

I was staggered. I knew, from what Jeffreys-Geography had taught us at school, that there were eight million people in London, but numbers spouted in a one-room school are vastly different to the abodes of hundreds of thousands of human beings, row after row, street after street. By the time the train arrived in Paddington Station my head was in a whirl. A host of passengers left the train and hurried by me to the ticket barrier, but I was too busy staring at the great heaving steam engine and silently hero-worshipping the driver and his fireman to notice them.

Suddenly, amid the hissing of the engine and the clouds of steam emitting from its cylinders, and the dull thrum of noise from the huge station all around, there was a voice at my side. I turned around and there was a policeman. He was not a big, burly, elderly man like Williams the Police back home, nor did he have a bicycle. This one was a young man and thin. 'Going somewhere, lad?' he asked pleasantly.

'Reeya,' said I, and dug in my pocket for my ticket while the policeman waited, his brow furrowed quizzically. He read my ticket and grinned. 'From South Wales, eh?' he asked me.

'No. Merioneth, but I caught the train in Newport.'

'Did you now? Well, I'm from Llantrisant myself. Come on, I'll show you the way to the tube. You have to go to Charing Cross . . .'

'*Fe allai siarad Cymraeg.*' I told him I spoke Welsh.

'Can you? I understand some, but I can't speak a word of it,' he replied.

Although the underground train was a frightening wonder to me as it flashed through London far below street level, I felt much better. There really were Welshmen in England. I was not all alone among the *Sais*.

The journey through Kent and Sussex seemed to take almost as long as the one from Newport to London. Even though the distance was nowhere near as long. In the morning light I peered through the windows at the fields and hedgerows and rich-looking, tidy houses. It seemed to me that in England everything had been put together very carefully and precisely. Compared to this the houses and barns in West Wales were a memory of scraps thrown down higgledy-piggledy by a careless God, jealous of the beauty of our hills. The few acres of arable, rich land that He had bestowed on us were merely a small repayment for our singing. Why, one square mile of Sussex fields seemed more rich than the whole county of Merioneth. There were no rocky outcrops to be seen, no barren uplands, no abandoned farms or cottages, but there wasn't much of the unintended, untended, fierce beauty of Wales, which is beauty in its true state.

Here, in England, the skies were the same blue as in Wales; the clouds the same shape, yet there was something different about the skies. There was not the lightening of shades of blue to silver on the horizon, nor did the clouds have the same sinister darkness of shadow on their undersides. The English clouds slid along; the Welsh ones had *charged*.

Finally, after one or two changes of train – I forget how many – I arrived in Rye and stepped forth from the tiny railway station, shouldered my sea-bag and, after asking directions from the ticket-collector, made my way along the High Street. Almost immediately I spied the top masts of four vessels. As I drew nearer I saw that two of the vessels in the river, further downstream, were upright, floating on the tide in the narrow creek, and two were keeled over at angles, where they had not yet taken the tide.

Folk of whom I asked directions were, it seemed to me, fresh as I was from West Wales, somewhat off-handed, but they replied kindly enough even though it was very difficult for me at first to understand their Sussex drawl. In West Wales a stranger would have been escorted to his or her destination, if only for the sake of a chat on the way.

It's all a long time ago and men have visited the moon, and here I am remembering the cobblestones of Rye quay, and how tufts of grass grew around the bases of the big iron bollards, and the old cast iron mooring posts made from ship's cannons, and a horse-drawn cart loading up with crates of bottled mineral water, and my first sight of the 'Dandy' ketch, *Second Apprentice*.

She was one of the two craft which were listing against the quay walls at a slight angle, high and dry above the tide and all about her hovered the smell of the sweat of the sea – the yeasty odour of corruption and new creation which salt water reveals every time the tide retreats at the bidding of the moon. Her port lee-board, a great wood and iron forging eighteen feet long and eight feet broad at the fan, was drawn up to her gunwale. She was just under a hundred feet long and her bowsprit stuck out another twenty feet further. As I lugged my sea-bag towards her,

my eyes strayed upwards. Her main and maintop masts
made a total height of about seventy feet above the deck.
The standing rigging seemed, to my unaccustomed eyes, to
be a veritable jungle of cables, ropes and ratlines. Her
mizzenmast was about forty feet high. On her stern hung a
drooping red ensign, almost black with grime.

I reached the edge of the quay and wearily dropped my
sea-bag on to the paving stones beneath my feet. I looked
at the work going on. The gangway on to *Second Apprentice*
was no more than a plank, about six inches wide and two
inches thick, down which crates of empty bottles were
being slid to the deck of the vessel. The shore-side part of
the operation consisted of a brewer's dray-type cart, a black
and white shire stallion with great hairy fetlocks over feet
as big as soup-plates, an old man atop the cart handing
down the crates, and a young lad with tow hair, a bit older
than I, sliding the crates down the plank.

I left my sea-bag where it was and approached the lad.
The stallion gave a sudden start and twitched flies with its
tail.

'Good day,' said I.

'Wot cheer, come to work, then?' The tow haired lad
stopped work, straightened up, and grinned at me. He was
an inch or so taller than me. His eyes were deep blue and
two of his front teeth were missing. He stared, grinning at
me for a second, then hunched his shoulders, braced his
arms, and set to sliding down crates again still grinning to
himself.

I stood there for a short while, as the lad slid the last of
this load of crates down the plank to a man on deck, who in
turn swung them over and stacked them on top of a net
suspended from above by a rope from the end of the gaff,
which was being used as a derrick. The man on deck was,
at a wild guess, around forty-five years old. He was small

and dark, with a complexion the colour of a roasted chestnut. He sported a black, bushy walrus moustache and wore a flat cap, an every-day jacket over a collarless shirt, corduroy trousers tied with string just below the knees, and boots. He peered at me through the smoke from a cigarette stuck in the corner of his mouth.

The old man on the cart said, 'Got a good berth there, son,' flicked his whip at the stallion and took off along the jetty at a good clip. The stallion was surprisingly agile and fast, considering his tremendous size. As he started to heave the cart his hooves slipped a little on the paving flags, and tiny sparks flew from his massive iron horse-shoes. It reminded me of a knife being sharpened on a grindstone.

The tow haired lad jerked me out of my moment's reverie. 'Wanna go aboard then, mate?'

I plonked my sea-bag down on the plank. It slid down to the deck. The little dark man with the walrus moustache grabbed it and winked at me. 'You must be the Taffy, right, son?' he said. 'The new nipper?'

'That's right, sir.' I teetered my way down the plank and landed on deck alongside the little dark man, who grabbed me. He saw I was on my feet, then he let me go.

'Take your gear forr'd, right?' he ordered. 'There's some tea in the galley. My name's Bert and I'm the mate on board this here ship. Tansy's . . . the captain's having a kip.' He thumbed aft. 'He'll be up when we finish getting this here little lot on board and stowed away down in the bloo . . . blummin hold, right?'

'Right, sir . . . er . . .' I started to say something.

The mate chimed in, 'Don't you "sir" me, Nipper. My name's Bert, right?'

'Right, Bert.'

'Right, Nipper, and when you've stowed your gear I'll

show you where everything is in the galley, right?'

'Right, Bert.'

'Right, Nipper, so now, off you go, on your toes, my son, and make yourself at home, right?'

'Right.'

'Right what?'

'Oh . . . right, Bert.'

'Right, Nipper, now you go up forr'd as fast as Chri . . . as your feet will let you, and get settled in, right?'

'Right, Bert.'

'Good lad!' Bert turned again to slinging the crates of bottles down into the hold. As I went forward I heard him mutter, 'Blummin youngsters . . . no idea . . .'

I made my way forward along the deck, a bit daunted by the seeming complexity of the tackle all around. The mainmast, where it went through the deck, was of immense girth, like a full grown tree. I saw the scuttle hatchway down to the fo'c's'le, threw my sea-bag down it, and followed it down into the gloom below.

When my eyes became accustomed to the dim light, I found that the fo'c's'le crew's quarters were a triangular space about twenty-one feet across at its widest, furthest aft. At its longest, amidships, it was about twelve feet in span. There were wooden berths, two on each side, with a big wooden drawer below each berth. In the middle of the triangular space was set a big shiny black coal-stove with its chimney going straight up through the deckhead (roof). Around the base of the stove there were four horizontal brass rails, one above the other, about a foot apart. These, I was to find out later, were for drying wet clothes. From the deckhead hung a large brass lamp with a green glass shade about eighteen inches in diameter. I was to get to know the fo'c's'le, the lamp and the stove intimately in the coming months. It was to be one of my chores to clean them daily, regardless of the weather, come hell or high water.

Only one of the berths seemed to be obviously occupied, so I unpacked my sea-bag and stowed my clothes neatly in the drawer under the port-side after berth. Then, that done, I took another look around the fo'c's'le. It was all very plain and simple – almost stark – with the rough-hewn timbers of the ship's side and bulkheads fore and aft as the only decoration. It was, however, very clean and tidy, with everything painted white, except for the sole (floor) which was scrubbed. I was soon to get to know that sole very well, too, every square inch of it.

The only daylight that penetrated into the fo'c's'le was what came down through the open scuttle (hatchway). In the day-times, when work was afoot on deck and the fo'c's'le lamp was not lit, it was a gloomy place.

Having packed my changes of clothes away and changed my boots for the canvas deck-slippers which Cei Powell had made for me, I clambered up the hatchway and emerged again on deck out into the afternoon sunlight. I headed aft along the deck towards the galley. This was little more than a wooden box, about six feet by five, and six feet high, strapped to the deck by iron bands.

As I reached the galley door another load of crates had arrived on the quay and Bert was again busy lugging them on board and swinging them down in the net into the dark hold below. I looked down into the hold over the hatch-coamings and saw a cavernous, gloomy space as big as the chapel hall back in Llangareth. It was almost full of closely stacked crates. Stacking them in the gloaming below was a tall, lanky lad of about eighteen. He wore neither shirt nor shoes; only a pair of black mole-skin trousers. Under the dust and straw his hair was fair in the English way. As I gazed at him, he suddenly looked up and stopped work, puffing heavily. 'Wot cheer, cock?' His grin almost split his

face in two. 'You the new nipper, then? My name's Ted.' I
had to listen very carefully to him to be able to understand
what he said. As it was, I must have looked so puzzled that
he repeated his greeting twice.

'Hello . . .' I stood there gazing down at Ted until Bert
broke in, 'Stowed your gear then, Nipper?'

'Yes sir, I've . . .'

'Bert.'

'Oh . . . sorry, sir . . . Bert, I've . . . I've taken the port
after berth . . .'

'Where's your working gear, son?'

'Oh, it's all right . . . Bert, I've stowed that, too . . .'

'Have you indeed? Stowed it away have you, Nipper?
Well, you just trot back down to the fo'c's'le and put it on,
right? There's work to be done, and look quick about it!
Tansy'll be along any minute and if he misses this blummin
tide there'll be all hell let loose! Now get a move on,
f'Crissake, we want our blinkin' tea! Right?'

'Oh . . . right . . . er . . . right, Mister Bert!' I fell back to
rush my way forward and below.

'Nipper!' Bert's cry brought me up all standing.

'Yes, sir?'

'I've told you . . . my name's Bert. Now, no more of that
highfalutin' nonsense! *Right?*'

'Right, Bert!' I flung myself forward and down the
hatchway. In three minutes or less I was dressed in my
khaki cotton shirt and bib-and-brace overalls. I made my
way self-consciously back to Bert. As I walked along the
deck I gazed across the river. A little 'stumpie' barge
leaning against the far bank, her decks deserted, lay so still
that she seemed to sleep profoundly, wrapped in a hay-
scented mantle of soft sunlight and silence, her furled sails
like closed eyes.

Bert saw me looking at the 'stumpie' barge. 'She's

waiting for a load of bricks tomorrow. Her blokes are both
at the local, having a pint,' he said, somewhat regretfully.
Then he grinned at me, sizing me up in my overalls.
'That's better, Nipper, nice and ship-shape now, right?' he
said quietly as he led me into the tiny galley. Inside, the
first thing that caught my eye was a big oblong stove, on
the starboard side, all shiny and black with polish, with a
coal-fire glowing in the centre hearth. Everything in the
galley was spotlessly clean, except where some fine grey ash
had fallen out of the grate into the metal ash-pan in the
hearth. On the forward and after sides of the galley there
were port-holes with brightly polished brass frames. The
cooking pans were stowed with their handles stuck down
behind horizontal wooden battens around the forward side
of the galley. Beneath the pans was a potato box to one
side, a vegetable box and a flour bin in the middle, and an
iron coal-box on the other side. Along the port side, beside
the galley door, was a long wooden work-bench, its top
dead-white and worn with decades of scrubbing. Above
and below the table were cupboards for canned and bottled
foodstuffs. Bert opened the cupboard doors. 'And make
sure you always stow the tins and bottles with their labels
showing, and the right side up, right?'

'Right, Bert.'

'Good, now we'll have a cup of tea, then, when you've
cleared up after that, you can give us a hand with the cargo.
We've got to catch the tide tonight, right, Nipper?'

'When can I see the captain, Bert?' I asked nervously, as
I filled the gallon kettle with water from the hand pump by
the zinc sink.

'Who . . .? Oh, Tansy will be around in a while, don't
you fret, Nipper.' Even as Bert said this a voice, deep and
gruff, rang out from somewhere down aft. '*Bert!*'

'Talk about the devil . . . there he is now!' muttered

Bert. 'Yes, Tansy,' he hallooed.

'Where the dickens . . .?' The gruff voice muttered loudly, 'The new nipper on board yet?' I heard the sound of purposeful footsteps treading the deck, coming nearer.

'In the galley, Tansy!' crowed Bert. 'Yes, he's here turned to . . .' Bert clapped one hand on my shoulder as I stood back from placing the heavy kettle on the stove top. He was a small man, not much taller than I, but his strength nearly knocked the breath out of my body. It was like being cracked with a snapped steel cable.

'Where?' the gruff voice asked again. The footsteps approached the galley door. The sound was closely followed by the captain of *Second Apprentice*, Albert Edward Lee, Esquire. He stood in the sunshine just outside the galley doorway, bathed in golden light.

At first I couldn't see the captain clearly, but when my eyes accustomed themselves to the glow around him he looked much younger than he actually was. He appeared to be about in his mid-fifties, but I later found that he was, in fact, *seventy-two*.

'Come on out here, Nipper, I want to have a word with you,' the captain ordered in a much less gruffy tone. I stepped outside, and the captain walked aft along the deck a little way, his hands clasped together behind his back. He had a sailor-man's gait, a sort of stiff roll, when he walked. When he turned and stood still, he held his body erect, his feet slightly apart as if he were bracing himself to his ship's movement. His head was lowered, so that he gazed at me from under his dark bushy brows. As I neared him he lifted and lowered one eyebrow. A suspicion of a smile played around his lips. As he stood gazing at me in silence for a few seconds, I, in turn studied him. He was about five feet ten inches tall, and at first to me looked skinny, until I realized later that his body was all muscle. His hair, what I

could see of it under his bowler hat, was black, streaked
with silver. His eyes were a piercing, startling green, deep-
set under bushy eyebrows. His nose was prominent, the
bridge laced with tiny blue veins, and his complexion was a
tanned reddish-brown. He wore full salt-and-pepper
coloured whiskers around his face, but no moustache. He
wore his shore-side suit of blue serge, jacket, waistcoat and
trousers and in his waistcoat pocket was stuck the stem of a
short clay pipe and a heavy gold watch fob. His shirt was
blue and white striped with a white celluloid collar, from
which hung a narrow black tie. His feet were shod in black,
highly shined boots, almost as shiny as the ancient suit he
wore. In his jacket breast pocket was tucked an off-white
handkerchief which looked as if it had been stuck there for a
month of Sundays. He removed his hands from behind his
back. They were like steel fox-traps, but their movement
was gentle.

'Hmm,' said the captain, after he had given me a full
twenty-seconds look-over. 'And how was your trip, son?'

'Very good, Captain . . .' I didn't know what else to say
for a moment, then I went on, 'I slept very well on the
train, well, for a while . . . and a lady gave me an apple . . .'
I tapered off, feeling embarrassed and childish. I reminded
myself to try to keep the tone of my voice low.

The captain smiled more broadly. 'An apple, eh? Well
now, that was nice of the lady.' He thought for a moment
or two, then he said, 'I hope as how you thanked her, son?'
Then, without waiting for my reply he shot a quick glance
over my shoulder at Bert, who was standing behind me.
'You shown the nipper around, Bert?' he demanded.

'Yes, well, leastways round the galley,' replied the mate.

'Good, good.' The captain's green eyes returned to mine.
I felt as though I had been jolted. 'Now, son,' he said in a
low confidential tone, 'Your father and me have been

friends for a long time, and if you behaves yourself and does your best you're going to get on a treat on board my ship. It's a lot of work, and at first you won't see much sense in some of it; but stick at it and you'll learn a lot.'

'Yes, sir . . .' I muttered.

'You'll learn more on this blooming ship than you ever thought of at school. It's a bit rough and ready at times and it's not always cakes and ale, but it's a good honest steady trade and it'll go on for a long while yet, because we can get to places where the steamers can't . . .' Captain Lee thought for a second, his eyes straying up to the rigging. Then he added, 'Or where it ain't worth their while to go.' He was silent then.

I thought he was waiting for some response from me. 'Yes, sir,' I said, dutifully.

The captain clapped his hand on my shoulder. It was a gentle movement, but his grip was like a vice-lock. 'Right,' said he, 'now off you go and give Bert and Ted a hand.'

'Yes, sir.' I turned to take my leave.

The captain's voice, still low, stopped me in my tracks. 'Just a minute, son.'

I turned around and faced him.

'You know the wages for makee-learners?' He didn't wait for an answer. 'Seven shillings a week and all found and a new set of working clothes every St Martin's Day?'

'Yes, sir, and Saturday afternoons and Sundays off, my Dad said . . .'

'When we're in harbour, Nipper, when we're in harbour,' he corrected me and turned to go ashore. As he stepped on to the gangplank he hesitated and again called back to me, 'Nipper!'

I was still busy watching him mount the narrow plank. 'Yes, sir?'

'When we're in harbour in *England* . . . don't want any of

them foreigners . . .' he stopped, then continued. 'My
name's Albert, and some people ashore call me Captain and
so will you when we're ashore, but my friends and my crew
call me Tansy. On board you call me that. Then I'll know
who you're talking to . . .' He tailed off and seemed to be
thinking of something else. 'Ted!' he bawled, after a few
seconds.

There was no reply. 'TED!' Now the captain's voice was
as loud as Bardsey Island fog-horn. Ted's muffled reply
came up from the dark cargo-hold.

Tansy hollered. 'We've got a nice leg of lamb for supper!
Nip'll give you a hand with it if you show him how. Get
supper up early, lad. We wants to be out on the tide!' This
last as Tansy walked up the shaky, six inch wide loading
plank as sure footed as a steeple-jack of a quarter of his age.

'Right, Tansy,' shouted Ted from the murky depths
below, then he called me. 'Come on, Nipper, give us a
hand with these bleedin' crates!'

'It's all right,' said Bert's voice behind me. 'You go and
make the tea, Nipper. I'll give Ted a hand. Give us a yell
when tea's ready.'

Later, when I'd cleared away everything in the galley, I
went out on deck with Ted and Bert, and clambered over
the hatch-coamings and down the ladder. Stacking the
crates was back-breaking labour for a none-too-big lad of
almost fourteen, but I was happy. I was in a ship among
friendly folk, and we were to sail with the tide. For the next
hour or two Llangareth was completely out of mind, at
least for the time being. While I made better acquaintance
of my new shipmates, down in the dusty, smelly hold in the
half-dark, and grunted over crates of empty mineral water
bottles, I completely forgot the pain of leaving Mam and
Angharad, Caradoc and Cei, Blind Sioni and Goodness
Gracious. The hills of Wales sang sadly to me no more for

a blessed while, and I was for a while no longer sick for my old home. Such is a boy's way.

By the time all the cargo of bottles were on board it was almost dusk topsides. Dusty and dirty, with sore hands from handling so many crates, and with an aching back, I clambered up the ladder out of the hold. Both Ted and Bert were already washing themselves in salt water which they had bucketed over the side from the incoming tide.

A few minutes later, refreshed a little, it was time to go into the galley with Ted, and peel potatoes and swedes, carrots and onions, while he set up the leg of lamb for roasting. While the meat was cooking Ted took me below to what he called 'the skipper's lobby'. This was another living space, smaller than the crew's quarters forward, but much more comfortably appointed. On each side of a narrow sort of hallway, wherein was the dining table, there were two small cabins, one for the captain and one for the mate. Here again there was a small coal-stove, black with brass trimmings, another hanging lamp, brass with a glass shade, and also a skylight with brass protection rods above and below it. The panelled bulkheads were of some tropical timber, and varnished. There was a brass ship's clock on the forward bulkhead. At each end of the table was a padded chair fixed to the sole, and along one side was a plain wooden bench. 'This is where we eat,' said Ted, as he set the table for supper. 'All muck in together, see?'

The only time I can remember when we had any kind of relaxation that evening, was when Ted and I sat outside the galley for a few minutes while the roast cooked, and over supper.

Tansy came back on board just after dark with his sailing orders sticking out of his jacket pocket. Soon after we all ate at the big table in the skipper's lobby. As Ted and I dished out the meal and sat down to eat, the oil-lamp over

the table just started to budge as the ship's hull responded
to the incoming tide. Tansy sat at the head of the table,
furthest from the companionway ladder and facing it; Bert
sat opposite him at the other end of the table. Ted and I sat
on the bench. Ted, being the senior of us two deck-hands,
sat next to Tansy and I sat next to Bert. Every evening
meal on board *Second Apprentice*, when she was in harbour
or at anchor, was taken so, in the small space between
Tansy's and Bert's cabins. Tansy said grace before we
started to eat, and Bert kept us laughing during the meal,
with his tales of all kinds of scrapes he'd been in through
his thirty-six years at sea.

But that first night aboard *Second Apprentice*, at supper,
although I must have been famished with hunger, I could
hardly eat for excitement, though I tried to hide it. The
captain, the mate and Ted all ate their food heartily and
swigged down their tea, and helped themselves to second
rounds. After that they soon tucked down a whole six-inch-
deep, foot-wide plum duff, but I could not finish my first
plate.

'Not much appetite, Nipper,' Tansy observed.

'No, sir, I . . . I ate on the train . . .' I tried to excuse
myself.

'A whole apple?' Tansy grinned.

'You'd better go easy, son,' commented Bert, who was as
thin as a boathook, 'you'll be getting too fat to shin aloft.'

Everyone laughed, except me, of course. I was too
preoccupied thinking about the ship sailing that night, and
how the next day would be my fourteenth birthday.

Then Tansy said, in a softer voice, 'Oh, I expect he's a
bit shy. First night away from home and all that, eh,
Nipper?'

Suddenly I thought of Llangareth and tears welled in my
eyes, but I managed to stop them falling. I was a man now

among men. I told myself that I must remember that, and to try to soften my pain I forced myself to think instead about the forthcoming voyage.

9

A Wet Shirt and a Happy Heart

In case, in this 'modern' world, much more complex and far more cynical than the world I knew as a boy, my tale reads something like the opening chapters of *Treasure Island*, I must try to explain the reality of it all, the actuality of life in the special world of trade-sailing the narrow seas around Britain in the late thirties.

While words can hardly express the romance of it all as it seems in retrospect, so too it is difficult to find sufficient expression for the hard, mean, incessant toil which underlay all the picturesqueness and beauty and fitness-for-purpose of the old coastal sailing ships. Towards the life they lived and in the ships they sailed, the mariners were deadly serious; they had to be, for not only were their lives and livelihoods at stake, not only were the ships the means of their very existence, they also provided the livelihoods of their families, and the mariners' responsibilities to the ships' owners had to be forever borne in mind.

Some of the people of whom I write might, on the surface, be thought of, in this more flashy age, as 'quaint characters' or 'salty old sea-dogs' or even as 'semi-retarded illiterates'. Some of them may have appeared so, they may even have sounded so, but they most assuredly were not. No one who had navigated, in command or as mate, the treacherous waters around the British Isles for more than a year or two could be anything but well-informed about the waters he sailed, intelligent, crafty and wily – and these two last in the best meaning of the words.

The fact that I never saw Captain Tansy Lee use a chart, or that he never opened a book apart from the Bible, the accounts book, and the ship's log, does nothing to detract from his intelligence and his experience so hard won over so many years of silent inner struggle and anxiety. The mate, Bert, while to all appearances seeming to be a happy-go-lucky skilled labourer, could stow two hundred and fifty tons of cargo in the hold so expertly that nothing would shift in the hardest gale, and the ship at all times while loading or unloading was kept on an even keel. Tansy and he could warp the ship out of a crowded mooring with the finesse of an orchestra conductor and the responses of a virtuoso. They both, the captain and the mate, had the true sailorman's ability to make even the most complex task or problem seem simple and easy.

In more recent years I was to see a few instances of sailing ketches and schooners, approximately the same size as *Second Apprentice* being prepared for sea, and making their departure. In all cases they were to have a much bigger, much more formally educated crew than did *Second Apprentice*; in all cases their equipment, such as sails and cordage, were to be of modern materials such as nylon and their navigational aids were to be of a standard undreamed of in the thirties. In all cases electricity was to have been introduced on board when the vessels converted to 'yachts', together with big diesel engines, and in most cases there was to be plenty of money among the owners and crews. In many cases there were to be voyage-sponsors hovering in the background to come to the rescue should the slightest thing go wrong with the preparations for the voyage or on passage. In most cases, too, there was to be such a lack of true knowledge and expertise, such a hullabaloo as soon as the merest of the unexpected occurred, as to make me wonder how the vessel would ever make any landfall anywhere, or even in some cases reach the offing.

Yet Tansy and Bert could, if necessary just the two of them, quietly warp *Second Apprentice*, engineless, out into the stream, with hardly a word spoken, and that no more than a murmur, punt out, hoist the sails and be underway with no fuss at all, in silence and grace. They could make a round-voyage – a paying voyage – anything up to a thousand miles and more, and be at their destinations within a few hours either side of their estimation. On passage they might emerge from a Channel rainstorm to find the captain of a big transatlantic steamer asking Tansy, in a blinking frenzy of morse on the big ship's signal lamp, what *his* position was. Nine times out of ten, with a cast of a lead to the sea-bottom, Tansy could tell the big ship master-mariner, within a half-mile or so, where he was, and ninety-nine times out of a hundred Tansy would be right.

The sailormen may seem 'quaint' to people of generations which have lost touch with nature, to people whose view of life and the world has been distorted by the false values ground out to them daily by the 'modern' media, but in actual fact they operated the most cost-efficient transport ever devised by man.

The sailormen were simple and many were unlettered. Some were unwise in the ways of the shore-world, but all of them, without exception, were true *men* in every meaning of the word. I was not only lucky to know them – I was also honoured and privileged.

A few words about the ship. For my landsmen friends I will try to make them easily understood.

Second Apprentice had been built in Sussex in the 1890s. Her hull, except for the bows and stern, was a box-like structure of oak with a flat bottom. She was ninety-five feet in length, twenty-three feet in beam and her hold was eight feet deep. She loaded a maximum of just over two hundred tons, and when deep laden her draught was seven feet six inches. This meant that when she was fully loaded as she often was in summer, there was only six inches of her hull above water level.

The bowsprit was almost twenty feet long, tapering from a diameter of about six inches at the outboard end to approximately eighteen inches inboard, where it was stepped into a double bitt (stout vertical timbers rising from the forefoot, through the deck to just about deck level).

The bowsprit bobstay was triced up while in harbour. The standing end of a short chain pendant was shackled to a plate on the cutwater at the water-line. The other end of the pendant had a single block shackled on to it. The standing end of the running part of the bobstay was shackled to the lower eye of the cranse-iron tack and then went down to the block on the chain pendant, back to a block on the bowsprit and then from there inboard. The bobstay was slackened off in port, and triced up by an inhaul. There was a patent iron windlass, hand-worked, for raising the anchor, which weighed about a quarter of a ton and more. The anchor chain (or cable, as we called it) was stowed in two lockers in the forepeak. Each locker had sixty fathoms (three hundred and sixty feet) of ⅝ inch cable, made up of four fifteen-fathom lengths. Thirty-five-fathoms of anchor cable was always, except in heavy weather, laid out on deck from the port locker. The reserve cable was in the starboard locker, with one link out from the chain-pipe on deck, ready to be hauled up. Very low gearing on the windlass permitted one man (or two boys) to weigh anchor in fair weather, and one man and a boy in contrary conditions.

Just abaft the windlass was a dolly-winch. This was used

for warping in and out of harbour. The wire on its barrel was $^6/_{19}$ inch, eighty fathoms (four hundred and eighty feet) long.

Stowed in the forepeak were also: thirty fathoms (one hundred and eighty feet) mooring rope of six-inch coir, thirty fathoms of towing rope of seven-inch coir, eighty fathoms (four hundred and eighty feet) track line of $1\frac{3}{4}$ inch cotton, sixty fathoms (three hundred and sixty feet) horse line of $2\frac{3}{4}$ inch cotton. (The track and horse lines were used for warping in and out of harbour.)

A little abaft the windlass was a scuttle (hatchway) with a sliding roof which led down to the crew's quarters in the fo'c's'le. There were two hatches to the hold – the fore and the main. The smaller forehatch was just forward of an iron horse on which the foresheets worked. On either side of the mainmast were barrel-winches for the halyards. A little further aft was another barrel-winch for working cargo with a block swung on the mainmast. Right across the deck, between the two hatches, was an iron lug-plate, on which the lee-boards worked, port and starboard. The main hatch, with three feet high coamings, had fourteen cover-boards, each thirteen inches wide, three inches thick, and fourteen feet long. Forward of the mizzenmast was an iron box in which the main-sheets worked, and to port and starboard were the lee-board winches, hand-worked. From them the chain falls to the lee-boards passed outboard through small sheave holes. To starboard of the mizzen-mast was a galvanized iron water tank which held about a hundred gallons, and which was strapped down on to the deck with iron bands. There was a skylight over the captain's flat, and aft of that was a small deckhouse. The open forward end of the deckhouse was roofed over and housed a brass decorated steering wheel. A small enclosed toilet was to starboard of the wheel. Abaft the helm-dodger was the galley, and to starboard of that was the companionway down to the captain's flat. On the port quarter were the boat davits, where the jolly-boat was rigged when the ship was underway.

As for the sail plan, it was very simple. There were three headsails, which were set out on the bowsprit; a staysail, a gaff-headed main topsail, the main and mizzensails and a mizzen topsail. A square sail was also carried: when the wind was directly astern this was set up from a yard. The whole square-sail rig, sail and yard, were sent up as far as the main houndsbands when required for running before a hard breeze. Then the mainsail was handed and furled. The mainmast was raked forward and the topmast had a pronounced curve, which to the uninitiated made it seem that the forestay had been set up too taut. The flying jib was hanked to the topmast stay, but the jib halyards all led to the masthead cap, so that the upper part of the flying jib gradually left the topmast stay, making the upper part of the luff of the sail appear to be bent aft. There was a good reason for this. It enabled the sail to be carried much longer in a stiffening breeze. If the flying-jib halyards had been led to the head of the topmast, the strain in a good blow, should the skipper keep the sail up too long, would have probably broken the topmast if not the main.

The sails on *Second Apprentice*, and on all the dandy ketches, were left their natural canvas colour, as distinct from all the other coasting barges, which had red-dyed sails. Another difference was that on ketches the topsails were set to port and the jolly-boat's davits were on the port quarter instead of the starboard.

Both the main and mizzen booms had roller reefing, but unlike modern practice, this was managed by means of a wire reeved around a 'gypsy' at the heel of the boom and then through a block aloft, which was secured to a burton from the houndsbands. Apart from this, all the running rigging was manila rope.

On each side of the mainmast were four galvanized iron shroudwires as well as a running backstay, which was set up on the windward side. Hemp ratlines were clove-hitched to the shrouds, one foot six inches apart. Also lashed to the shrouds, outboard, were two lifebuoys painted in white and red, with the ship's name painted on them in black. These were within easy reach of the deck. Above these, the kerosene-fuelled navigation lamps were fitted, red to port, green to starboard. The mainmast heel was set into the keelson, and, unlike most of the other types of coasting barges, the masts were not made to be lowered for passing under bridges. For this reason the boomies or dandy ketches were considered by the authorities to be fully fledged sea-going vessels, and so could trade 'foreign'.

The mizzenmast was stayed forward by a burton (a 'forestay' which could be tautened by heaving on a line led through a block), and had two shrouds either side. When taking on or discharging cargo the main boom and gaff were swung out over the ship's side (usually to starboard) out of the way. A small, thick gaff was used as a derrick for hoisting and lowering cargo into and out of the hold if no shore derrick and crane was handy.

The ketch rig first came into use in the early 1700s in the Royal Navy. Special vessels were needed to carry huge bomb-mortars, which weighed several tons and which, when fired, almost shattered with their recoil the very hulls which carried them. The mortars, therefore had to be mounted well forward in the ship. In full-rigged ships it was found that when the mortars fired their heavy shells the shock did tremendous damage to the forward mast, yards, and rigging. The foremasts were then removed. This left a vessel with only two masts, a main amidships and a mizzen aft. In time, square-rig sails gave way to fore-and-aft-rig. This is the reason why the two masts in a ketch or a yawl are known as the main and mizzen, while in a brig or schooner they are more sensibly called the fore and main.

The dandy ketches, like *Second Apprentice*, and their cousins the sprit-sail barges and the mulies had much in common. All three types had a box-like hull and they all used lee-boards when hauling to windward, but in the ketches the hulls were far more fit for heavy seas. They had higher bows with a holder sheer, much more powerful for throwing off steep seas. In the ketches, the lines of the hull forward were finer, and they carried a false clipper cutwater (a heavy triangular-sectioned timber balk for parting the seas). *Second Apprentice*'s cutwater was decorated with gold scroll-work. This, apart from the gold-leafed ship's name on each bow and on the counter, was the only decorative work on the otherwise all-black hull.

Aft, *Second Apprentice*'s lines were less sharp than forward and they finished in a well-rounded counter stern. Some of the other ketches which we saw, especially those built in Kent, had a square transom aft.

Along the sides of the deck ran a deep bulwark, about four feet high, to keep as much sea-water where it belonged, in the sea and not so much on deck when the ship was deep-laden. As we shall see, these bulwarks were also handy in stopping the crew from being washed over the side in heavy weather.

The construction of *Second Apprentice*'s hull was . . . massive. Some idea of this can be gained from the dimensions of her main timbers (which I noted during my time on board and quoted in a letter to my family). The keelson (inner keel, along the length of the hull) fourteen inches by fourteen inches, Oregon pine. The floors (bottom frames) – eight inches by six inches, oak, on twenty-one inch centres. The keel, twelve inches by four inches, elm. The ceiling (the deck above the floors) fourteen by three inches, pine. The futtocks (side frames) six inches by six inches, oak, on twenty-one inch centres. Outside planking, double, two inch thick, pine carvel-built, caulked with hemp and oakum. The stem and stern posts were nine inches by twelve inches, oak. The stem was twelve feet six inches long.

As near as I recall the sail areas were as follows: mainsail, two hundred and fifty-five square yards, No. 1 flax canvas. Main topsail, one hundred square yards, No. 2 flax canvas. Foresail, ninety square yards, No. 1 extra G flax canvas. Mizzen, forty square yards, No. 3 canvas. I cannot recall the areas of the three jibs, but combined it must have been about one hundred square yards. This gives a total of about *five thousand three hundred square feet*, all to be handled by one man and two boys. The square sail was about one hundred and eighty square yards in area.

On the stern rail were fitted two sweep irons. Into these the rowlocks for the long sculling sweeps (oars) were fixed, for moving the vessel when there was no wind, or for maintaining a slow headway over a current when the tide carried the ship.

The steering gear was a very massive worm-gear arrangement connected by rods and chains to the steering wheel, which was about three feet diameter made of teak. It had eight turned spokes, and was decorated with brass strips. Below the steering wheel, on the deck, were two ringbolts to which the wheel could be lashed down in an emergency in case the wheel-brake failed. The compass binnacle was also brass, and was secured to the deck immediately forward of the wheel. Inside the binnacle was a small oil-lamp, which exhausted through a little chimney in front of the binnacle. From the top of the deckhouse protruded the chimney from the galley stove. This was known as the 'Charlie Noble', but no one could ever tell me why. The deck locker on the stern, where various spare blocks and tackle, coal shovels and deck-brooms were stowed, was known as 'Yarmouth Roads', after the mooring ground off the east coast port. I suppose that in the dim past someone with a wry sense of humour must have named the locker so because he thought that all the odds and ends found their way to Yarmouth.

From about 1850 onwards, large numbers of sailing ketch-barges had been built on the English east and south-east coasts. Their main trade, in the heydays of sail before the First World War, and to a much lesser extent between the Wars, had been hauling coal from the staithes (small jetties) of north-east England to the harbours and beaches along the east and south coasts. Flat bottomed, the ketches could run right up the beaches on the tide, with a kedge anchor run out astern to haul themselves off again on the next high tide. Once on the beach they unloaded their cargo on to horse-drawn carts, or if the weather threatened to deteriorate they dumped the coal on to the beach, to be picked up at leisure by the purchasers. Often the skippers sold the coal-cargo piecemeal to the rural locals. This was a great benefit to many isolated communities. It meant cheap coal, and they could exchange for it their farm produce which was eagerly sought after in the ports of northern England, so near to the great industrial centres.

Several ketch-barges made transatlantic voyages, mainly to engage in river trading in what was then British Guiana, and one or two of these were still to be at it after World War Two.

Most of the barges which voyaged far abroad were schooner or barquentine rigged. The largest of these, *Eliza*

Smeed, loaded seven hundred and fifty tons and it was said
that she logged ten knots easily. She ended her days driven
ashore in a hurricane on the beaches of New Jersey, on a
voyage from New York to the West Indies.

Now, in the late 1930s, the ketches took whatever cargo
they could get. It might be coal from Yorkshire down to
the Thames or round into the English Channel to one of
the many havens there; it might be pitch to France, cement
or bricks to anywhere, Portland stone to London, or farm
produce, grain and such, from a creek on the east coast to
the Pool of London for transhipment on to lighters or on
to big steamers bound abroad. It might be cow-hides – a
stinking cargo – or gravel, or scrap-iron, or even manure for
fertilizer – and everything was loaded and unloaded by
hand.

On my first trading voyage we were lucky. Ours was a
comparatively easy cargo – about two thousand wooden
crates of empty mineral water bottles closely stacked and
lashed in the hold atop about fifty tons of scrap iron, all
headed for Germany.

By modern standards there was very little ease or
pleasure in the lives of the crew of a small trading sailing
vessel. What there was of both those abstract notions was
almost always serendipitous – an occasional delay in the
delivery of a cargo, the ship caught in harbour on a
Sunday, a chance day of fair wind and fine, sunny weather
– but mostly it was hard slog, slog, all day and all, or much
of, the night. Even when we were held up for cargo, or fog-
bound, or at anchor waiting for a favourable wind, there
was still maintenance work to be done on board, wood and
iron to be scraped and painted, bilges to be pumped out,
masts to be painted, rigging to be oiled, wires and cables to
be spliced, sails to be repaired, and for the boys, there was

always cleaning, cooking, cleaning, in between all the other jobs. Even in the fog there was a look-out to be kept, the bow-bell to be tolled every minute.

Most of the coasting sailing barges were, despite their low freeboard and flat bottoms, very seaworthy craft which could take any amount of punishment from the often vicious winds and seas of the English Channel and the North Sea and still remain tight as bottles. Many a time I was to see *Second Apprentice* still being driven along with all her working sails aloft, when motor-craft were seeking shelter, or were making very hard going.

The captains of all the coasting barges were highly respected. Most of them had been at sea all their lives, and many of them had held command since their early twenties and were well-known in practically every port in the British Isles. Many of them were recognized in European ports, too, from Hamburg to Bordeaux, and a few even further afield. When he went ashore the captain always wore a good shore-going suit, and when he returned on board he usually went down into his cabin and did not emerge until the ship was ready for sea.

A sailing vessel trading only in British waters required only a master qualified by hard-gained experience. He needed no official certificate of competence unless he was to be the skipper of a fishing smack of twenty-five tons or over. If a boy wished to eventually rise in the Trade by gaining a Master's Certificate he sought out a berth in the dandy ketches, like *Second Apprentice*, which were considered by the authorities to be fully recognized as sea-going vessels, and whose masters needed Board of Trade Certificates. A berth in a dandy ketch was, by the late thirties, very hard to come by. For that reason I was very fortunate that my Dad and Tansy had been friends.

At the other end of the scale from the captains were the boys. Even though we lived almost cheek by jowl with the master, a great chasm separated us. Boys from poor families, or from orphanages usually went to sea first on a fishing boat – and generally the only thing they possessed were the clothes they stood in. On board the bawley or the smack he worked all the hours that God ever sent, and his quarters below were no more than a filthy shelf in a floating slum. His pay was no more than would just keep him alive.

Between the two extremes there was a widely varying range of payment and living conditions, but for all at sea under sail-in-trade life, whether underway or in harbour, whether in fine weather or foul, there was in the main little but arduous, unremitting toil.

Among all the seamen I met whose craft had been converted from sail to power I cannot recall any one of them ever complaining about it. Without exception they all considered it a blessing, but they were also extremely proud of the ability and skills which they had gained under sail. When they spun a yarn, it was invariably a tale about blown-out sails, or clawing off a lee shore with no engine below.

In the fishing boats they still carried on the indentured apprentice system for boys. They had an even grimmer existence than did we lads in the ketches. Their main job was to coil the trawl-warp down below in the fetid, tossing, stinking warp-room each time the long, wet, freezing cold, tarry warp was hauled in, which might be several times a day. The only thing to remind him of the light and the sky and the sea outside was the steady clink, clink of the pawls on the windlass barrel and the hiss of escaping steam from above. In between spells in the dark, heaving warp-room, he peeled the potatoes, made tea, helped pack the fish catch in boxes, helped stow the heavy boxes in the hold, coiled lines on deck and if there was a fog he stood for hours on the freezing bow tolling the fog-bell. The fisherboys had only one consolation for their baleful existence – they had a tiny share in the profits from the catch. It rarely came to more than a few pennies, but the thought of how their share would be spent ashore kept many a poor little fourteen-year-old going as the never ending warp came snaking like a cold, wet serpent in the gloomy warp-room. In the ketches we had no share in the profits, but a good skipper would work a small bonus into a boy's pay if a fast passage had been made. It was hardly ever more than a shilling, but it made all the difference to a good or a bad voyage.

By the late thirties the coastal sailing vessels still in trade were mostly owned by companies, but there were still a few, like *Second Apprentice*, which were part-owned by the masters. British vessels are apportioned, for God only knows what reason, into sixty-four shares. This has been so from time immemorial – probably since before Stonehenge was built – and it still is so. The other thirty shares, apart from Tansy's thirty-four, were owned by a ship's chandler and sailmaker in Harwich, a coal merchant in Deal and a captain's widow in Ramsgate. In the days before the Government started to get its sticky fingers into everything that worked well this was in many respects a good thing, a fore-runner, if you like, of syndicalism. For instance, if a skipper was trying to skimp on the crew's food and pared down on the meat for meals, then the butcher who arranged the supply of meat, was going to want to know why. Our sails, when we replaced them, which was rare, were obtained from the sailmaker in Harwich at a decent discount, because he was making sails partly for himself. The same with blocks and rope and such from the chandler. The coal merchant arranged cargoes of coal from Gateshead, County Durham, to Kent or Sussex for *Second Apprentice* whenever we were seeking a cargo, so the ship was very rarely without gainful employment. As for the widow, each time our ship was to call at Ramsgate, she brought delicious meat pies down to the jetty for us in china bowls, covered with blue cloths . . . and she had a pretty young daughter.

The food was always the responsibility of the owners. There were a few cases of skippers starving their crews, but these episodes were soon advertised around the coast, and those captains would be lucky to find themselves another crew, or with anything but an incompetent rabble clambering on board, desperate for work and incapable of securing a mooring line properly, much less make a fender from old, worn-out rope.

At a guess, the sailors in the coasting trade, while they were probably the hardest worked labouring people in or around the British Isles, were also probably the best fed, at least while the ships were in harbour. At sea things were different, as it was not easy for a young boy to prepare a gourmet meal in a bucking, tossing, tiny galley only five by six feet square, with no refrigeration on board. After a few days at sea the ship's biscuits were broken out. These were about four inches square, grey coloured, smooth on one side and rough on the other. They were called by the sailors 'Portmadoc pantiles', because they looked a bit like roofing slates, but I was proud that the little port in West Wales, once the home of a great sailing fleet, was still remembered here, far away in south-east England. Later I was to find that Portmadoc was remembered the world over, wherever a sailing craft wandered – with English spoken on board and ship's biscuits in the galley locker.

Within a few hours of joining *Second Apprentice* I had learned the dandy ketches' slogan: 'A wet shirt and a happy heart'.

10

Underway

That first evening, on board *Second Apprentice*, no sooner
was the supper eaten and the pots and pans cleared out of
the skipper's lobby, then preparations started for getting
underway. By then the ship was well afloat on the tide
which was just about to turn. There was a fitful south-
westerly breeze, which meant that it was more or less
against us until we got out of the river and gained the
offing. The night was fine, with moonlight illuminating the
stream between fleeting clouds.

The captain, mate and deckhand were in no hurry, or at
least to me they seemed not to be. Ted delved into
Yarmouth Roads – the big decklocker aft – and brought
out the side lights, green and red. They were brass lamps,
about a foot high. In the galley he filled their kerosene
reservoirs with oil and lit them, then he jerked his head at
me signalling me to follow him. Soon he had both lamps
lashed to the side-boards which were secured to the main
shrouds. The red and green lights cast an eerie glow on
each side of the ship, the green one on the leaves of the
trees which lined the jetty, and the red one on the waters of
the river. Little midges and other flying life darted about in
their beams, like sparks off a slow-match. These emerald
and ruby iridescences to each side of the dark ship gave to
the scene an aspect of unreality, like a display of subdued
joy by the ship, as if she were glowing with anticipation of
returning to her own element, the sea.

Meanwhile, Bert had secured the last of the cargo-hold
cover-boards and covered them with tarpaulins, which he

wedged in firmly to sockets in the hatch-coamings with a sledge hammer. Next, he and Ted, with me watching, and helping where I could, gathered up all the running rigging, which had been temporarily displaced to be out of the way while the cargo was being loaded, and put it back in its proper position, flaking it out on deck or belaying it to the correct cleats. Then all the spare ropes and spars were laid out neatly fore and aft along the top of the main cargo hold.

That done, Bert went aft to the captain's companionway and called softly, 'Right, Tansy, all squared away!'

There was a muffled, gruff reply. A minute later Tansy emerged from down below, still wearing his bowler and his watch fob. His clay pipe was between his lips, with the bowl upside down. 'Nipper,' Tansy peered at me, 'you stay alongside me, seeing as how it's your first trip.' Then he turned to Bert and nodded with a slight movement of his head.

Bert moved aft, while Ted ran forward. Silhouetted against the red, green, and silver moon glow, they moved like sprites in the night. Ted let go of the forward mooring warp, which he quickly ranged aft along the starboard side-deck, and hopped to the main-topsail halyard, ready to hoist the high sail over the mainmast. Immediately the forward mooring warp was let go the breeze caught the masts, spars and rigging and slowly pushed the bows out into the stream. Bert then let the after mooring warp go, hopped on board, and we were underway. As soon as the tide moved the ship forward Ted hoisted the topsail. I thrilled as I stood beside Tansy at the wheel and the moonlight shone on the white sail far above us.

The anchor was still hung out over the bow, below water, but clear of the bottom. As the ship approached the other bank of the narrow river on the starboard tack the anchor caught the bottom mud, and brought the bow to a halt. The ship pivoted on the anchor and the stern carried on swinging towards the far river bank. To my novice's eyes this was very disturbing, as I thought we were going to collide with the bank. But then as soon as the wind caught the port side of the topsail, Tansy spun the wheel to starboard. Bert and Ted were on the anchor windlass and pumping away for all they were worth, raising the anchor again. The ship moved forward on the port tack, towards the jetty-bank, from which we had departed minutes before, but about fifty yards downstream.

This manoeuvre was repeated about a half-dozen times, until we had a fair breeze to make the harbour-exit on a broad reach (that is with the wind at right angles to the sails). The anchor was left cock-a-hoop (hard up against the bow), while the mainsail was hoisted. As I watched the man and the youth hoist the heavy main-gaff right up to the houndsbands, Tansy said to me, 'We calls that gilling.'

With the mainsail set, the ship seemed to give a start and a sort of sigh, as her pace quickened. Now we were passing the outer harbour light, and ahead of us I could see only the gleaming sea, restless under a gibbous moon. As I turned to Tansy for a fleeting moment, *Second Apprentice* felt the clear scent of the sea, and she became a living thing, the sum of all the life which had ever been bestowed upon her by generations of sailormen. It was impossible that she could be merely a sailing barge on her way to the Rhine with empty bottles and scrap iron. She was a quinquereme, a galleon, a caravel; she was a carrack bound for the rainbow lands of gold and precious stones across a sea of silver and azure, with a cargo of dreams and poetry. Tansy repeated, 'We calls it gilling, Nipper.'

'What's that, sir?'

'Tansy,' the captain reminded me softly.

'What's that, Tansy?' I asked him, my eyes back absentmindedly on the white mainsail now pregnant with the wind and shimmering ghost-like under the moon.

'What we did with the anchor back upstream. There's another way to do it, called dredging, but we calls it *drudging*, because it is a real blessed drudge, especially for them who have to raise and lower the anchor every time we want to come about.'

By this time the mate and Ted had the foresail hoisted, and were busy hauling up the two jibs. Tansy looked around into the night, then he said to me, 'Hold the wheel a minute, Nipper. I'll just go and hoist the mizzen.'

I stared at the great brass-bound wheel in Tansy's grip, not moving. I must have looked like a rabbit gazing at a snake.

'Come on, Nipper, it won't bite you,' said Tansy. 'Catch ahold of this here spoke and keep her heading just like she is. See the compass?' I stretched a little on my toes and peered into the binnacle. I was accustomed to the tiny compass on Morgan Whistle's lugger. This was a much bigger one, but the principle was the same. The heading was east-by-south-east.

'Yes, sir.'

'Tansy. Well, keep her on that there heading,' ordered the captain.

'East-by-south-east, Tansy.'

'Good boy!' Tansy's face shone softly in the subdued glow from the light of the compass binnacle for a second, then he was gone into the shadows aft. I gripped the wheel with a tight, nervous fist, and stared for all I was worth at the compass card, which hardly moved, even when Tansy hauled the mizzensail up. Soon the captain was back again at the wheel. 'Now,' he said, 'you've had a long day, Nipper, what with travelling and all. You go forward and get a good sleep.'

'Oh, I'm all right, Tansy . . .'

'That's an order, Nipper.' His voice was stern.

'Yes, Tansy.' I started to make my way forward on the gently heeled deck, marvelling at the tautened shrouds and the bellied mainsail, which looked like a sea-shell seen through shimmering water. I heard Tansy's voice behind me. 'Careful how you goes, son. Good-night!'

'Oh . . . good-night, sir . . . Tansy!' I saw Bert and Ted working away up forward. Before descending down the scuttle to the fo'c's'le I paused to watch them as they brought the anchor on board to lash it down on the cathead. They were both wet with spray. When the anchor was safely catted Bert went aft to relieve Tansy. Ted looked up from securing the anchor with the iron cat-stopper. 'You'd better get your head down, Nipper. You've got a long day tomorrow.'

I looked out into the night, at the moon's reflection leaping from wave to wave between the blackness of the cloud shadows, and dimly to starboard; over the green coruscation from the side-light playing on the sea; at the coastal lights, a steady gaze here, like a nurse watching her charge, a slow gleam there, like a fond farewell, and quick stabbing flashes in the low blackness of the horizon; reminders that the sea does not gladly suffer fools or idlers, and to watch to our duties.

Reluctantly, yet sleepily, I headed down the ladder into the fo'c's'le, where Ted had already lit the swinging lamp, and where the dying stove gave off a soft golden glow on the sole. Wearily I climbed under my two blankets and laid my head down on the pillow, close to the ship's side. Even though the side planks were four inches thick, I could hear, as the bows rose and descended gently, the trickling wavelets as they washed against the moving hull. It was like the sound of young girls gossiping and giggling. I fell to thinking about Angharad and Branwen Powell back home in Llangareth. Then I remembered Mam and Caradoc and Cei, but before I started to cry I fell asleep, half sad in my homesickness and half mad in my joy. That is the way that boys are.

In between being half-wakened a couple of times in the next few hours by thumping and clattering overhead, I slept soundly all through the night until Ted roused me at daylight. 'Come on, Nipper, work to do!'

I sleepily clambered out of my berth and squared away my blankets. Ted was cleaning out the ash-pan of the stove. The fo'c's'le was rearing up and down, and the bows were banging away quite merrily. I hung grimly on to the ladder.

'You missed all the bleeding fun,' said Ted, without looking at me.

I looked at him. He was still wearing his blue shirt and tattered oilskin jacket. His hair was tousled. 'How's that, Ted?'

'We was running free all night, from just after you turned in. We dropped the main and hoisted the square sail. We came up past the Downs (the Dover Strait) like a dose of salts. Then, when we was off the Foreland we got a north-wester, and we've been biting the bloody wind ever since – heading hard to windward. It's a bit lumpy up there. You wants to wrap up nice and warm – cold as a fish's tit . . . and you'd better get aft as quick as Christ'll let you. Tansy's waiting for his breakfast.'

When I reached the top of the fo'c's'le scuttle it was as if I were on a ship other than the gentle vessel of the night before, or rather it was as if the ship were in another world. The first sensation I had was a stream of cold spray all over me, but I was in my oilies, so there was little harm done, apart from the stinging shock of North Sea water.

The ship was heeled over so much that the port bulwark was half the time half under water. The mainsail was close-hauled (hauled in tight so that its luff and plane grabbed and bit into the wind) and pulsing like a living thing against a grey, overcast sky. The only land to be seen was a thin blue line on the horizon on the port quarter.

Over my head and behind me the staysail and two jibs drummed away like an army of martial angels, and the wind in the rigging zinged. I peered skywards. Tansy still had the topsail set on the main, and it was as full as an elephant's belly. Aft, the mizzensail had been reefed a couple of points so as to avoid having too much weather helm (the tendency of the aftersail to keep pushing the ship's head into the wind). I clumsily made my way aft along the sloping deck and passed the helm as I headed for the galley. Tansy's hand was on the wheel, and he sat on an upturned barrel, with his pipe still upside down and his bowler perched on his head.

'Morning, Nipper.'

Even as the captain greeted me gruffly Bert emerged from the after companionway and hailed me. 'Had a good kip? Wait for Ted in the galley. He'll show you the ropes for breakfast, and after that you and him scrub down the decks, right?'

Breakfast was porridge, cooked in a great iron pot, smoked haddock and bacon, with two fried eggs apiece, and of course, tea. It was my first try at cooking a meal in a small galley which was heeled over and jerking with every judder of the mainsail and jolting with every shudder of the bows against the seas, but somehow or other, under Ted's supervision I managed it all right without spilling too much porridge or tea. By the time we had shipped the fiddles on the table in the skipper's lobby there was quite a decent spread. (Fiddles are wooden battens which are pegged into the sides of the table-top to stop eating gear from sliding off when the ship is heeled or rolling hard.) As Bert sat down to eat we could hear the noise of the thousands of empty bottles in the hold, forward of the bulkhead, all clinking away. 'You a good bottle-washer, Nipper?' the mate asked.

'You have to do that before we put the bottles ashore in Germany,' broke in Ted, his face serious.

Bert looked at Ted. 'Don't tell him that, you'll put him off,' he said, also serious. 'I told you not to tell Nipper about washing them bottles until we got to Remagen . . .'

Now they had me worried. I stared at them both, then I burst out, 'What, wash all those bottles? Why, there must be a million of them!'

'Well, you wouldn't want them there Jerries filling dirty bottles with mineral water, now would you, Nipper?' Bert replied. They were both silent, as they piled into their food and tea, and left me shattered at the prospect of cleaning all the bottles. They kept the jape up right until the crates of bottles were slung ashore, and had me worried about it every time I thought of it for the rest of the trip.

Scrubbing the decks took an hour or so. Ted and I did this despite the water streaming over the decks every time the ship plunged into the cold humps of the North Sea. As the forenoon wore on, though, the sun came out fitfully, and then, even though the sea-water was painfully cold on my bare feet, the sights and sounds of the wind and the sails, and the hull driving through the sea, and the rigging humming with effort, were glorious.

Towards the end of the deck-scrub we sighted a spritsail barge heading north, also beating into the wind. As we caught up with her the sun shone. The sprittie was about seventy feet long, and her bluff bows shouldered the green-blue seas aside, occasionally rising to come down again with a resounding crash, which sent showers of iridescent spray whizzing over her foredeck, drenching her decks and hatchcovers and soaking the lower cloths of her dark red mainsail, already almost black with brine. As *Second Apprentice* overtook her we saw her name on her counter – *Lady Mary*.

'She's one of Everard's boats,' commented Ted, as he casually turned away to stow the deck-scrubbers in the after locker.

I watched the play of purple shadows on *Lady Mary*'s russet sails and the shining whiteness of her jib as it strained at the bolt-ropes. Her brightly varnished topmast gleamed as it whipped to leeward under the pressure of the wind in her huge topsail. Her weather rigging, on the far side from us, was as taut as steel bars and her sails were all hard curves, except for her mizzen, which was half brailed up to the mast.

As we pulled ahead of her, the sprittie came about (went on the other tack, so that the wind would be on her other, starboard, side). She was only about fifty yards or so away from us. I could clearly see her helmsman pushing the wheel over hard – she had no deckhouse. *Lady Mary* wound into the wind with a thundering slatting of canvas which we could hear plainly even over the drumming of our own. Her great sprit spar (which held her mainsail out) lurched to and fro for a few seconds, her head paid off from the wind helped by her foresail held a-weather with a bow-line, her topsail began to fill, her foresail was released and smacked over to leeward with a sudden explosion. Then she stood out on the starboard tack, a vision of graceful curves and shadows, her golden transom rising and dipping in the creamy froth of her wake as she streamed away from us towards the English coast in the west. I see her in my mind's eye now, so long ago and far away.

At sea, Tansy wore – under his yellow oilskin coat if it was wet – an older, more worn version of his shore-going suit, but the same bowler hat. His sea-going suit was single breasted and when the light caught it edge-on it shone green. At sea he wore calf-length rubber boots inside which he tucked his trousers. When the weather was warm enough – which was not very often – he doffed his jacket and shirt collar and rolled up the sleeves of his thick flannel shirt to his elbows. His trousers were rigged with both suspenders and a two inch wide leather belt with a great brass buckle. On his left forearm, the muscle like a steel cable, was a single tattoo, blurred with age – crossed flags, the British Union Jack and the American Stars and Stripes, and below a scroll on which were engraved the words, 'Death before Dishonour'. With his clay pipe and waistcoat he was a typical barge skipper, one of the last inheritors of a tradition going back almost to the dawn of human navigational history.

'Where does Tansy come from, Ted?' I asked as the deck-hand and I prepared dinner that day.

'He lives in Sandwich, leastways he's got a cottage over there,' Ted replied. 'His missus died four years ago. He don't hardly go there any more. Got a nice daughter, though – Daisy. She comes down and visits us sometimes when we're in Kent or Sussex. A real, bloody good hand is Daisy, but she don't stand no nonsense, leastways not from the likes of us.' Ted stirred the soup on the stove, tasted some from the spoon, smacked his lips and went on, 'Like I said, he don't go home much now – stays on board most of the time when we're in harbour. Well, at holiday times it saves him having to pay a bloody watchman, don't it?' Ted stirred the soup again, balancing himself against a beam overhead as the ship bucked and jolted against the head-seas. 'He don't stand night watches, Nipper. Tansy, I

mean. It ain't the custom for skippers to do that, not when
they got two other bleeding helmsmen on board.' Ted
stuck out his thin chest slightly as he said this. 'But he
always keeps the forenoon watch while Bert – he keeps the
morning watch from four till eight, see, gets his head down
– has a kip – and I clean up. Course, now you're on board
it'll be a bit easier for me. We been without a bloody
nipper for over a month, ever since the last one fell from
the gammon iron (at the top of the mainmast) and cracked
his skull.'

I was astonished. I hadn't heard of this accident before.
Ted grabbed the soup dixie and started ladling out a rich
leek broth. 'Oh, he was a silly little sod, wouldn't listen to
no one. Came from bloody Stepney, didn't he? Reckoned
his old man was a waterman on the Thames lighters, but he
was as thick as two bleedin' planks.'

'Do you think I'll be able to take a trick on the helm,
Ted?'

'Well, you wants to ask Tansy about that. I expect he'll
let you take it while he's on watch, for the first couple of
trips, anyway. Here – take these down to the skipper's
lobby . . .' Ted handed me the dixie and spoons which
somehow, God knows how with the ship bashing away and
jolting like a startled carthorse, I managed to set out on the
table without spilling more than half of the contents of the
dixie all over the companionway ladder, which I then had
to clean up.

Over dinner, Bert told me that I could spend an hour or
so on the helm, and this I did, after the meal was cleared
away and he had relieved Ted. The afternoon sun shone
gloriously over a greenish-blue sea. As I gripped the wheel
and held it steady (it was surprisingly sensitive) I could
hear behind me, on the other side of the galley bulkhead,
the pots and pans banging and rattling in their battens as

they jarred and racketed to each plunge of the hull. Each time *Second Apprentice* met a sea, up, up the foredeck climbed, yawing and surging and quivering, and then, with a clear, sickle-like swoop it plunged down into the seas. I could plainly hear, above the thrum of the sails and the screeching of the dry blocks, the flaring bows as they cut down into the water below them and *squelched.* Then there was a pause each time the bows reached the bottom of their scend, where the divided waters rose above the bowsprit and came down heavily on to the foredeck like a volley of grape-shot. That, each time, was followed by the tinny clinking rattle of thousands of bottles in the hold below, a hundred grunts and squeals and swishes from two dozen blocks and twice as many lines, a yaw as the vessel slid off the sea, a punt, a kick, and then *Second Apprentice,* before my wondering young eyes half-blinded by spray, gathered herself together again to repeat the motion. Pickle, smash and rinse, pickle, smash and rinse. Beating to windward, it's called. All the time the endless seas tramped towards us from the north, one after the other in serried millions, never-ending.

That evening, just before supper – it must have been about seven o'clock – Tansy came out on deck, leaned against the port weather bulwark and stared at the horizon for a minute or two. He came over to Bert, who was about to take the helm over from Ted, and said, 'We'll bring her round now, Bert.'

I stared around at the horizon and the sea. I saw nothing at all was different to what it had been an hour before.

Tansy took the wheel, and turned it to starboard. The bows turned away from the wind, Bert and Ted eased off the sheets, and the ship headed more or less south-east, with the wind on her port quarter, almost running free (going directly away from the wind).

Quite suddenly, it was as if *Second Apprentice* was in another time and place. Now the wind apparently eased from half a gale to a modest breeze, the seas gently caressed and nursed her hull with fond massages from astern, and the ship's bow rose in and out of the troughs sedately, fitting into each trough cosily, rising on each crest modestly.

'Now we'll have a nice easy run in the Maas,' murmured Tansy. 'If this here wind keeps up we should off Voorne in the morning at first light.' With the wind aft, and in the calm shelter of the helm-dodger, he turned his pipe bowl right side up, and, as Bert and Ted adjusted the main, fore and mizzen sheets, he puffed away contentedly. 'Go and get the supper up, Nipper.'

Before I went into the galley door I looked all around. Dusk was upon us. It was a fine night, with little cloud for that part of the world. From astern of us, out of the blackening horizon, came the music of the elemental symphony of wind and water. The breaking tops of the seas glowed whitely in the glare of our stern light, like little corpses rolling in their shrouds. The ketch moved gently enough now to cause a shower of silver sparks to break from under her stern and dissipate in her wake each time her counter lifted atop a sea. Sometimes *Second Apprentice* paused for a moment as the wind varied, and then the seas seemed to stop, too, and brood on some reflection, before once more taking up their charge.

Now the noises were much more subdued than they had been all day. They were mainly the noises of the moderate wind and what it encountered, rigging or spars or canvas, or the play of a slack rope, the bubbling of the water along the side, or the slight groaning of the hull timbers as they worked, each against the other. Nothing is ever still at sea.

I stepped over the sill of the galley door and set to, boiling five pounds of potatoes for supper.

Around the table later, there was little sign of all the activity topsides, all the wonder and immensity of sea and sky. In the gleam of the swinging lamp, reflected on the varnish of the bulkheads all around us, with the little coal-stove glowing, the talk was mainly of ports along the Rivers Maas and Rhine, where we were now bound, of cargoes taken in and discharged, of friends in Holland and Germany, and of when we could expect to be back in England. That is the sailor's way.

After supper was cleared, there was not much for me to do but stand by Bert at the wheel and wonder at our passage. We had no newspaper or magazines on board – they were too expensive for the meagre funds of the captain and crew – and Tansy would not have allowed a wireless-set on board, even if one could have been afforded. 'Too much bloomin' noise on board already,' he had told a fellow captain who had proudly displayed his radio receiver to him. Fortunately I had with me my *Oxford Book of English Verse*, which I read for a while in the dim light of the fo'c's'le lamp, but I wanted to see the night, even though it was quite cold topsides. After an hour or so of silently gazing at the sails and rigging dimly lit in the fading moonlight, it was time for me to turn in. I fell asleep trying to recall the names of all the ropes and tackles that Ted had shown me that day. It didn't take me long to slumber. I had been on the go practically since dawn, making breakfast, dinner, tea and supper for four hungry men, one of whom (Ted) ate like a horse, cleaning the galley each time a meal was finished, scrubbing the decks and the fo'c's'le and the skipper's flat, tidying both the captain's and the mate's tiny cabins, giving a hand wherever I was asked to, and making a tremendous effort to learn and remember a bewildering number of different things, their proper places, and their uses.

The next morning, just before dawn broke, I was roused again, but to a very different scene than the previous morning. All around the sea was almost calm. The wind was a mere zephyr, but still from the north-west. Above, the topsail bellied slackly, but the main hung half-empty, while the jibs drew almost no wind at all, shielded as they were by the bigger sails. Dawn came up in fiery red splashes which bathed the eastern horizon and shot stabs of golden light through the tops of light blue seas with a sandy cast to them. As I headed for the galley, Bert, on the helm, lifted his chin ahead and grinned at me. I looked forward of the bowsprit . . . and saw my first foreign shore. It was a long, sandy rise shining in the early sun, all along the south-east horizon. On it, a couple of miles away, a stark white lighthouse held up an admonishing finger before my astonished eyes.

Second Apprentice was holding a course more or less parallel to the shore, which was about two miles off, and we were heading for the headland which, as Bert explained, led around into the mouth of the Maas.

By the time I had four kippers grilled and a dixie of porridge and a gallon of tea prepared, I could hear Bert cursing at the wheel. Next I heard Tansy's footsteps mounting the companionway from his cabin. Right away, Bert's language moderated.

'What's up, Bert?' I heard our captain ask the mate.

'The bloomin' wind's changed, Tansy – we're headed!' I poked my head out of the galley door. Suddenly we had got an inexplicable steady breeze right in our teeth, from the north-east.

'No sense in it,' I heard Tansy mutter. 'It don't fit this

season, and it don't fit the sky.' All the while the mainsail
and jibs slatted away, until Bert shoved the wheel over and
we headed north-west again, out to sea, away from our
destination.

'Someone's got it in for us, Tansy,' I heard Bert say.

'Reckon so,' agreed Tansy, as the easterly breeze rose to
a hard blow and *Second Apprentice* heeled over sailing in
the diametrically wrong direction from her destination.

'Be just right, this here wind, if we was out on a pleasure
sail,' commented Bert after a while.

All at once, the breeze dropped and we were left in a
dead flat calm, rolling away, with the ship's bows turning
where they willed, and no headway on the vessel.

'Damn and blast!' cursed Bert.

'The Lord provideth,' said Tansy quietly as *Second
Apprentice* pitched and tossed on a windless sea, three miles
out from the beckoning, tantalizing river-mouth.

11
Magic Moments

For an hour, as we clumsily consumed breakfast *al fresco* around the galley door, the ship wallowed and rolled like a drunken dinosaur. Bert and Ted had already handed (lowered) the mainsail to stop the gaff from slatting about, but the foresail and jibs were left hoisted. Every time *Second Apprentice* heeled this way or that in a sickening lurch the canvas slammed over with a great hollow *thud!* In the galley it was as much as I could do to keep everything from sliding off the stove-top and table on to the deck. Every so often the ship's bows came round and headed into shallow hills of undulating sea. Then her movement became wonderfully gentle as she slowly pitched and tossed for a few minutes; but as the bow turned again off the seas she gave a sudden lurch sideways, sending me and everything in the galley toppling again into strenuously agile confusion.

After an uncomfortable breakfast noshed standing on deck braced against anything handy, Bert and Ted unlashed two thirty-foot-long pulling sweeps from their stowages along the side bulwarks and shipped them in the sweep-iron rowlocks just forward of the helm-shelter. Then they commenced to row the ship, with Tansy steering.

As Bert hauled on his sweep he called to Tansy, 'How's the tide?'

Tansy stooped and peered through the skylight, just in front of his feet, to see the time on the lobby clock below. He ambled over to the side-rail and looked directly down at the sea for a minute. 'She'll be on the flow in about an hour, Bert.' Often, on many occasions since, I have seen various yachting skippers reckoning up the tide, usually a scrambling and fretting as they read out the figures in the local tide tables, their electronic calculators beeping, and always I remember Tansy and *Second Apprentice* in the North Sea off the Maas so long ago. It was as if they were both part of the tide and locked into the tidal influences. Tansy just *knew* the tide was going to change.

For an hour Bert and Ted heaved and pushed away at the sweeps, each giant oar as long and thick as a young tree-trunk; then it was my turn to relieve Ted for half an hour of back-breaking toil. My sweep was so long that it took me three or four steps backwards and the same forwards to get the full range and half the power of the oar. The ship hardly seemed to move. We were merely holding our own against the outgoing tide for the first half an hour. When the tide turned, though, it was clear that we were moving at about one knot, and with the tide helping us, the toil at the sweeps eased off greatly. All we had to do now was maintain steerage way over the tide.

While all this was going on we were practically surrounded by other craft, big and small, sail and power, entering and leaving the Maas. There were a couple of small tugs lying off the mouth of the estuary, but a tow cost money, and *Second Apprentice* was working on a small enough profit margin as it was. A tow, unless the ship was in grave jeopardy, was out of the question. We might just as well have expected the Crown jewels for Christmas.

As the inflow of the tide decreased the speed of the current of the River Maas, so our ship moved a little faster through the water, and by noon we were well inside the Maas estuary. When the tide slowed down again, in the early afternoon, Bert and Ted were still pulling away at the sweeps. Tansy steered the ship over towards the north bank of the river just downstream from Maassluis town.

As we approached the low, grey-coloured bank I could see no houses on the shore, nor any land behind the river-bank wall. This puzzled me until Tansy told me that the wall was in fact a dyke and the town behind it was all below sea-level. There was nothing to see but high grey walls lining the river banks, and hundreds of barges, sail, power and dumb-lighters, tugs and other work-boats, moored all along the sides of the river, as far as I could see.

Just as *Second Apprentice* turned course to head for a mooring, a slight breeze sprang up, again from the north-west, blowing directly in from the sea along the river, setting up a crinkled sea. The opportunity was taken. With hardly a word spoken, the two long sweeps were pulled inboard and laid along the deck. Bert and Ted hauled on the mainsail halyards, heaving the sail up for all they were worth. Tansy sheered off and headed upstream and we made slow but steady progress against the river current for the rest of the afternoon.

I was amazed at the number of craft navigating and moored along the Maas: everything from the biggest class of ocean steamers down to tiny sailing smacks; there were two long processions of vessels heading both ways along the river, past hundreds more anchored and moored along the banks and in the great docks of Schliedam and Rotterdam, which seemed to sprawl for miles and miles. Often, where ships had been taken down through the locks to below-sea-level berths we could only see a forest of mast-tops over the top of the dykes.

Going upstream on the Maas, though, was not a sight-seeing trip for me or anyone else on board. There was still the ship's work to be done; oiling the windlasses, scrubbing the galley and toilet, polishing the brasswork on deck and down below, scrubbing out the fo'c's'le, the skipper's flat and the captain and mate's cabins, changing the officers' bed-linen, laundering, and preparing the supper. There were very few minutes of relaxation, and of course, all the while I was wearily anticipating having to wash all the empty bottles in the hold when we reached Remagen. I'd even worked out the number of bottles by now – thirty thousand, give or take a few hundred.

Second Apprentice 'went to' moor ('brought up' is the correct term) just before dusk off the town of Ridderkerk, which is on a branch of a stream joining the River Maas to the River Waal. Bringing up was more or less the same process as getting underway, only in reverse order. First the mizzen was handed, then the main, and the lee-boards hoisted while the captain eased off the headsail sheets. The jibs were handed as the ship crept up to the mooring under topsail and foresail only. Next the foresail was lowered, rolled up and lashed like a sausage, and hauled again up the forebrace clear of the foredeck. As the bows slowly approached the mooring buoy, Ted went over the bows, clinging on to the bowsprit with one hand, mooring rope in the other. When the ship was near enough he reeved the mooring line through the ring on the buoy, and passed the fag-end back up on board. That done, the topsail was lowered with a clatter, and another mooring line, with a shackle in an eye on the end, was passed over to Ted, who shackled it on to the mooring buoy. Then the first, looped mooring line was either eased off or brought back on board. It was not easy, handling four-inch tarry coir ropes while hanging over, under, or on to, the bowsprit, but Ted made it look easy, and within a few weeks I was doing the same thing myself.

The Dutch customs inspection at Ridderkerk was no more than a handshake and a greeting between the inspector and Tansy. They were obviously old acquaintances. Tansy must have been to Ridderkerk many, many times in his life at sea.

Like any boy I would have loved to have been able to go ashore. I stared longingly at the little town, so clean and fresh in the clear May evening. There were trees and flowers growing all along the river-bank and people, young and old, strolling along, but I was only allowed ashore, for my first six months, on Saturdays. In any case by the time the ship was moored and the supper cooked and cleared up I was so weary that I could just about drag myself forward to the fo'c's'le and turn in, like everyone else on board, with the prospect of rising at five o'clock the next morning and getting underway again.

The daily routine of ship's chores was almost always the same, whether at sea, up a river, or along side, except that along side it was much more strenuous; the crew handled all their own cargoes out and into the vessel. First there were the decks, the galley, and the toilet (or 'head') to be scrubbed white and a score of bits of brass to be polished. Then there was breakfast to prepare. After breakfast was cleared up Bert told Ted and me what our tasks for the forenoon were; chipping paint, varnishing, tarring, splicing or sewing, or if the weather was too wet to work on deck unlaying old rope for Bert and Ted to make up fenders or sennits or baggy-wrinkle. These last were pads made of old rope which were laid around the standing rigging-wires, where the sails tended to chafe against them. The standing rigging always had to be kept taut and we were forever cleaning and painting the ship's structure, even when underway in calm waters. Along side, if we were waiting for a cargo, the ship's side was scrubbed and painted where necessary, and every block was overhauled and greased as far as possible.

Hull bottom-cleaning was carried out twice a year, and it was two days hard labour for a man and two boys to scrub and then apply two coats of black varnish to the whole three thousand square feet or so of the under-water hull. Daily, every few hours at sea, there was the hull to pump out, for wooden ships always take in a certain amount of water, no matter how tightly they are built. No harm in that – salt water keeps the wood fresh.

It was little wonder that at the end of a long day, even in a place as pretty and attractive as Ridderkerk, none of the crew showed much eagerness to go ashore, and were only too pleased to crawl into their berths.

Later, I was to find that sometimes it was a relief to be out at sea in bad weather even in winter, because, apart from standing watches in fog, snow and rain, the weather conditions and the movement of the vessel made most kinds of work impossible, and then, when I was off watch, in between preparing and clearing up meals, I could catch up on the sleep and restore some of the strength I had lost or expended working in port.

The next morning we got underway as soon as the night sky started to lighten. There was no breeze, so it was sweeps again for Bert and Ted, while I cooked breakfast. That lasted until about seven o'clock, when a nice steady south-westerly breeze roused itself. We were not alone – about a dozen other sailing barges, and many more motor barges, all started off upstream and downstream at the same time as *Second Apprentice*.

The Dutch barge skippers mostly sailed with their families on board, and their vessels were real little family homes, with flowerboxes around the windows of the deck-houses and children scampering around the decks. The Dutch boats were invariably clean and shining as new pins. They always seemed as if they had been freshly painted that very day. They were big vessels, many of them much longer than *Second Apprentice*, with huge, bluff bows and a tremendous sail spread. What with the flowers and the youngsters and women on deck, and usually with lines of laundered clothes hanging out on the sterns, when a flotilla of Dutch barges got underway it was more like a regatta than anything else.

Quite a few of the Dutchmen knew Tansy and Bert. When they encountered us on their way downstream, or passed us going up-river, they shouted greetings and waved. Going up the Maas and the Rhine in *Second Apprentice* was often like a triumphal home-coming. Many a time at a mooring someone rowed over to our ship and offered a bottle of schnapps, but Tansy always gently and courteously refused. He would not countenance booze of any kind on board. On these occasions Bert usually looked on silently ruminating. Both Bert and Ted liked a drink, but they drank only ashore, and that was invariably beer, which was all they could afford.

That day's wind took us a good fifty miles by dusk, up as far as Zaltbommel in Gelderland. All the way, as I worked, I stared fascinated at the life of the river. There were vessels from practically every country in Europe – German, Danish, Swedish, Norwegian, Belgian, French, Swiss and Austrian, even, much more rarely, Polish, Finnish, and Hungarian. Bert explained the different ensigns as the barges motored or sailed past.

Up-stream from Rotterdam we saw few, if any, of our own flags as the British small-craft trade with the Continent, especially under sail, had been almost throttled to death on the outbreak of, and during, the First World War. Now there were very few British vessels heading up and down the Rhine, apart from the two or three engaged, as we were, in the mineral-water and scrap-iron trade.

There was a trickle of coal going out from the German Ruhr, but not much – Welsh coal was cheaper and better for use in ship's boilers. There were also a few cargoes of wine from the Rhineland, but in pre-Second World War days the British drank much less wine than they do now, and especially German wine.

Besides the depredations of the Great War on British sail, the Northern Europeans, and especially the Danes, Swedes and Dutch, who had been neutral during the conflict, had built up fleets of motor coasters powered with diesel engines. These were hardy steel vessels, which might take little or no account of weather conditions. By the late thirties they had seized practically all of the European coastal trade, even into the Mediterranean, and they were small enough to use a great deal of the European inland navigational system of rivers and canals. Diesel fuel, in those days, was cheap and plentiful. Each cargo of oil landed in Northern Europe tolled the death of yet another sailing craft, or at least the conversion of a thing of beauty into a mastless hulk which plodded the coastal waters and the rivers as if ashamed of itself.

On the way up the Maas and the Rhine we saw dozens of sailing craft hulls which had been converted to power, and not one did we see that was not ugly; not one did we pass without feeling a strange pride, despite their overtaking us ten times out of ten. Subconsciously we knew that *Second Apprentice* was part of the elements, of the winds and the waters, and that she was not forcing them, but bending them to her will without hurting or destroying them. She and we were as much a part of the sea and sky, the river and the trees, as the birds on high.

The next day we were headed (that is the wind was against us), but despite this, by tacking back and forth across the wide river we were able to make good about thirty-five miles, up to Druten. On that day Tansy let me take the helm in the forenoon, after I had finished my morning chores. I was surprised how easily the ship came about through the wind. There was not much tending of sheet-ropes because we then carried no jibs and the foresail, topsail, mainsail, and mizzen sheets all worked on horses (iron bars across the ship) and so they worked themselves. At first the slam of the iron horse travellers, to which the sheet-ropes were attached, was alarming, but I soon got used to it, and after a while gloried in sending the ship's bows through the wind as sharply as I could. It was a bright sunny day, and I can see the owner's pendant now, streaming back in the breeze from the topmast cap, and woolly round clouds driving across a blue sky, and on each side of us the tidy, green fields of Holland, with Friesian cows, all black and white, grazing on the slight green slopes, so different to the dark, rugged hills of Wales.

All the time we were tacking up-stream we were accompanied by other sailing barges doing the same thing, as far as the eye could see ahead and astern, and many a racing match developed. We always tramped past the smaller vessels, but we were hard put to keep up or pass Dutch ships of the same length as *Second Apprentice*, and I don't recall us beating any bigger vessel, though I expect we probably did, because some of them were under-sailed for their size. The Dutch botters, heavy and ungainly as their hulls appeared, were surprisingly fast and handy, and they could turn in practically their own length. When they went about they seemed to pivot more than travel through the eye of the wind.

The following day *Second Apprentice* was headed again for much of the time by an easterly breeze, but we managed to make Millengen, just on the Dutch side of the frontier with Germany, passing Nijmegen on the way, where there were, it seemed, a thousand river craft either moored or busy loading or discharging cargo.

Millengen was an appealing town, and we arrived there in the late afternoon. Much to my envy, Ted got ready to go ashore with Bert to buy fresh vegetables and a leg of pork. By 'got ready' I mean that Ted slicked his hair back with some water and put his shirt and shore-going boots on. I went topsides to see them row ashore in the jolly-boat, which I helped to lower into the water. My face must have been as long as a wet Sunday in Aberdeen, so long that Tansy called over to me, 'Nipper, you lost a shilling, or what?'

'No . . . Tansy . . . I . . . I . . .'

'What's up, son?'

'Noth . . . nothing.'

'Want to go ashore for a spell with Ted?' Ted sat in the boat grinning.

'Oh . . . could I . . . please?' I was still in my grubby working gear.

'Well, it's not a Saturday, but seeing as it's Holland . . . and you've been a bright spark, considering . . . yes. But hop to it and be quick . . .' Tansy turned and clomped down the companionway to his cabin.

It took me no more than three minutes to fly forward, slide down the fo'c's'le scuttle and change, as fast as I could, into my shore-going rig, the one I'd arrived on board in at Rye five days before. With my working clothes still strewn about my berth, and my boots in my hand I took off up the ladder, still buttoning up my shirt. I tied up my bootlaces while I was still in the jolly-boat, with Ted rowing it to the landing stage. There I stepped foot on a foreign shore for the first time in my life, in Millengen, the last town on the River Waal in Holland, before it becomes the Rhine.

We three, the gallant crew of the British Registered Vessel *Second Apprentice*, rolled up the steps from the landing stage and crossed the quay. It seemed strange to be on dry land again, on a deck which was not moving. Just before we turned a corner to go into the town, so neat and clean, I turned to take a look at our vessel. She sat gracefully at her mooring like a mother-swan patiently awaiting the return of her cygnets from a waddle on the bank.

Once out of sight of *Second Apprentice* the first place that Bert made for, with Ted and I traipsing alongside, was a bar. Unlike an English waterside pub it was very light and airy inside. The walls were covered in white tiles with blue pictures on them, of sailing ships and windmills and such. Bert boldly plonked an English shilling down on the marble counter. The owner, a stout, bald man wearing a blue and white apron, a bow tie, and a huge blond moustache, perked up, inspected the shilling, nodded his head slightly and slowly, and poured Bert a beer, at the same time greeting him in very guttural English. It was obvious that Bert was a regular customer of the establishment. The mate also bought Ted a beer, and a lemonade for me. We sat back like freshly arrived ambassadors to the court of the Kublai Khan, in the unaccustomed luxury of padded chairs, taking in the sights and scenes all around us and through the windows of the bar, watching the people go by, some of the men and women, boys and girls too, wearing wooden clogs. Practically all the men smoked big-bowled pipes or big cigars. To my surprise many of the boys, even smaller than I, did so, too.

On the way to the greengrocer's and the butcher's I saw quite a few strange sights, like dogs pulling little milk carts, and people carrying loads suspended from wooden yokes which they wore over their shoulders. It was a bit like a modern tourist picture of Holland, only then, in the thirties, that is the way it really was. I had felt strange in England, where I could barely understand what was said, but here, in eastern Holland, I felt like a visitor to Mars. The language spoken was rapid and guttural, but Bert seemed to make his way quite easily by simply turning English back to front. 'I the potatoes and carrots want . . . I the beef for the stew want . . .' The shopkeepers smiled and seemed to understand perfectly as they reached for exactly what Bert had ordered.

All the way along the streets and in the shops, Ted ogled the girls. Since he was not a bad looking lad, as English lads go, the girls usually returned his look with a bright bold smile. This made Ted go red in the face, look away, and talk to me about his favourite soccer team, Arsenal, and how they were doing in the league. I noticed he didn't swear while he was anywhere within hearing of a female, even though he probably would not have been understood.

We could only have been ashore for an hour or so – it was even yet bright day when I rowed the jolly-boat back to the ship – but I still recall clearly the surprises and wonders that I saw in Millengen; the clean, tidy houses, most with flowers in boxes around the walls, the well-tended gardens, all ship-shape and Bristol fashion, and the trees in bud along the river bank, the green grass and the flowers, so new and fresh after a week at sea seeing nothing but wood, iron, canvas, soup, salt beef, potatoes, carrots, plum duff, tea, rope, sky and water.

From the Dutch-German frontier to Remagen as the crow flies is about a hundred miles, but by river, with all the twists and bends, this increases to about one hundred and eighty. It took *Second Apprentice* another four full days to make the passage up-stream against the current. We had a fair westerly breeze most of the way, but at times, especially in the lee of the hills along the western side of the river, we lost the wind. Then it was again a case of what we called 'Armstrong's Patent Propulsion System': in other words getting out the long sweeps and rowing all three hundred tons or so of *Second Apprentice* and her cargo against the might of the Rhine as it swept down through its often beautiful valleys. Sailing past places like Duisberg and Dusseldorf, the scenery was nowhere near as pleasant as it was on most of the river. The smoke from the furnaces of those great industrial cities blackened the sky and often made night out of day, besides settling a layer of soot all over the ship and her sails, which had to be cleaned off each time.

We passed through customs inspection just inside Germany, and the inspector was friendly to Tansy, but his crew were very surly looking and off-handed with us. The customs boat wore a swastika on the cross-trees as did many of the German vessels we saw. South of Dusseldorf, we passed very close to a couple of motor barges with their decks crowded with people, mainly youngsters it appeared, all wearing brown uniforms, shouting and singing at the tops of their voices, seeming to be having a rattling good time. The adults with them also wore brown uniform and swastika brassards. Some shook their fists at us – some waved. A band was playing on deck very loudly and oom-pah-ish. 'What price the Salvation Army now, Tansy?' joked Ted.

'Silly blighters . . . silly, stupid beggars . . .' Tansy replied, quietly.

Most of the German bargees were friendly to us when we passed them, or moored by the bank in the evening, and the officials who came on board to log us in or out acted very correctly. One or two, who wore war medals on their uniforms, even saluted our Red Ensign when they came on board or left the ship.

We had a broad reach most of the way up-stream from the frontier to Remagen (that is the wind was at right angles to the ship, usually the fastest point of sailing). We clipped along at a good rate when we were not shielded from the wind by a high hill. We arrived at the confluence of the Rivers Rhine and Ahr nine days after sailing from Rye. We had carried almost two hundred and fifty tons of cargo without using one drop or lump of fuel, apart from what we put into the lamps and stoves, and without any wear, tear, or damage. The only cost had been captain's and crew's wages and food. The soap, paint and other material used on the voyage would have cost about £3. For a total expenditure of less than £12 we had transported our two hundred and fifty ton cargo almost five hundred miles from dock to dock.

At the confluence of the Ahr we were met by a man with two big stallions. He had arrived at the behest of a pal of Tansy's by telephone from Bonn. Our tracking ropes were attached to the horses' harness, through brass rings on the top, and the horses, with the topsail helping them a mite, towed us along the Ahr River, plodding steadily at about two knots, the few miles up the river to the Apollinaris loading dock.

As we approached the dock, in beautiful rural surroundings, with trees and meadows all around, Ted appeared on deck with a metal bucket and a piece of wire with a bit of rag seized on the end. He put them down beside me, as I stood at the galley door staring at the passing scenery. I looked down at the bucket.

'That's the bloody bottle-washing gear,' said Ted. 'You'd better get some hot water ready and put a fucking decent gob of liquid soap in it, too, Nipper. We'll be humping the bleeding bottles out very shortly.'

I put the largest kettle on the stove and did as Ted had bidden me, wearily reckoning up how much time it would take me to clean the thousands and thousands of bottles. As *Second Apprentice* approached the dock nearer and nearer I saw many children running down to the river bank, there to stop and stare at us, or shyly wave. Then, with a dull, soft thump we were alongside the dock, Ted and Bert cast on the mooring lines to the dock bollards and my first voyage was over. I stepped out of the galley and looked around. I saw the big shed where the mineral water was stored ready for loading, and a steam crane on the jetty, and how our cross-trees had been steeved up so they would not be damaged by the overhanging trees on the river bank, and how, on the way up the River Ahr our hold-covers had been taken off and all made ready for work to commence as soon as we docked.

We arrived at the Apollinaris dock in the middle afternoon. The unloading started right away, as soon as the ship touched the dock and was secured. Ted and I went down below, hefting the boxes on to the skip. Then, on deck, Bert and a German lad transferred the boxes from our skip on to a kind of pallet, which the steam crane on the jetty hoisted up. The pallet was then unloaded by Germans ashore. It was impossible, Ted explained to me, for the steam crane to hoist the boxes straight out of the hold because its boom was not long enough to reach over the top of the hold.

When darkness fell the Germans, being nothing if not efficient and thorough, rigged up an electric floodlight over the hold so that Bert, Ted and I could go on working. By the time the hold was empty of boxes my back and shoulders were almost breaking and my hands were so blistered that I could hardly haul myself up the ladder

when the last box had left the hold. I was so thankful and
relieved that I ·didn't have to wash the bottles that I
completely forgave Ted and Bert their jape.

Over a mug of tea, which ·Tansy had made while we
finished work, we found that the scrap-iron was to be
unloaded a mile further up the river. That would be early
the next day, then *Second Apprentice* would shift back to
·the. mineral-water dock to load with full bottles of that.
liquid so necessary, evidently, to the upper drinking classes
of England.

By the time we had drunk our tea, it had started to rain,
and was becoming a downpour. Weary as we were, the
mate, Ted, and I hefted the heavy hold-covering boards
into position so that the hold would not flood too much
with fresh rainwater, which does wood no good. Then Ted
and I set to making supper. It was a quarter to midnight
when we finally cleared up the galley and dragged
ourselves forward to the fo'c's'le. It was cold down there.
We'd been too busy all day to light a fire in our quarters,
but I soon got warm under my two thick blankets, and fell
asleep, exhausted.

We unloaded the scrap-iron further upstream very early
the next day. That was easier than the boxes of empty
bottles had been – there was a long boomed crane which
picked up the great jagged pieces of boiler-plate directly
from the bottom of the hold, so all Ted and I had to do
mostly was secure strops around the iron. It was very dusty
in the hold and we had to be careful not to tear our hands
on the jagged metal, but it was a walk-over compared to the
empty-bottle boxes of the day before, or at least I thought
so until we started loading the full-bottle boxes, all four
and a half thousand of them, back at the Apollinaris dock.
That was what the Americans call a real goddam ball-

buster, and by the time Ted and I had the boxes all securely stowed under Bert's expert eye I was just about ready to die, but I put thoughts of expiring out of my mind and got on, somehow, with peeling the potatoes.

We sailed at first light next day, and now that we had the current with us we carried on downstream day and night until we reached the German-Dutch frontier, which, with the fair breezes we encountered, took us a mere day and a half. From the frontier we made it out to the estuary in another day and a half, emerging from the Haringvliet mouth of the Schelde River. Out in the North Sea we found a good north-wester blowing, so we were on a close reach for most of the two-day sea-voyage back to Rye, until we passed by the Foreland and into the Straits of Dover, when we were headed by a south-wester. That meant a couple of tacks on either board for a whole day.

It was a glorious day, the sunlight clear and strong. As we ploughed the Straits the waves of the Channel seemed to know that *Second Apprentice* was coming home. The waves met her charging at them to dash them into myriads of sparkling gems that hovered about her at every surge.

We finally made our way into Rye harbour entrance five days after leaving the dock at Remagen. The whole round trip of about nine hundred miles had taken *Second Apprentice* just two weeks and I had made my first foreign voyage. The following day was a Saturday, and I was given leave to go ashore in Rye for the afternoon, with a strict order from Tansy to be back on board by nightfall. I felt rich as I went ashore with one of my remaining two shillings' pay in my pocket, and I must have looked at the other boys in the street and in the cinema with something like disdain. I was a fully fledged seaman now, so I thought. I strolled along with a slight swagger, or leaned

back manfully in my cinema-seat. The prospect of all the
thousands of boxes of full mineral-water bottles waiting to
be unloaded on Monday morning completely left my mind
for a few blessed moments.

12

In My Element

The amount of work expected of a young boy on board a ketch-barge never ceased to amaze me. I had known from conversations with old sea-farers at home, that the boy was also cook as well as deckhand, look-out, steward, cargo-handler, and makee-learner helmsman, rigger, sailmaker and painter, but I had never realized quite how much continual effort was involved, nor how much of this was taken up by the cooking. The worst of that job was that unless I thought about it deeply, I could never see any result. No sooner was a meal ready and served than it was consumed. There was left only a pile of plates and pots to be cleaned, and that in itself was another job. We had no such thing as washing detergent. Soft soap was, in our straitened circumstances, always in short supply. I used to do most of the galley cleaning with salt water and sand.

With the amount of work to be done by everyone on board it was vital that the crew be properly fed. After the first trip, when I had worked in the galley under Ted's tutelage and with Bert's eagle eye often on me, I was left more or less alone to get on with it as best I could, though the mate and deckhand were always willing to help me if I had a problem.

On the short passages we more or less ate as we would have done ashore: porridge, bacon and eggs, and tea for breakfast, plenty of bread brought from ashore, best butter, potatoes, onions, carrots, cabbage and fresh beef, lamb or pork. There was always a good supply of tea, condensed milk and sugar, too.

On the longer sea passages, for example when we sailed up to the north-east coast or south to the Channel Islands, where we might expect to be (and often were) becalmed for a few days, it was a different story. Then we stowed away salt fish – usually cod or haddock – potatoes, rice, dried peas, 'Portmadoc pantiles' (hard-tack biscuits), margarine, and salt beef. Unlike some of the other coastal sailing craft, we salted down our own beef. Tansy never trusted the quality of barrelled salt beef bought ashore. Before a longish trip he took time off from all his other duties, such as dealing with the paperwork, the factors, and a couple of dozen other entities, to go along to a local butcher (who was usually a pal of our butcher-shareholder in Harwich). There he selected his own cuts of beef, flank, brisket, chuck or sirloin. When the white-aproned butcher's errand boy showed up with the meat in the basket of his bicycle on the jetty, I carried the beef down below to the meal-table in the skipper's flat, still in its muslin wrapping. There, Ted and I rubbed coarse rock salt into the beef until all the salt had been absorbed. Tansy never let Bert take part in the beef salting, though I never found out why. It might have been to do with an old sailor's superstition that only virgin-boys could do it, otherwise the beef was supposed to go off. As far as Ted was concerned, I wasn't so sure that Tansy was on the right track. From the yarns he spun to me when we were alone in the fo'c's'le Ted was far from a virgin, *if* he was to be believed. Our beef almost always stayed good, so I presumed Ted was exaggerating about his conquests.

After we had salted the beef, we took it back topside, to where a big salt-barrel was lashed on the port side of the deckhouse. This was known, for reasons that may be imagined as the 'harness barrel'. The brine inside the barrel was so salty that a wooden tackle-block would not submerge in it. The beef was held down in the brine with a broom handle until it stayed completely immersed, and it was left to pickle for several days before it was taken out and cooked. Then it was either delicious or rank; it was a matter of luck. We had a lot of luck. We never called it salt beef; the sailor's name for it was 'old horse'. The name for salt fish was 'yellow peril'.

The food on board *Second Apprentice*, and, I was told, on most of the coasters, was of good quality and the helpings served were more than fair. It had to be so, with everyone from the captain to the ship's boy eating at the same table, from the same dishes.

By the end of a hard day's work loading or discharging cargo, or standing watches at sea, everyone had a good appetite. Ted ate like a shark, anything and everything put before him. I have never seen anyone since who could eat like tall, thin, wiry, Ted. A great steaming helping of roast beef, potatoes, and greens, all piping hot, along with duff pudding, rhubarb and custard for afters, and two or three pints of hot, sweet, milky tea, would disappear as if by magic after Ted sat down to his evening meal, and he always asked for second helpings of plum duff. Both Tansy and Bert had good appetites, too. Cooking for them was, as they would put it, 'a dockyard job'.

After we had been at sea for a few days the baker's bread, bought ashore, would either be used up or mouldy. Then the 'hard-tack' was broken out. The 'Portmadoc pantiles' were so steely that Bert, who had lost a few teeth when a boom had smacked him across the deck in a past, well-recounted gale, used to take a jack-knife out of his jacket pocket to crack the biscuits. He soaked the pieces, as hard and sharp as slivers of glass, in his mug of tea for a minute or two before he attempted to consume them. It was said that if you fed pantiles to a pig it would cause internal bleeding and the animal would roll over and die. The biscuits were so rock-hard that after eating them for a few days our gums became sore and started to bleed. Then we couldn't eat them any more, and had to make do with watered porridge for our cereal intake. This never happened to Ted. He could consume hard tack for ever and a day with no evident difficulty. When he cracked the hard tack he even looked like he enjoyed doing it.

There was much more to cooking salted food properly than at first met the eye. If it wasn't pickled properly, and then steeped in fresh water for a good spell before cooking, it brought out salt-water sores on our bodies. Salt fish and beef were mostly boiled, but after a while I learned how to make minced beef for shepherd's pies, fried fish cakes and suet dumplings. Those dumplings, with boiled beef, carrots, potatoes, and onions, made a good nourishing stew, which we all thoroughly enjoyed. 'Bloody good grub' was the invariable opinion of Bert and Ted.

With rice I made curried beef and rice, and rice pudding liberally dosed with currants and sultanas. Sailors called that 'soldiers in a snowstorm', or '1812'.

In bad weather, in the tiny, hot galley, with the door shut to keep out spray and wind, it was like all hell let loose. I had to sit on the seat over the coal-bin and try to keep the pans from skittering off the heaving stove-top. I was scalded quite a few times, but fortunately never seriously. The wind blowing down from the mainsail blew the smoke back down the chimney, or 'Charlie Noble'. When the galley was full of fumes I was forced to poke my head out of the door in order to breathe, then I usually got a good dollop of freezing spray over my face and a gallon of sea-water swirling over the galley deck. Then I had to mop that up as well as try to keep the pans on the stove.

In rough weather when the food was ready, a difficult

job was to get it down below and on to the lobby table
without losing it, or getting it dowsed in cold sea-water.
After a couple of minor disasters I learned the tricks and
managed quite well. One of these accidents was quite
funny, though at the time it didn't seem so at all. I was
juggling a tray of boiled salt fish and a dixie of soup down
the companionway. Topsides it was blowing the Devil's
pants off. Below Bert and Ted had just gone down for their
supper. Ted was already seated, waiting, fork and spoon in
hand in the glow of the lobby oil-lamp. Suddenly, the bows
hit an extra big sea. The ship lurched like a Grand National
courser going over the sticks. I lost my footing and went
slithering down the companionway with an almighty crash.
The tray and the soup-can went flying out of my hands and
smack into Bert, covering him from head to foot in fish and
soup. Fortunately he had his back to me, taking off his
oilskin coat, and still wearing his souwester hat, so no real
damage was done, but he was lucky. Bert took it in his
stride – he merely turned to me with the 'yellow peril' and
soup dribbling and dripping from his oilies, and growled,
'That grub smells nice, Nipper, but next time put it on the
table, please.'

I scrabbled around for the pieces of fish, and put them
back in the dish. They were still reasonably warm and
edible, and the sole of the lobby was so clean and scrubbed
you could have eaten the fish from it. Bert and Ted both
declared that it wasn't worth the trouble of cooking another
meal, and they made do with the rescued yellow peril while
I mopped up the soup. I was thankful that Tansy was on
the helm when this happened. By the time he came off
watch I had another piece of fish fried up for him. I never
forgot the lesson. I never again tried to carry more than one
hand could hold from the galley down to the lobby in
rough weather. Ever afterwards I always bore in mind the

old sailor's saying, 'One hand for yourself and one for the ship'.

On the very few occasions when the salted meat went bad, we used some of it for fish-bait, with varying degrees of success. On one trip to Bordeaux with cattle-feed we were becalmed for more than a week with a barrel of stinking beef on board, and caught nothing but a couple of small fish. We had to make do with potatoes, margarine, and hard-tack, until we finally arrived off Royan. There Bert went ashore in the jolly-boat and fetched back a box of tomatoes and a leg of lamb. Tansy never went ashore in France if he could possibly avoid it. He never said why, but his expressions whenever a Frenchman was in sight showed that he was not exactly francophile. I'll never forget how good those fresh tomatoes and roast lamb tasted, though, after more than a week on hard-tack and boiled spuds.

It was on board *Second Apprentice* that the value of fresh water was driven home to me. At home in Llangareth fresh water had to be pumped from a spring, but except sometimes in deep winter, there had always been plenty of it. At sea fresh water can be worth its weight in gold – sometimes worth more. In *Second Apprentice* we had a hundred gallon tank on deck, beside the galley, and another three hundred gallon tank down below in the 'cupboard' as the after end of the main hold was known. One of my jobs was to keep the deck-tank full by pumping water up from the main tank. Before I could do that, however, I had to ask Bert to unlock the pump handle, which was secured by a padlock and chain. Then, when the deck-tank was topped up, I had to ask Bert for the ready-use tank spigot handle, which was detachable. Without the tap-handle no water could be drawn from the ready-use tank. More often than not Bert, in his capacity as mate, stood over me while I drew what fresh water was necessary for whatever galley

job was in hand. For the captain and mate the daily fresh
water ration was one and a half gallons in a bucket, and
they took alternate first turns at washing and shaving in it.
It was the same for Ted and me, except that we had to
make our water last two days, which was considered by all
to be fair, because neither Ted nor I then shaved. In
harbour, where most of the dirtiest work was done, it was,
of course, different. Then we could find a tap or a pump
ashore somewhere and wash away to our heart's content, or
if the ship were in a fresh water river and the water was not
too filthy, we could sluice ourselves in that.

Apart from galvanized steel buckets, the only other toilet
facility on board *Second Apprentice* was the lavatory, or
'head'. This was in a very poky little closet open to the sky
alongside the helm position. It consisted of a wooden box
inside which was a sort of large metal funnel, mouth-up.
To the bottom of the metal funnel was fixed a pipe which
led at an angle straight down through the ship's side just
below sea-water level. Ullage was sluiced down with a
bucket of salt water. It worked very well until the ship
started to labour in any kind of heavy seaway. Then, unless
we were very wide-awake, and jumped up in time with the
ship's movement, our transoms were liable to be sluiced
with a few gallons of cold sea-water swashing up the pipe.
Of course I didn't know about this. The first time *Second
Apprentice* started working heavily, in the North Sea going
hard to windward on our way to the Maas, I had gone into
the 'kaasy' as the bargemen called the 'head', and all three
of my shipmates had waited gleefully for me to come
shooting out again, my trousers around my knees,
spluttering and dripping salt-water.

'We always uses the chains at sea,' said Bert.

'The chains, Bert?'

'Yes, up forward on the bow. You'll probably get a wet

arse up there, too, hanging on the cathead, but at least it'll be when you expect it!' (Which explains why the ship's toilet is called the 'head'.)

Sometimes, if we had good salt beef still remaining in the harness barrel after a voyage which had been faster than we had expected, we let the townsfolk know, and they came down to the ship to buy it from Tansy; his reputation for the excellence of his salt beef was so good. This was particularly so in the ports of Ramsgate and Margate. Tansy always put the proceeds of these sales straight into an old biscuit tin where he kept the food kitty, for further food purchases.

There was always plenty of coal on board, which is not surprising, considering the amount we used to carry as cargo. We also did very well for cheeses, as we took a couple of cargoes of Edam and Gouda from Holland to Harwich that first summer. We didn't pilfer the cargoes; what we had was given to us by the Northumberland coal wharfingers and the Dutch cheese merchants. Tansy used to take gifts, such as a couple of boxes of Whitstable oysters with him, to present in return for the gifts we were given. Tansy being as he was, as straight as a die, would never have countenanced anything like pilfering, not even one lump of coal or a basket of coke.

Although stowing and unloading cargo – boxes, sacks, coal, housebricks, stone, was hard enough work for young boys, the heaviest job, as far as I was concerned, was anchoring and pulling the anchor up again when getting underway.

Going to anchor, the first job was to haul several cables (say one hundred and fifty feet) of anchor chain out of the lockers down below, through the spurling-pipe, and range it along the deck forward of the windlass. Another several cables were then hauled up and laid in two wooden mangers, one on each side of the forward main hatch. As the ship approached the anchorage the anchor, which was catted up to the bow (that is hauled up with its shank horizontal) was lowered until it hung vertically from the hawse-pipe, then the anchor was 'apeak'. This done, Bert stood by with a crow-bar. When Tansy nodded his head to order the anchor let go Bert released the cat-stopper tumbler – a sort of big pelican hook – with his crow-bar, so releasing the anchor. Down through the hawse-pipe the chain went, with a roar. If extra chain was needed to be let out, to increase the scope, I flung a turn over the windlass barrel, and the weight of the chain already over the side heaved it out steadily. We had to always be careful we didn't lose a finger, or even a hand, especially on a dark windy night at an open anchorage, with *Second Apprentice* yawing and veering, pitching and tossing like a maddened steer. We had to watch our feet, too, that they were clear of the wildly running chain as it surged through the hawse-pipe.

The worst job of all – the most exhausting – was heaving up the anchor, especially if we had let out a lot of scope. It needed all the strength of Bert, Ted and my puny self. The windlass was worked with a lever, like a pump, and it brought the wet, cold chain on board link by link. The chain piled itself up on deck as it came in and had to be cleared every so often back into the manger. This we did with a chain hook, something like a meat-handler's hook, or like Long John Silver's hook.

After interminable pumping, the anchor chain was at last straight up and down. Then we hoisted enough sail to move the boat, depending on what the wind and sea were like, and from what direction they were coming at us. Then, as all three of us pumped up and down on the windlass handle, Tansy sheeted the sails in and worked the ship's head off the wind, so using the ship's weight to drag out the anchor from the sea-bed. All the time we pumped away on the windlass handle until the anchor stock broke the surface of the sea. Then, with the anchor still half under water before the bow, we hoisted more sail, so as to get clear out to the offing. As the ship moved we hauled in the anchor and catted it, that is we slung a line with a hook on the end of it around the anchor stock and hauled the anchor up on to the cathead high enough so that another chain, called the cat-stopper, could be fastened on to the anchor, to prevent it from being accidentally let go. That done, the hook was shifted to the anchor crown and the anchor was then 'fished' tight on the outboard side of the bulwark, where it was secured with yet another line called the shank painter, then with an iron chain called the cat-stopper. By the time that was done all of us were sweating, no matter what the weather, and breathing very hard indeed.

Often we also let out a second anchor, called the bower. Then there were two anchors to be weighed, and sometimes they might both, the main and the bower, be fouled on other crafts' anchors which had dragged over ours, or over which ours had dragged. The work involved in unsnarling such a cock-up on a moonless night with the rain blowing hard in the wind, especially if the wind was blowing onshore, leaving the captain little sea-room in which to manoeuvre the ship may be imagined. This happened on more than one occasion, in the wide, open harbour of Dover especially. What with heaving up our own two anchors and perhaps another besides, and at the same time hoisting the sails, a good foredeck hand needed to be a cross between a circus strong man, an acrobat, a steel-erector and a ballet dancer all at once. After six months on board *Second Apprentice* my back, belly, leg and arm muscles were like steel cords. I was, as the sailors say, 'like an Afghan hound – all prick and toe-nails.' I, too, developed an appetite like Ted's. The only difference between our eating capabilities was that I couldn't tackle the hard-tack as voraciously as he.

It was just as well that my muscles developed as they did, because hoisting anchor or the big heavy main-gaff, with the huge mainsail weighted on it needed all the strength that Ted and I could muster.

Being at anchor, especially in open roads when we were windbound – waiting for a favourable wind – meant standing night anchor watches. In the summer these were quite pleasant, and I sat on the forward windlass humming to myself or trying to remember a poem or a passage I had read, all the while keeping a look-out for other vessels coming to anchor, or our own or other vessels dragging. In winter-time, though, anchor watches could be purgatory. I stood or stamped up and down the foredeck (if Ted wasn't asleep down below) or the side-deck trying to keep warm, or in the rain or snow, trying to keep dry, with my oilskins streaming wet and trickles of cold water oozing down from the scarf tied around my neck. It was useless to seek shelter – there was none – and if there had been it would have obscured the necessary all-round view. My favourite anchor watch was the morning, because it was the shortest. At day-break I could dowse the anchor light and turn in. My least favourite anchor watch was the middle from midnight until 4.00 A.M. The nights were at their darkest, there was little or no movement in other ships, and the hours never seemed to end. The worst time of all at anchor watch was during a fog. Then, every noise from outside the vessel was to me a nightmare; it might be a big power vessel bearing down at us, we might be dragging our anchor; we might even be drifting near to the shore; I never knew for sure what was happening for much of the time as I strained my eyes searching, trying to penetrate through the thick fog and ringing the fog-bell every minute or so. Sometimes in a fog the cold was so damp that it penetrated even a set of oilskins and two thick wool jerseys, right through to my bones. During my first few months on board I woke Bert several times with false alarms in fog, but he never chastised me for it. He always said that it was better to be mistaken and safe than to be cocksure and dead.

There was still a lot of work to do, even when the ship was fog- or wind-bound. There was still the galley and the cleaning, the scraping and painting, and every time the tide changed the anchors and cables had to be tended, to make sure, as our bows changed their attitude to the wind and the ship and all the other ships in the anchorage slowly swung around, that we did not foul any other vessel's ground tackle, hull, or spars. Even so we had several close shaves, and it was only by fast and judicious use of the sweeps that we were able to keep clear. We had to keep good anchor and tide watches; repairs were expensive and money was in short supply. But it wasn't the thought of having to spend money that made good seamen; it was that to them, there was only one way to do anything: properly and well.

The easiest cargoes to handle in and out of the hold, were bulk cargoes like grain or coal. They were usually loaded on board down a chute. Then all we crewmen had to do was wait at the bottom of the chute, but well clear of it, for the stuff to come hurtling down a whole wagon at a time, and redistribute it around the hold evenly with our shovels. It was so dusty when the commodity poured down that we had to wear neckerchiefs around our mouths and at times could hardly breathe. The worst for dust was coal ('all or nothing'), and the fine black powder got everywhere. Our shovels were eighteen inches across the blades and with them we could lift about twenty pounds at a time at first, but that soon dropped to ten pounds.

Getting the coal and the grain out of the holds when we discharged cargo was a different matter. Then we used skips. These were shallow boxes with an iron lifting ring at each corner. They were lowered down the hold one at a time by Bert operating the spare gaff as a derrick by means of the dolly-winches and blocks and tackles. As each skip came down we loaded it with our shovels as fast as we could. When the skip was heaped full – about half a ton each load – Bert hauled it up and on deck. There, most times, the gaff tackle was unshipped from the skip, and the shore crane-tackle was bent on and up it went, on to a pile of grain or coal ashore, or into a railway wagon or horse-drawn cart or lorry, depending on where we were.

Flour, potatoes, and cement were shipped in bags, each weighing forty pounds. By the time a thousand or so of those had been chuted down the hold and humped up on to stacks as tight as we could get them you may imagine how our backs ached. At that time cement had started to be shipped in thick paper sacks, but the manufacturers had not quite developed the sacks strong enough to be sure that they didn't break when they slid down the chutes. Usually, cement powder flew everywhere. Each time the hold was unloaded and empty, it had to be cleaned out, to be ready for the next cargo, whatever that might be. That was a good two hour job for Ted and me, first with brooms and shovels and then sluicing away with a hose. After that the hold-bilge had to be pumped out.

The worst cargo of all was house-bricks. We carried them usually to the Channel Islands from Southampton or

Portsmouth. None of the brick-loading docks had a crane, and it meant handling fifty thousand or so bricks by hand each time we loaded and discharged. This involved five people. One man on the wagon ashore, who threw the bricks down, five at a time, to his mate on the jetty. He, in turn, threw the bricks, still in fives, down to Bert on deck. Bert then slid the bricks down a wide plank into the hold, where I caught them at the bottom of the plank. I was supposed to throw them, in my turn, five at time to Ted, who stacked them in the hold, but at first my hands were too small and soft. I could only manage three bricks at a time, consequently the pile of bricks grew at the bottom of the plank. Then, while the men topsides took a short breather, I had to carry on clearing the heaped up pile at the bottom of the plank. It was months before I could handle five bricks at a throw, ten thousand throws a load. We were not provided with gloves, and we wrapped our hands in rags, but by the end of the day, after fifty thousand bricks had passed through them, I had hands like bloody pieces of meat. It took weeks for them to harden enough to handle bricks without stinging and bleeding.

I don't blame the skipper or the mate for this. It was partly my fault that I suffered so. I was too proud to complain. If Ted could do it, so went my reasoning, so could I. In a way I was right, because after a few months I could stack bricks as fast as he. On subsequent visits to the Channel Islands in the years since, I have often looked at the neat brick-built houses which were constructed just before World War II and wondered if the inhabitants had any idea of the torture involved in getting those bricks to the islands.

The cargo back from the Channel Islands was usually cattle- or sheep-hides. These were dried, heavy, and the sharp edges were another excruciation to handle with unhealed hands. We didn't usually have many hides, and they generally were accompanied by barrels of animal offal, which always stank to high heaven; so much so that when we docked to unload them in Poole or Gravesend other craft slipped their cables and shifted berth or went out to anchor, to get away from the stench. When the hold was at last clear of hides and offal Ted and I scrubbed away for hours to get rid of the foul smell.

It wasn't all hard drudgery, though, and there was many a fine day out in the Channel, with the wind fair and easy. The times I enjoyed the best were when, after a few weeks, Tansy let me take regular tricks on the helm. At first these were always during his watch, the forenoon or the dog watches, so he could keep an eye on me. One fine sunny day, in September I think it was, there was a cold snap in the air, and we were bound cross-channel with a cargo of bricks for Jersey. I was tending the helm, while Tansy sat on his up-turned barrel, smoking his pipe, alongside of the wheel. The wind was almost dead on the beam, from the north-west, steady and not too strong. *Second Apprentice* was wearing every stitch she had but her squaresail and she was hammering along through the short, choppy seas like a steam engine, on a broad-reach. Astern, the coast of England still guarded us; ahead there was nothing but blue seas stretching, it seemed to infinity, shining and cold. The sky was clear, except for a few solitary gun-puffs over on the western horizon.

I was half wide-alert, watching the curve of the sails, the lines of the luffs, the gentle pitching of the bowsprit, and half daydreaming about the immense silence of the sea and of its voice. I was thinking how strange, what a paradox it was, the sea, its voice, and its silence; yet how true. The noises we could hear as *Second Apprentice* ploughed on towards the rim of the world were not of the sea. They

were of the encounter between the sea and what it met –
the ship's hull, her rigging, the strain of her timbers. The
sea is more reserved unto itself, more solitary, than any
other phenomenon known to man. I reflected that the land
lay inert; the land, except for what life in its myriad forms
imparted to it, was dumb. The sea had a life of its own.
Even if there were not one living thing in the depths of the
sea, even if all life left the Earth, yet the sea itself would
live, and the sea would speak still in her masked voice of
silence, like one of the oracles of the Gods, the essence of
mystery, eternal.

I was wakened from my half-reverie suddenly, as a
seabird cried over the starboard quarter. I turned my head
to see it. Tansy was no longer there on his bucket. He must
have crept away down the companionway and left me to
steer the ship alone. There was no one else on deck. I was
in command of the ship. Silently, without a word, the
accolade of trust had been bestowed on me, and I knew
then that I was considered to be more of a man than I
thought myself to be. Almost mechanically, I peered down
into the compass binnacle. The ship was a point off the
course. Joyously, proudly, I shoved the helm over and
lifted my head, and checked the wind and the sails. They
seemed, at that moment, to share in my pride and joy.
There was an instant urging in the wind, an instantaneous
stiffening of the sails' curves, a prompt angling of the hull a
little further to leeward, a brisk acceleration of the
bowsprit's pitches and tosses for a minute or so. Then the
wind eased back into its regular strength. The ship
regathered her sedateness about her and plodded on. But I
knew that *she* knew, and that in the bygone moment we had
been one entity, the wind, the sea, the ship, and me. I was
in my element.

13

Ted

To many a City gentleman, as he watched the sailing
coasters ply London Pool, the Thames Estuary, or the
Solent, the life of a sailor must have seemed replete with
romance, perhaps with a spicing of hazards. Many an office
boy, on his way across Tower Bridge with a message, or a
clerk going home after a boring day at the office of a law
firm, must have felt a pang of envy when he saw two or
three spritties, ketches or stumpies rafted together, waiting
for a change of tide, or for the arrival of cargo to be loaded.
The captains might be seated together on the stern of one
of the craft, yarning as he thought, telling tales of far away
places and sunny shores; more likely they were comparing
notes as to what cargoes were waiting, where, or what
vessel had foundered, and why, and who had survived, or
what ship had been laid up in the breaking yards, or what
trade our heavily subsidized continental competitors had
broken into.

As his eye ran over the hulls, our City man would
perhaps have noticed the red sails of a sprittie brailed up to
the mainmast and wondered why they looked so sloppy and
untidy. His eyes would have ranged over the mainsail of a
ketch and noted the varied hues of the patches on her
mainsail. But the main cause of his envy would have been
to see the evident casualness with which the crewmen
carried on their tasks. Unless they were manoeuvring the
vessel, or handling cargo, the bargemen rarely hurried.
They must have seemed to move slowly, as if they had all

the time in the world, as if they had brought into the very heart of the twentieth century the leisured pace of centuries gone by as they ambled along the decks seemingly aimless, or poked their heads out of the deckhouse door.

We could hardly have expected our City man to realize the truths of the matter; that the mainsails were brailed up loosely in readiness for shifting the craft; that the ketch mainsail had been patched because new mainsails cost money; that the crewmen moved slowly because they were probably exhausted after unloading a two hundred and fifty ton cargo of cement by hand in the little time available between tides, or while a dumb lighter was available; that the cook was gasping for air after sweating in the poky galley for hours.

Sunday in port was the only day when we perhaps deserved to be envied. If *Second Apprentice* was anywhere within reach of the south-eastern suburbs of London, Bert went home to his wife and family, but Tansy, Ted (who had no home), and I stayed. In the morning Tansy put on his best shore-going suit and went to chapel, if we were anchored or moored within decent reach of one; if not, he stayed in his cabin and read his Bible. Sundays were the only day when I didn't tidy and clean his cabin. On the shelf beside his bunk the only objects were a faded picture of his dead wife and a collection box for some Methodist Mission in West Africa. The only other books he had in his cabin, beside his Bible, were the ship's log and the accounts book, in both of which he made his entries in beautiful copperplate handwriting. Two of my weekday early morning jobs were to see that his ink pot was half full and that his boots were shined every morning, even at sea.

While the captain was at chapel or down in his cabin on Sunday mornings, Ted cleaned up the fo'c's'le and topsides; I looked after breakfast and prepared the midday meal. In port this was always a bit fancier than the weekday fare, perhaps pork with apple sauce or a stuffed hen, with a gooseberry tart and custard.

After dinner, when everything was cleared up, Ted gave us a few tunes on his mouth-organ as we all sat on the cargo-hatches. If we were laid alongside other coasters we might go and visit them, or their crewmen might come on board *Second Apprentice*. Often there was someone with a banjo or a concertina, and the bargemen came on board usually after the pubs had shut at two o'clock. Then the landsmen must have really envied us, as they strolled along the jetty with their families on their Sunday afternoon outings. Sometimes, if there were several ships lying together, perhaps the spritties *Camria*, *Genesta*, or *Sirdar*, which all had lively crews, there would be quite a gathering, with anything up to twenty sailors and captains, mates, deckhands, boys, ship's cats and dogs (on the shore), and, on rare occasions, even a wife or two and a few sailor's offspring, all enjoying Ted's rendering of 'Lambeth Walk', or 'Tipperary'. He was a discordant musician; his music was barely recognizable, but everyone enjoyed themselves anyway. Someone would bring out a tin whistle, someone a Jew's harp, and soon a pretty full orchestra was under way. They always, out of courtesy, played Tansy's favourite tune – 'Good-bye Dolly I Must Leave You'. We young lads soon found ourselves humming or whistling along with the music, and we forgot the back-breaking drudgery of the weeks gone by and to come, for a short while at least.

In this way I met many of the bargees and coastal sailors, some from as far away as Ireland, Scotland, and Liverpool. Some of them had been, in their younger days, before the First World War, seamen in the old square-riggers, the Cape Horners like the ships of the Garth Line, and some had even, as boys, sailed on the American Black-Ball Line, the hardest-driven ships ever in the history of sail. I cannot remember any one of them who was at all loud or boastful, though God knows they had the background to be so. I was always surprised, and, I suppose as a boy would be, a little disappointed, to find how modest, pragmatic, and conservative they generally were. After several voyages, I came to realize that these traits were very necessary to ensure happy and safe passages under sail, and I eventually realized that those traits were almost invariably balanced by a bigness of heart, a generosity of soul, an almost childish freshness of outlook and a knife-quick sense of humour which was both ribald and mischievous. They were expert at practical jokes.

A few of our sailor-visitors loved a drink, but (perhaps fortunately) their pay did not run to much more than a pint or two of beer a day when they were in harbour. The common landsman's impression of professional sailors as a rowdy, drunken lot is completely in error. It might have been true of some of the seamen from bigger ships, suddenly let loose on the shore after weeks of being pent up in the dreary confines of a steamer or under the rigid discipline of a warship, but very rarely was it true of coastal or estuarial sailormen, and especially in the cargo trade. Their pay was too low, their work was too arduous and the risks were too great. As the sailors used to say, 'Only fools and passengers drink too much.' As for the long-passage sailors in the old days, the reason they took to hard drinking in between passages is simple: it was to insulate themselves from the appalling conditions of their existence ashore. It was not easy to be a homeless, shipless sailor on the waterfronts of Liverpool, London, San Francisco, Valparaiso, or New York. It still is not.

We were also visited by various shore-side friends of Tansy's, a farmer, a butcher, a ship's chandler, perhaps an inn-keeper or two, but to me those visits were nowhere near as enjoyable. The main topics of conversation of those occasions seemed to be supplies, cargo, and money, and the tradesmen rarely, as the sailors almost always did, seemed to treat me as anything other than a small, unintelligent being either to be patronized or at everyone's beck and call.

Sometimes, if we were moored anywhere near Sandwich, Tansy's daughter Daisy came to visit us. She was in her middle teens, and it was obvious to me that Ted had taken a shine to her. Daisy, however, treated him with a certain aloofness, and she sought out my company. I don't know why this was – I was nowhere near as tall or handsome as Ted. I suppose it must have been because I liked her as a person just as much as I liked her as a girl. She reminded me of Branwen Powell back in Llangareth, on whom (I realized when I'd left Wales) I'd had a secret crush for a couple of years. Also, unlike Ted, I didn't try to change the subject when she talked about what were supposed by Ted to be 'girlish' things like books and poetry, music, and painting. By any standards, Daisy was showing promise of becoming a real beauty. She was slim, she had golden hair, she had April in her eyes, and music on her tongue. Several times I ached to ask her to come for a walk, but always I desisted for Ted's sake. I had to go to sea with Ted, sometimes cooped up with him for days on end, and I depended on him to 'show me the ropes' when it came to most jobs on board. I think I acted on intuition – I don't think I was any wiser than my years would allow. Daisy, anyway, was a year older than I, and at fourteen, one year is like ten years at thirty. But Ted and I always looked forward eagerly to Daisy's visits, and we both spruced ourselves up for hours before she arrived, though I doubt if anyone would have noticed it except ourselves. The other thing we looked forward to was the dainties which Daisy brought each time she visited us – things like jam tarts, and apple pies, treacle toffee and home-made jellies. What I appreciated most were the books she bought me – everything from *Mr Midshipman Easy* by Captain Marryat, to *Nostromo* by Joseph Conrad. After our first conversation, Daisy always brought me at least half a dozen books and a few newspapers. I devoured them eagerly, at sea, hunched up under the fo'c's'le lamp in between cooking, cleaning, tricks on the wheel or cargo handling. As Tansy had told me, I was to learn a lot more on board *Second Apprentice* than I had at school.

Another source of books was the Mission to Seamen launch, *Flying Angel*, which cruised the Thames Estuary, bringing a small lending library, along with spiritual comfort for those in need of that intangible commodity. Each time *Flying Angel* came alongside the clergyman on board stayed on the launch, in consideration, I suppose, of the old sailors' superstition about having a 'man in black' on board one's own craft. Tansy chatted with him for a few minutes over the side-rail. Ted and I seized the opportunity to dash on board the holy-roller's launch and down below to a tiny cabin where books and papers lay higgledy-piggledy in a large crate in the custody of a severe-looking young man wearing rimless spectacles. Ted sorted out several comics, those which weren't too tattered, and I scrabbled around for anything above the level of *With Gordon in the Sudan* or *What Katy Did*. Sometimes I came across treasure trove – books like *The Autobiography of a Supertramp* by W. H. Davies, or *The Call of the Wild* by Jack London. (After I read the first page of that, I have remained a devotee of London.) The variety of old magazines which the Seaman's Mission launch brought around never ceased to amaze me – there seemed to be everything from *The Tatler* to *The Farmer and Stockbreeder*

via *John O'London's Weekly* and *Titbits*. Sometimes the
magazines were years old, but we enjoyed them all the
same. I once even discovered one of Havelock Ellis's
manuals on sexual behaviour which had evidently escaped
the eagle eye of the Mission librarian. I shoved the book
under my jersey quickly and smuggled it on board *Second
Apprentice*. Ted and I eagerly tried to decipher its esoteric
Victorian language. At first I was pleased with my find. I'd
actually interested Ted in a *book*, but after one or two
sessions hunched over the book with furrowed brows of
deep puzzlement, Ted gave up on Havelock Ellis. 'Too
bleedin' long-winded,' was Ted's verdict. 'Blimey, if I
wanted to get a bit of khyfer and stopped to read all that
bloody gubbins my bird would have it away on her toes
before I got through the first fucking page!'

Apart from girls (or day-dreaming about them, rather)
Ted's only other shore-side interest seemed to be cowboy
films and soccer. His prize possession on board was an old
football, which, when we had a rare idle hour, we used to
kick around on the quay-side, sometimes with the lads and
men from other craft joining in. This we did rain or shine.
His dream was to be centre-forward for Arsenal, or, failing
that, outside-right. His job on board, and the life he led, he
seemed to consider to be temporary things – a brief episode
before a life of soccer and women, which was to somehow
miraculously come about 'when I'm bleedin' twenty, by
Christ'.

I had very early learned the unwritten law that on board
a ship of any kind a person's private life, his origins, his
family, were completely his own concern and that I should
never ask any questions about those matters. It took several
months before, from what he volunteered to me, I could
piece together scraps of Ted's life-story.

Ted's mother, so he said, was Irish and she had been an

assistant cook in a big household in London. 'Bleedin'
house full of toffs up in the West End,' as he put it. She
had fallen for a soldier, who, when she discovered that Ted
was to be bestowed on the world, promptly deserted her by
wangling a transfer overseas (one of the conveniences of the
Empire). How Ted knew this was a mystery to me. It
seems that Ted's mother farmed him out to foster parents
soon after he was born, and his mother paid for his keep.
Eventually when he was about four years old his mother
disappeared. Whether she had gone away with another
man, killed herself, or returned to Ireland no one ever
knew. Ted was sent to an orphanage near London, and
had remained there until he was fourteen and old enough
to work. 'Bloody place – I was in trouble half the time –
you know, smoking in the shit-house and that kind of
thing, and I spent bloody hours nearly every day polishing
the floor in the hallway – at the posh end of the house, see?
Polished my bleedin' arms down to the fucking elbows, I
did. They used to make us all dive into a bath full of cold
water every morning when we got up. Never knew why. I
suppose they thought it would stop us getting a hard on –
that and the bleedin' cocoa every night. They laced that
with some stuff to stop us wanking, but Christ, you could
hear the bloody beds squeaking and rattling all soddin'
night.'

From the orphanage Ted had been sent to work in a pub
as a live-in porter, cleaning up and carrying crates of beer
down into the cellar, but after a week or so he had been
discovered drinking ale on the job and had been 'sent up
the road' (fired) immediately. The relative of a youth whom
he had befriended was the deckhand of a shrimp bawley
sailing out of Southend in Essex. He got Ted a job as deck-
boy. Ted's duties were to help cast out the shrimp nets,
make tea, haul in the nets, and help to cook the shrimp on

the way into port. If that sounds a fair employment for a
young lad, see how Ted expressed himself about it: 'We
was out day and bleedin' night, the bloody boat was only
twenty-four feet, and sometimes the fog was so thick and
the rain so fucking heavy you could have stuck your arm
out and made a hole in it. The skipper was a right stingy
geezer, as mean as old Bill, and he docked our pay any time
we ripped a net, or was late getting back into South-
bloody-End. I didn't have nowhere ashore to stay, and my
pay was bloody sixpence a trip, so I couldn't afford a doss-
house. I slept in the fore-cuddy, about as big as an ordinary
fucking dog-kennel, and got fish and chips from ashore for
the first few weeks. The bleedin' skipper found out that I'd
been pinching a handful of shrimp to eat, and docked me a
week's bloody pay. Then I started cooking for myself on
the little stove where we used to boil the sodding tea-water,
and when he found out about that he charged me for
lodging on board, three bob a week, the fucker, and him
not married neither. Pity any poor woman that married a
geezer like that. She'd be paying him bloody lodgings and
giving birth to fucking cash registers, and living on bloody
boiled shrimp for ever and a fucking day! Come to think of
it the sod had a face like a bleedin' boiled shrimp! Then a
mate of mine got me a berth on a mulie, so I told the
shrimp skipper to stick his bleedin' bawley where the
monkey sticks his sodding nuts. It was tons better on the
mulie, though. I was on board her for about six months.
But the bleedin' cargoes – all the shit from every bleedin'
horse in the Household Cavalry and at Whitbread's
Brewery, and from Carter Paterson's furniture wagons. It
wasn't bad working with the brewery people, though; they
always used to send a crate of beer down with the horse-
shit. The grub was much better too, and the mulie had a
proper fo'c's'le. It was like a bleedin' home from home. Then,

through another pal, I met Bert, and here I am. Of course, I won't be at sea all my life, no fear! I am going to find a nice little *pusher* (girl) and have a home and kids and everything . . .'

At first I was wary of Ted. He was a rough looking kind of youth, despite his handsomeness, and I had been warned in Wales, time and again about the dishonesty of Londoners and how they would rob their own mothers. But Ted never stole anything from me in the eighteen months or so that we sailed together. True, he might, in jest, hide my sea-boots, or surreptitiously cut the buttons off my watch jacket while he stood talking to me in the darkness on deck, and hide them, but those were normal kind of japes among lads anywhere. Neither, as far as I know, did Ted ever pilfer from the cargoes we carried, although sometimes the stuff we carried, like bags of sugar or boxes of tomatoes, could easily have been broached and some of the contents sold ashore. That would have been very risky, because most of the waterfront folk in the small ports in Britain were finely attuned to any activity that was in the least bit unusual. No doubt word of any misdeed would have reached Tansy's ears before the ship sailed, if not upon her arrival at the next port, or upon her return to the scene of the crime.

Ashore, to Ted, however, was a different matter; ashore was a different world and to him landsmen merited a different set of morals. Never, I think, did Ted go ashore for a walk in the town and around, in the summer-time, but he returned with his pockets full of apples or plums filched from some good yeoman's trees. Never did he go shopping on an errand for Tansy when he did not come back with a couple of bars of chocolate or a bag of sweets, or a packet of Woodbines which he had shop-lifted. Ted ashore was like a magpie. Anything that wasn't cemented to the ground, lashed or nailed down was fair game to him. He never stole from shops where he bought things for Tansy or Bert. That would have been against his peculiar sense of morality. Instead he went to the bigger department stores, such as Woolworth's or Marks and Spencer's. How he was never detected and caught is a wonder. When he slithered down the fo'c's'le-scuttle and triumphantly displayed combs and pencils, sweets and chocolate, cigarettes and even, once, a fancy shirt, I always wondered how he managed to hide it all. Once, in Ramsgate or Margate, I forget which, I had a bad cold and no money to buy cough lozenges (I sent most of my wages home every time I was paid). Ted disappeared into the rain ashore 'to buy a paper, Tansy, I want to see how Arsenal got on.' He returned a half hour later with two packets of cough-drops filched from a newsagent's counter. How Bert never knew that Ted was doing this is a mystery, because it was obvious that on a deckhand's pay he couldn't afford a shirt like the one he stole. Perhaps Bert did know, and turned a blind eye. That would have been Bert's way, except that I was pretty sure the mate would have had a 'quiet word' with Ted.

Ted borrowed small sums of money from me from time to time – sixpence here, a shilling there – but he always paid me back as soon as he himself was paid his wages.

We could draw advances on our pay at any time in port, but I was wary of doing this in case I couldn't send my Mam her regular five shillings a week. That left me with two shillings spending money or roughly three-pence halfpenny a day. That wasn't bad, in those days, for a lad of fourteen, because a bar of chocolate was only twopence, and the entrance ticket to a Saturday afternoon cinema show was never more than threepence. However, by the end of July, I had started to save up for my railway ticket home to Wales at Christmas, so that just about halved my own weekly pocket money, down to one shilling. Out of that I had to buy an oilskin coat (I'd lost mine over the side through my own negligence) and a new pair of shore-going boots; the ones I had worn from Wales were ruined by salt through wearing them at sea. (The romance of sail-in-trade!)

Ted's cursing lessened a great deal once he got to know me better. I observed that it was his habit to swear a great deal mostly when he was with people, especially other boys, whom he didn't know very well. I put it down as a cover-up for shyness or for inarticulateness. Where others said, '... er ...' or '... hmm ...' Ted said 'bleeding', 'bloody', 'fucking' or 'sodding'. He meant nothing by it. His upbringing would have made a saint curse.

When Ted went up on deck the colour of his language changed directly from blue to pink. When Tansy came up on deck it changed again, to pure though halting lily-white.

Ted was, despite the often dirty labour, a very clean lad. Even on the coldest days as soon as work was finished he sluiced himself down, bare to the waist, in sea or river water hauled over the side in a bucket. I soon found myself doing the same, though I hated the coldness of the water. The shock seemed, somehow, to be too much of an intrusion into the depths of my being. Perhaps I had been subconsciously thinking of Ted's orphanage cold-baths.

After a while I never read anything but papers or magazines when Ted was in the fo'c's'le. It made him uncomfortable when I was reading a book, and I did my best not to sound at all much-read or more informed about what was going on in the world than he appeared to be, but it was a hard job. I had to be on my guard all the time I was with Ted, so as not to lose his fragile friendship. To put him at his ease, I never lost any opportunity to ask his advice on how something should be done – perhaps coiling a line or how to make a knot, or a splice. This pleased him greatly, and then we were very close pals. Indeed we became such good friends that at Christmas that first year, in 1938, I invited Ted to go home with me to Wales, but Bert had already made arrangements for him to visit his family in London. I had to be careful how I invited Ted. He was sensitive to any suspicion of pity about his circumstances. For weeks I boasted to him about how much more wealth, how much more friendliness, what better footballers, what pretty girls, we had in Wales, until he was ready to put a bet on it, and even agree to come to Llangareth to see for himself. Fortunately, because of Bert's invitation, he couldn't come. I would either have lost the bet because I'd lost the argument with Ted, or I would have lost a friend, so in the end it all worked out for the best.

Ted was one of the nimblest-fingered sailors I ever saw. His deck-seamanship – there is only one word for it – professional. In the fourteen months or so that he had been on board *Second Apprentice* he had learned from Bert, and even, in some cases, surpassed him at, making eye-splices and long splices in wire rope; and his knowledge of knots and hitches was surprising in one so young. The average bargeman used only a few knots – the reef, the sheet, the figure of eight, the bowline – and about the same number of hitches – the clove, the timber, the Blackwall, the Liverpool, the round-turn-and-two-half-hitches; but Ted knew knots and hitches that even, at times, surprised Tansy, and he could run up a foot or two length of baggy-wrinkle out of scruffy old rope in no time at all. Ted loved working with ropes and wires. He disliked keeping watches at the helm. He said it bored him. Often I stood an hour or even two of his watch, while he stood for me in the galley.

Ted was the kind of person who always has to be doing something with his hands, and is not happy unless he can see the results of his effort. When he made a sennit, or a fender from old rope the looks of absolute concentration on Ted's face, while he was busy making it, and of satisfaction when it was done, were sights to be remembered. Whatever Ted had made looked like it had been purchased brand new at a chandler's.

Apart from making things, another activity Ted enjoyed was shinning up the main shroud ratlines whenever a job had to be done at the mainmasthead, such as lashing up the topsail when it was handed, or keeping a lookout for a buoy or a marker. Then Ted looked completely *en rapport* with all his surroundings. Unconsciously he then was what all boys who ever dreamed of going to sea would like to be: fair, handsome, healthy, strong, mostly willing, clever in his own way, ingenious in a pinch, well liked and good humoured.

If everything went well Ted would advance in life, slowly perhaps, but he would advance at least to a mate in the Trade. He might even rise to Master some day, if he could keep his language, his childlike impulses and his man's passions under control. If he could not, then he was doomed to a life of toil, privation and debauchery. This was one of the things about himself that Ted knew, as he confessed in the small dark hours, but the one thing he did not know was fear or self pity of the whining kind. Ted was doomed to be one of those who are man enough to scorn any who might pity them. His life, hard as it was, was his own and to live it was, to him, a privilege. He was a child of the sea, and knew of no other affection or love. He was one of a type whose tradition goes back to the youth of the world, a type without which the mighty civilizations and empires of the past could have been only dreams; without which the human race would probably still be sitting by fires in caves.

It could be said that Ted's cultural replacements are the skinheads and the punk rockers of today, but they are a lot less innocent than Ted was, not quite as colourfully profane, and much less believing. They have learned how to make themselves heard, but they have also learned how to whine and complain. That Ted never did – he would have rather thrown himself over the side. He knew all about cruelty, cold-heartedness and exploitation – if anyone ever knew about men's inhumanity to man, Ted did. But he never once showed spite in his heart, nor even resentment. Even when he cursed the memory of some bullying or meanness towards him or others it was always with a hint of wry humour. Now, men of Ted's ilk are middle-aged and those of them who survived the war are comfortably ashore, probably fully paid-up members of some trade union or other.

The generation after generation of boys and men who laboured on the seas in vile conditions for a pittance have all gone, forgotten except by a few, a very few, who are honoured to have known some of them, and who loved them.

14
Bert

Sometimes *Second Apprentice* made very pleasant lodgings, as when she was moored in a little rural creek or river like the Stour, the Hamble, or the Medway. Sometimes when she was made fast to a tree birds sang in her rigging and spiders weaved gossamer webs in her shrouds so that they looked like ratlines for elves, fairies and goblins, and green, red or golden leaves, conkers and acorns fell on her deck. At other times, we hauled the bower anchor and sank it into softly waving green grass. Then Ted and I ran on the banks and swung on low tree branches. There *Second Apprentice* might wait for a whole tide mirrored in a pool, her decks spangled with dew drops under the moon, her black rigging and sails towering into the night sky, probing the domain of the driving clouds and the swinging stars. Then, when we lads crept silently down the fore-scuttle, the fo'c's'le was snug, warm, and without draughts. The oil lamp lit up brightly in a second or two, the vessel in the calm water undisturbed, without dirt or noise, and no landlord's bill to pay. On those days and nights, very few and far between, I would not have exchanged homes with the King of England.

Gradually, as the weeks of my first year on board passed, the ship became more and more my home, and ever more to me she became a part of the men in her, so that the men in her became part of my home. Abaft the deckhouse, *Second Apprentice* was like a replication of her captain – quiet, tidy, stern yet at ease, severe yet relaxed, and honest as she was sturdy. Forward of the helm she took on certain aspects of

Bert's personality. At sea or in port, to a trained eye everything about her mid-ships section was ship-shape; everything was how, where, and when it should be, all the halyards, the sheets, the burtons, the lazy jacks, the downhauls and falls, the clean decks and paintwork, all was exactly as it ought to be in any well run ship. But to the novice or the landsman, unaccustomed to the ways of working sail-craft, it would have all seemed a chaotic pickle, with a plethora of ropes of all different lengths and sizes hung, strewn, and coiled in all sorts of places, so that he would wonder how anyone could ever sort out the mess. So it was with our ship's mate, Bert.

Everything that Bert did on board *Second Apprentice* he did with a perfection that is almost unattainable this side of the pearly gates. If Bert heaved the weighty gaff of the heavy mainsail up in a howling breeze the halyard needed no extra swinging; it was up, chock-a-block. If Ted and I with our combined strength could not lift another link of the anchor cable and Bert grabbed the windlass lever, the anchor came up. If Bert made an eyesplice in a two-inch diameter wire rope it was finished as neat as a roebuck's eye, and that wire would part before the eyesplice failed. If Bert stowed an awkward cargo of barrels, sacks, boxes, or timber, and the weather played up hell on the passage, the cargo stayed stowed.

But perfection breeds paradoxes. Everything that Bert did, he seemed to do awkwardly. Even when he walked along the deck it was with an awkward gait. Even when he ate his meals he seemed to be all odd angles, and his missing teeth did nothing to help him seem at all symmetrical. It wasn't the shape of his body; hard labour had kept Bert trim enough, as it did most of the working sailors (except a few of the very old cooks). It wasn't lack of dexterity; I saw Bert many a time flick a round-turn-and-two-half-hitches over a cleat or a mooring post so fast that my eyes could not discern his movement. It wasn't that he did not have a sense of fitness or tidiness; God knows he instilled that into us lads so deeply that it remains with me until this day. In his movements he resembled one of those men who, despite the neatness of their form, no matter how much they spend, can never find and wear a well-fitting suit of clothes. It took me several days of working closely with Bert until I finally discovered what it was about him which made his movements seem so awkward. It was very simple. Bert was left-handed, 'clack-handed' as the sailors put it. It was also obvious after observing him for a while, that his left-handedness did not stop at his elbows, but extended up to his brain, and therefore it affected the way he saw everything. Trying to learn from Bert was a little like looking in a mirror. You know that what you see is your reflection, and you take it for granted that this is what you look like. It is only after a few weeks or months of acceptance of this that you realize that what is in the mirror is actually the reverse of what you look like. The image is true, but only for your reflection, not for you. Everything that Bert taught us or showed us, every technique, was correct for *him*. But we had to reverse the whole process so as to make it correct for us. The miracle to me was that it worked. Bert, once he had taught us anything, no matter how complex, made it stick in our heads, and I for one never forgot it.

As mate, it was one of Bert's duties, by the unwritten rules, to teach us youngsters practically everything except the domestic chores. Those, like street rhymes and hop-scotch, were taught by our immediate predecessors on the ascending age-scale – in my case, by Ted.

There were no formal lessons in seamanship and navigation, as there would have been on a big ocean-going vessel. It was all 'hands on' training, as the Americans so vividly express the method. If I wanted to know how to do something I did it, and Bert stood over me to correct or congratulate me. To do this he had two stock phrases: 'Not that way, you silly bugger', or 'Good show, cocker! Now do it again!'

One of the first aspects of navigation that Bert taught me was the 'Rule of the Road' – the rules governing the navigation of a ship by night and day when other craft are in the vicinity. He did this by making me repeat rhymes over and over again until I could have repeated them backwards:

When both lights you see ahead,
Starboard turn and show your red.
Green to green, or red to red.
Perfect safety, go ahead.
If to your starboard red appear
It is your duty to keep clear
To act as judgement says is proper
To port or starboard, back or stop her;
But if upon your port is seen
A vessel's starboard light of green
There's not so much for you to do
For green to port keeps clear of you.

and: Steamers have white lights on the mast,
A sailer no such light will cast,
But if she shows red over green
Then a sailer you have seen.

and: Two black balls or red on red,
Then you know her rudder's dead.

and: Green on red, three whites on high,
And you know a tow goes by.

and: If moving white light you discern
Then you know you see her stern.
One or two white lights and stopped,
Be sure her anchor she has dropped.

and: Green over white – trawling light,
Red on white – catch fish they might.
Two black cones their points a-kissing,
By day you're sure that she is fishing.
A third cone, point up, like a cuckold,
Then your course well clear will you hold.

and: Three black balls to heaven bound
Shows that vessel is aground;
If by night to ground she's wed,
Two white lights and red on red.

and: A sailing craft, cone pointed down,
Her engine's pushing, homeward bound.

Nothing could be more simple, nor easier as a method to learn and remember the basic safety rules of nautical traffic. The official written rules were so complex as to be almost beyond the comprehension of the average barge makee-learner.

Other rhymes were:
For two sailing vessels meeting with the wind on different sides:

When the wind is on your port
Then of wisdom don't be short,
Like the ladies of the street,
You'll avoid them when you meet.

For two sailing ships with the wind on the same side:

If you are closer to the wind (always pronounced 'wynd')
Of her stay clear and peace you'll find.

For a sailing ship and a powered vessel meeting in confined
waters:

No matter if you're a big three master,
If she's got power she is faster;
A barquentine or sleek square rigger,
If she's got power she is bigger.
To yourself always say.
'She has power – and the right of way!'

For a sailing ship and a powered vessel meeting in open
waters: (Note, except for the last line this rule no longer
applies.)

When well clear and in the offing,
The steamer's cap to you she's doffing;
To you the right of way she'll give—
But keep well clear and you will live!

Right from the first trip, when we arrived at Remagen, I
helped Ted to rig the cargo derrick under Bert's supervision.
Even after six months on board, after we had rigged it
innumerable times, Bert could still do the heavy job alone
faster than we two lads. A spare gaff, which was lashed to the
bulwark when not in use, was mounted on the mast, by a
locking ring on its heel. Then a single whip was led from the
dolly-winch at the base of the mast through a big block on

the outer end of the gaff. A cargo hook was moused to the end of the whip. That was the heaving line. Then two guyropes were bent on the outer end of the gaff. One of these led through another block lashed up high to the shrouds. To the end of that guyrope we lashed a heavy weight – the bower anchor was usually employed for this, but if we were alongside a lighter, at anchor ourselves, then we used anything that weighed heavily enough – bags of potatoes or sacks of coal. This weight was known as the 'deadman'.

The cargo was hoisted up in skips by Bert working the dolly-winch handle. This hauled up the hooked whip which pulled the loaded skip up above the hatch. The shoreguy was then heaved by the man or boy on the jetty and the gaff-end was pulled over the cart or wagon being loaded. This movement pulled the shroudguy, thus hauling up the deadman weight. The skip was then lowered on to the cart by Bert unwinding the dolly-winch. The carter unloaded the skip and shoved it, empty, back toward the ship. The return of the gaff-end over the hold was aided by the weight of the deadman as it sank again. Then Bert unwound the skip-whip, thus lowering the empty skip once again into the hold, where Ted and I waited to reload it. Each haul and return of the skip, once we got into the swing of things, took about three to four minutes, and each loading of the skip, depending on what type of cargo we were handling, took between five to fifteen minutes. So it went on, up and down, all day, mostly in sweaty silence except for the rattle of the dolly-winch, the squeaking of blocks, the puffing and hooting of railway engines, the neighing of horses and the shouts of Ted, each time the skip was loaded and ready to be hoisted: 'Heave away, Bert!' or 'Up she goes, my hearty!' and Bert's yell each time the skip was swiftly lowered: 'Watch your heads!' or 'Come on, I thought you'd filled the bloody thing!'

Getting ready to sail was, for us all, a relief from the grinding work in harbour. Then Bert was in his glory. If we were all seated at a meal, perhaps breakfast, waiting for the tide to rise, Bert disappeared early from the table, usually without saying a word, or 'Well, I'd better go and have a shufti up top . . .' By the time I had cleared up the pots and plates, and Ted had squared away the skipper's lobby and the fo'c's'le, Bert, always humming to himself when he worked alone, had the cargo hatch covers, all heavy long boards, in place, and the loose gear such as the huge sweep oars and the punt-poles, and loose mooring lines, all lashed down on top of the hatches, the running rigging lines all flaked out on deck ready for hoisting, and the topsail sitting on the main truck ready for hauling up. When the time came to let go the mooring lines, Ted or I was already at the top of the shrouds, ready to let the topsail loose from its gaskets. If there was a strong wind blowing this was a risky business. I always remembered that my predecessor had been killed doing that job when he had fallen, or been blown, to the deck fifty feet below. As if I needed reminding, Bert always warned us, as we shinned up the ratlines, 'Take heed – one hand for yourself.'

Only when the mooring lines were ready to be slipped, and the last topsail gasket was being taken off, did Tansy appear on deck. He stood by the helm studying the mastheads for a minute or so, gauging the weather, then he silently nodded. The mooring lines were thrown off the bollards or the buoy, or the anchor was brought on board, the last gasket came zinging off the ballooning topsail, and it was hoisted up, gaff and all, until it was apeak. The power in the topsail, considering its size compared to the main, was amazing. No sooner was it apeak and sheeted home than *Second Apprentice*, all ninety feet of her, if there was any breeze at all, started to gain steerage way. By the time I had regained the deck the mate and Ted were already hoisting the mainsail. I guess that from the time Tansy took hold of the helm and nodded his head until we were under full working sail, in anything but a hard wind, was no more than about twelve to fifteen minutes. That was main, main-topsail, foresail, two jibs, mizzen and mizzen-t'sail. Often I caught glimpses of people watching us from the shore, or from other ships moored along the jetties or at anchor. Then I always felt proud and important, and not at all envious of the watchers.

Bert always kept his eyes on the sails and rigging when we were entering or leaving harbour, and much of the time at sea. I suppose that is one of the main differences between true sailors and town dwellers – the sailor's head is generally *up*. If there was a tricky exit, or a headwind entering a narrow harbour, Bert watched the sails and rigging, leaning over this way and that to watch a luff, or to check the run of a sheet, his blue eyes squinted almost closed, and one hand stroked his walrus moustache. Being novices, Ted and I generally followed the captain's gaze in tight corners, but Bert always watched his charge, the rig, and when he moved, to correct the set of some sail, he moved like quicksilver. I guessed his age at about forty-five, but when he was in a hurry his movements were those of a lad of twenty. Bert usually had a cigarette, lit or not, stuck in one corner of his lips. He was the dandy of *Second Apprentice*. He, being the only married man on board, changed into a wife-laundered shirt every two days, but he never wore a collar unless he was going ashore for a message, a pint in the evening or to his home. Both he and Tansy, in port, generally went to a pub where they were well-known, for a bath once or twice a week. We lads, not being rich enough or, in my case, old enough to drink, had to make do with a cold sluice in a bucket, or if we were near a freshwater supply a hot water 'rub-down' from a large bucket heated up on the galley stove.

Bert always wore, except at the meal table, a flat cap, in the peak of which was stuck a faded, tattered Armistice Day poppy. The cigarettes he smoked were 'Woodbines' at fourpence for ten, and he gave me the cigarette cards each time he opened a new packet. They were of footballers, and I treasured the whole set for years, until I lost them twenty-eight years later, in the *Two Brothers* disaster. They would be worth a small fortune now, although that's not the reason I saved them – we'll come to that in time.

The only occasions that Bert didn't smoke on deck were when we carried ammunition at the early part of the war, explosives or fodder. Then when he needed a fag he puffed away down in the skipper's lobby, safely away from any danger of fulminant fumes. Ted told me that Bert smoked and wore his cap even in bed, when he was asleep, and I believed him until one morning I discovered Bert sleeping off a hangover. But that was on only one occasion.

Ted smoked 'Gold Flake' cigarettes at sixpence for ten, but he didn't give me the cards. He swapped them ashore, and on board other coasters, for two cigarettes apiece.

It was obvious to me, after a few passages that Bert loved *Second Apprentice*; he must have done for he'd had one or two offers of a captain's berth on river-plying spritties, but he was content to stay with our ship. In effect, when we were in harbour or when Tansy was not on watch, Bert was completely in charge of the ship's sailing and working. Bert never seemed satisfied unless the ship had called from him his utmost exertions, and he had called from her all her power and strength. Both he and the ship repaid each other by a faithfulness, a loyalty which was often to be tried to the limits of endurance and beyond. He watched every flutter of the sail-luffs as if they were entering his very being. Every murmur of the water alongside seemed to delight him. He was, when his hands were not occupied in some task, always resting them for a moment on some piece of the ship, as if he was fondling her. In those moments his eyes veiled momentarily, as if he were suddenly dreaming, as if he were at that instant living more intensely than we have ever known, as if the ship was his ideal of beauty and perfection.

I once mentioned this offhandedly to Ted. 'Let's face it,' said that stalwart, 'he's bonkers about the bloody ship. If his missus could see him – blimey, it's like he was on the vinegar strokes – she'd do her bleeding nut!'

Whenever the ship was underway and Bert was on the wheel, he was somehow bigger and taller, and it was only when Tansy came on deck that he reverted to his real dimensions, and the colour of his complexion and clothes faded. But that was only in the imagination of a small Welsh ship's boy. Ted said that, 'Tansy had tasted bloody salt water before Bert was bleeding breeched. Bert's one of them blokes what always has to have someone over them. Tansy's a master, and that's why they work so flipping well together, see?'

'What do you think I'll be, Ted?' I asked him.

'A bloody tally clerk, that's what you'll be, if they don't bleedin' hang you first!' Ted grinned when he said that. I was reading a book. His face fell serious in the low glow of the fo'c's'le, 'You reading all that fucking bullshit. Fill yourself full of that and you won't know which way is sodding up!'

Towards the winter of 1938, we arrived at Greenwich on a Sunday morning with a cargo of coal and Bert took Ted and me to his home nearby. It was a grey, overcast day. I was astonished at the transformation in Bert when we stepped ashore from a neighbouring coaster's jolly-boat. From being a man in charge of all he surveyed, from looking as if he cared for everything he saw; from being an erudite source of esoteric information about everything from airing holds to refitting windlasses, from avoiding the Goodwin Sands to wearing the North Foreland, he was suddenly transformed into just another rather funny looking little man in a shabby mackintosh, black boots, a flat cap and moustache much too large for his face. As we waited for a bus he no longer talked of 'sheeting home' and 'being in irons', and the ships he'd sailed aboard which had been 'stiff as a church but mean as a pawnbroker's clerk'. Now all his talk was of how his wife might be annoyed with him for taking us home to lunch without first warning her. 'She'll do her flipping lid. I hope the babby's got over that whooping cough . . . I'd have taken you for a couple of pints, but if the missus smells it . . .' As we boarded the double-decker bus (the first one I'd ever been on) he turned to me as he reached the top of the stairs. There were other people waiting impatiently to go down the stairs to dismount at the next stop. Bert said, 'How about you blokes giving me a hand in the garden this afternoon? Last time I was home the missus played up merry hell because it's in a bit of a pickle . . .'

We alighted at the end of a long street, as straight as a rifle-shot, lined on both sides with houses which all adjoined on to one another, like a long row of stowed mineral-water boxes, all looking exactly alike. They all had the same shape of gable-roof, with the same kind of wooden fretwork under the eaves, and the same type of iron railing in front of the tiny gardens, which looked, from the end of the street, like a long array of dwarfs' spears.

As we wended our way to Bert's house, he told us that he was related to one of the old river families, who had been in the barge business since the days of Henry the Eighth, 'and probably before that. I started my working life on a dumb-

barge owned by my father, and went from that to a sprittie –
that was before the last war. Then, when old Jerry started
his fenangles I volunteered for the Navy and went into
mine-sweepers. I was lucky, I never got into any real
trouble. We was based in Scapa Flow and pretty well out of
the way of it all. But it got me hooked on the sea. When I
was discharged I didn't want to be on the river no more, see?
So I looked for sea-going coasters. I was in several of them,
first as deckhand, and then as mate. Let's see, there was
Torment; she was a sprittie but she sailed up as far as
Yarmouth and Lowestoft, then there was . . . *Sepoy*, till we
lost her off Cromer – 1933 that was . . . *Goldfinch* . . . she
was a schooner, a real beauty, that one . . .'

Bert reeled off the names of ships one after the other. It
was like a roll of honour of many of the most famous British
coastal sailing vessels between the Wars. As he reeled off
each name so we passed yet one more front gate exactly the
same as the one before. The contrast between our
surroundings and Bert's account staggered me.

Ted stared around him all the way; I suppose he was
looking for any girls that he could ogle. His luck was out. It
had started to rain, and the young lasses were probably all at
the cinema with their boy-friends who had good jobs in the
City or at the bank or Post Office.

After walking along the endless street past the houses all
lined up and expressionless as Grenadier Guards, Bert
grabbed one of a hundred iron gates, this one covered in faded
green paint. 'Here we are, lads,' he murmured perkily,
'welcome to home-sweet-home!' He fumbled in his pockets
for his door keys and finally extracted them, attached to the
ring on top of his clasp knife, the one with the small marline-
spike down one side, which both Ted and I coveted.

Bert inserted his key into the green painted front door. A
thin treble voice called out loudly from the depths of the

house. I fully expected, when the door opened, to see a cargo
hold yawning open in front of and below us. Instead there
was a dark narrow hallway which smelled of cooked cabbage.
Up one side of the small hallway was a flight of narrow
stairs. On the other wall, which was disguised with
wallpaper covered with a design of lattice-work and roses,
and three china ducks in full flight, was a coat-hanger.

'Hang your hats up here, boys – hulloo, angel!' Bert cried
loudly in a rising voice, as if he was ordering the topsail
handed. This was despite the fact that neither Ted nor I had
hats. The treble voice quavered again from a room at the
back of the short passage, 'Who's that with you I've told you
not to bring any of that crowd from the local why didn't you
send me a letter saying when you'd be home I promised my
Mum I was going to see her today who's this?' Mrs Bert was
a pale, thin, wispy-haired woman with a bird-like face. I
guessed she was in her late twenties. She was dressed for the
street and looked as if she needed a long sea-cruise. As she
inspected Ted and me her expression softened just a mite,
'Hmmm – that lot from the ship?'

'Yes, Nora . . .' Bert was about to reply when a noisy wail
came through the back-door, which led directly from the
kitchen, where we were, into the back-yard. 'How's the
babby . . . ?' Bert trailed off.

Mrs Bert sniffed. 'Oh, Hermione's all right. Look I'm late
already I promised Mum I'd be at her house by one o'clock I
thought you might be home I've left your dinner in the oven
if they want anything . . . ' She looked generally in our
direction, 'You'd better show them where everything is and
they can help themselves only don't touch the ham and the
butter or the jam and the sugar and leave the milk and the
lamb chops alone . . . ' With that Mrs Bert exited herself out
of the back-door and soon returned with a tot's push-chair
in which was confined by a red leather shoulder-strap a

runny nosed infant of eighteen months' age, at a wild guess. With quick jerky movements, as Bert looked red in the face and Ted and I stared in amazement, Mrs Bert manoeuvred the push-chair around the kitchen table, past the sideboard, out through the inner kitchen door and, slamming it behind her, was gone. Bert's offspring's wail diminished in direct ratio to her mother's progress through the front passage, out of the green-painted door and the green-painted iron gate into the street.

Bert removed his mackintosh and his cap and sat down. 'Well, boys, make yourself at home. Plenty of stuff in the cupboard. Have a fry up if you want to . . .' He poked his fork at the gas-stove.

Ted and I cooked up some fried bread and egg, with milkless tea, and hungrily consumed it in very short order. As we finished our repast Bert said, 'Well, like I told you blokes, there's nothing like a nice little home ashore, with a missus and family. I was a bit wild when I was your age, but since I found Nora and got tied up I've never been so well looked after.' Bert's face was deadly serious as he said that. Ted's face was a study in surprise. I did my best not to burst out laughing. Above us assorted nappies and blouses on the clothes-drying rack dripped water on to my collar.

After dinner was cleared away Bert showed us his family photograph album – one oval sepia picture after another of chubby looking Victorian and Edwardian ladies with their hair done up in buns and lace around their necks; stout, serious, respectable looking, black-dressed, moustached and bearded gentlemen in waistcoats and watchfobs, holding bowler hats on their knees, and lacy-drawered little girls all desperately trying to look like Alice in Wonderland. Then we helped Bert tidy up his small back-garden. There wasn't a lot to do – dig up an old bicycle frame half-buried in the earth and clear up a few leaves – but it was good to be out in the fresh air, even if it was a couple of miles away from the sea.

When we got back on board, Bert was once again his old self, the mate we knew. After having supper, when we were alone in the fo'c's'le, getting ready to turn in, I asked Ted how he'd enjoyed his outing. Ted stood by his bunk in his longjohns. 'Oh, all right,' he grunted. Then he said quietly, in a flat voice, 'I'll tell you one thing, Nip.'

'What's that, Ted?'

Ted's voice dropped even lower, 'I've changed my bloody mind about getting married . . . G'night!'

15
Tansy

I spent two summers and two winters on board *Second Apprentice* and still those two winters, of '38 and '39, strike me as the physically hardest times in my life. In the winters we plied mostly between the Solent and France. As soon as we entered port we set to unloading the cargo. We might get a couple of hours' spell waiting for the next cargo to arrive, during which we performed the ship's chores. After that it was back down the hold for hours on end, using Tilley oil-lamps, carrying into the dark hours so that we could catch an early morning tide. When there was little or no wind, or when the wind was a 'muzzler', that meant first working our way around the Isle of Wight, using the four tides a day to 'dredge' the ship with the anchor. We might drift, or row, with Ted and me on the sweeps to maintain steerage way over the tide-stream, then drop the anchor and wait a while, hammering in the cargo-hatch covers securely, lashing down the jolly-boat, or doing any of a thousand other tasks. When the anchor was weighted again there was more labour on the windlass and the sweeps until we were clear of the Nab, or the Needles if the wind was easterly, and out clear into the Channel. Sometimes the cross-Channel run was easy; a hundred and thirty odd miles on the starboard tack with the wind steady at twenty knots; sometimes it was a plain, twenty-two carat bastard, with shifting winds and calms before a hard blow, and sometimes it was an exquisite hell of icy-cold north-easterly wind, hail, rain, and sleet.

Whenever the weather was fair, Tansy, unless he was on watch, mostly stayed below in his cabin, but as soon as there was a promise of any liveliness he came on deck. There, in his oilskins and bowler hat, he plodded up and down, always on the weather side, with his stumpy pipe upside-down between his teeth, eyeing the topmast truck at intervals. Sometimes, after he had gauged the weather, he sat just inside the galley door drinking a pint of hot tea, or if it was well into Ted's or my helm-trick he might take over the wheel from us, to give us a spell.

While the weather was fair or uncertain, Tansy was rarely talkative. It was only when the die was cast and a rising wind and a lively sea showed a determined intent to give us a good dusting that he opened up and warmed to us lads. Then it was obvious that like all sailors of any experience, Tansy owed nothing to, and was owed nothing by, the sea. The wind was there to be used and the sea was there to be sailed over, and there was little that he or anyone else could do about it, so he might as well accept it and get on with it. He seemed neither to enjoy the heavy weather nor to abhor it. It was all part of life to him. He accepted it. He got on with his job; we should get on with ours, and the weather should follow the course which the Almighty had set for it, and get on with *Its* job, too.

Often in very heavy going, the helm-watches for us lads were cut down to an hour at a time. It was almost as much as I could do to hold the kicking wheel and every time a sea caught the rudder and battered it I nailed my soul to the helm, hung on like a stout centurion and prayed to the seven gods of the sea. Then Tansy, when he saw this, reached his arm around and calmly took the wheel. There was no magical transformation. The wheel didn't stop kicking and neither did the seas give up battering or the wind cease howling, but somehow something happened . . . the ship quieted.

It took some time before I realized the difference between the mate and the captain. In Bert's case he was in love with the ship. In Tansy's case the ship was in love with *him*. That was why, when Bert walked the deck during the night-watches, his footsteps clomped and reverberated all through the ship; when Tansy walked forward there was hardly a sound. With Bert the ship flirted and worked; with Tansy she loved and obeyed him.

In time, I always knew when the weather was going to deteriorate. There was a barometer on board, down in the skipper's lobby, but there was never any need to look at it, to see if it was dropping. As the atmospheric pressure fell so did Bert's spirits, and so, correspondingly, did Tansy's rise.

'You're a lucky chap, Nipper,' said Tansy. We were bowling along on a dead run up-Channel with cement for Newhaven from Southampton. It was a blustery October day of clouds shoving up to Dover with the wind. We were running free, with the mainsail handed and the squaresail boomed out on its yard and pulling like a hero. To our north the coast of England lay misty blue on the horizon while out to seaward all dark cloud and grey seas. I liked being at the helm when we were running free. It demanded a lot of concentration, but there was an urgent feel to the forward thrust of the sails, the rigging and the hull, which I imagine would have pleased any youngster. The wheel, while it needed more attention than when we were on other points of sail, was less demanding of brute strength, and so a lot easier for me to handle.

'Why's that, Tansy?' As I queried him my eyes stayed on the pennant aloft and the squaresail. 'Why do you say I'm lucky?'

'Well, you weren't grown up when you came to sea . . .' He spoke as if my five months on board had been five years. 'That's the best time of life to start at sea, like you were, just out of school. You know enough to be able to understand what's being said, but you don't know much about other people's . . . the way they do things ashore. The worst learners at sea are those who come to it late.'

'Why's that, Tansy?' The stern slid off a sea, sideways. I

heaved the wheel over to steady the ship. I was chewing on a liquorice stick. It was a habit Ted had introduced to me. They were much cheaper than toffees.

'Because they're always comparing the way we do things and the way it's done ashore, and of course, there can't be much comparison, because the way we do things and the way they do them are as different, leastways most of the time, as chalk and cheese. I mean if a bloke who's worked in a factory, say, comes to work at sea, he's not used to taking the weather into account, whereas we have it always in mind, all the time, even when we're on the beds for a refit ... Why, I once had a West-Londoner come to work as a deckhand, in his early twenties, he was. He'd been highly recommended to me by someone. We were at anchor off Whitstable, and I happened to tell Bert that we should clean and check the anchor cable soon. The chap overheard me, it seems ... A while later Bert and I went ashore to get a few oysters and have a couple of pints. We were sitting in the pub, nice and cosy, when someone from another boomie comes running in all hot and bothered and yells to me that someone is weighing our anchor. Of course Bert and I knocked off our pints and dashed outside the pub, and there was the ship, drifting out with the tide! Our factory friend was still pumping away at the anchor windlass weighing the hook! By the time we pulled the jolly-boat alongside she'd drifted about a couple of cables. Good job there was hardly any breeze ...'

'What about the other crewman ... I mean didn't he try to ... ?'

'We didn't have a nipper on board at the time. That was before Ted came to us.' Tansy gazed at Ted, who was splicing a line in the lee of the hatch-coamings, sitting on deck, still bare foot and still no shirt. 'Good job, really,' said Tansy, 'Ted would have crowned him.' Tansy was silent for a few seconds, then he said, 'No, to be good in the trade you have to start off in the trade. It's different on the big ships, because they have so many people milling around that the good ones can cover up for the dead-legs and idlers, and the officers are not often much the wiser.'

'How did you start off, Tansy?' I gave the wheel another half turn, all the time watching the sails, checking the strain on the running backstay now set up.

Tansy walked over to starboard and knocked the ash out of his pipe over the side of the bulwark, then he returned to my side, smiling. 'Me? Oh, I first went to sea in my father's lugger. We lived in Deal, you see, Nipper. I was six when I first started out, because there weren't much schooling for fishermen's sons in those days. That was in 1872 . . .'

I whirled my head to look at Tansy. He was staring at a sailing vessel far on the southern horizon. His green eyes slitted, he murmured, 'She's an east-coaster, probably out of Essex, I'd say.' I was hardly hearing him. My mind was staggered. I blurted out, '*1872?*'

'That's right. There were lots of luggers working out of Deal then. We used to launch them from the beach, then drag them back up, when we took the catch in, with horses, up above the tidemark.'

As he reminisced about the Deal lugger fleet I reckoned up in my head, 1872 . . . that was . . . 'Why, that's sixty-six years ago!' I shouted.

'That's right,' said Tansy, as he refilled his pipe. 'And when I was ten I went to sea in my first Rye trawler, my first real deep-sea boat. We used to fish off the Diamond Bank, off Dungeness, and land our catches at Ramsgate, because we could always get in there no matter what the state of the tide.' Tansy caught my eye. His green eyes shone. He grinned. 'Do you know, Nipper, the cook on my first Rye lugger was a lot older than I am now . . . and he'd started off at sea in the Navy, and he'd been a powder-monkey at the battle of Trafalgar . . .'

I started. '1805?' It was incredible. At school it had been

the best remembered date in British history, along with 1066.

'That's right. His name was Fletcher . . . Bill Fletcher. He'd been born on board one of the men o' war. They used to allow women on board in those days, when they were in harbour. The "matelots" didn't get any shore-leave, you see. Do you know what a powder-monkey was?'

'They used to bring the gunpowder to the gunners, didn't they?'

'That's right, Nipper. Well, Billy was on board . . . *Royal Sovereign*. That was Collingwood's flagship,' he added casually, as if he were recounting something of the day before.

'What was your next ship, Tansy?'

The captain laughed quietly, as if to himself. He left the helm-shelter for a moment to look astern. Satisfied that the weather was holding steady, he regained the shelter. He took out his pipe, already charged, and lit it with an 'England's Glory' wooden match. Then he gave one or two puffs to get a good draw, and said, 'Now I don't want you to get the wrong ideas, Nipper. What's gone is gone. We were arrested for smuggling brandy into Gravesend. The luggers, some of them, used to meet ships out at sea, and get a few dozen bottles or so, and take it into port under a catch of fish. But the Excise people got wind of it, and they came on board and the game was up.'

'What did they do?'

'The laws were stiff. The Excisemen sawed the lugger in half and jailed the captain. He got two years penal servitude. The crew – there were four of us – two of the older ones got six months hard labour, and us other two lads got the choice of going to prison for six months along with two dozen strokes – they still used the cat o' nine tails in those days – or joining the Navy. My pal Bob went to prison. I joined the *Andrew*. Mind you, I wasn't sorry. Rough it was, especially at first, it was easy compared to the fishing. That was in 1886 and do you know this is the biggest joke of all . . . ,' Tansy clapped my shoulder lightly, '. . . the first regular ship I was put on board was a blessed Revenue cutter in the Channel! It was funny. They still ran the Navy like they had in Nelson's days, at least they did on board the smaller ships. We used to wear tarred straw hats and when we armed for a boarding-party our side-arms were cutlasses. Only the officer had a pistol as well as his sword. Our ships were brigs and they were sailed hard, I can tell you, and never a lanyard out of place. It was more than your life was worth to misplace the smallest thing.' Tansy shook his head pensively. 'The discipline was . . .' he searched for a word, '. . . a bit much. Still, I was lucky after all, because we did get regular home-leave, even if it was only once every three months. We used to have big red kerchiefs, then, that we wrapped our things in when we went home; perhaps something we had made ourselves as a present for home, and a couple of gold sovereigns . . . if we had any pay due after stoppages. A lot of the men used to spend their wages on stuff like prick . . .' (Tansy pronounced it 'perique') 'tobacco. You know, it was rolled up, like a huge cigar. Then they soaked the tobacco in rum from their ration, and either chewed it or smoked it in their pipes. They used to cut small slices off the roll, so it was almost the same size as a penny. That's where the name "Navy Cut" for tobacco comes from, you see, Nipper?'

'Did you board any ships, Tansy? What were . . .?'

'Oh, yes, quite a few. There were some cases of smuggling, but mainly we were, in those days, in the late eighties, after what they called the copers. They were mostly coasters which bought booze from ships out at sea – there were a lot of Hollanders and Germans who supplied booze – and the copers then sailed around the fishing fleets and sold the liquor – duty-free and cheap – to the fishermen. They, or at any rate most of them, because they couldn't legally take the booze ashore, simply drank it all at sea, so they were drunk half the time, a lot of them. There were many sinkings and bad accidents caused by booze from the copers. At last the

Admiralty decided to put a stop to that trade. Of course, we couldn't arrest the copers, they were out of territorial waters, you see, but we scared them like billy-o. Our skipper used to sail straight at their bows or sterns, and us with every stitch of sail up. We used to rig ramming-gaffs out on the bow, and when we smashed them into the copers' rigging . . . well, there was quite some damage, you can bet a fiver on it. We used to rip their mizzenmasts and bowsprits right out of the copers' hulls. It scared them to death. We sank a couple. They didn't often return for a second dose, I can tell you. If they ever complained to their own governments, we accused them of dangerous navigation, and then they lost all means of livelihood, because their government took their fishing licences away from them. So you see, Nipper, we had them all ends up, but it took a couple of seasons to stop the coping trade. It still hadn't completely fizzled out when I was drafted to a barquentine and we sailed out to the Ashanti war . . .'

The Ashanti war! My mind boggled at the thought. It was as if Tansy was talking about Caesar's invasion of Britain.

'That was . . . let's see now . . .' Tansy stared at another ship which had hove into view, a steamer heading down-Channel. The smoke from her stack was thick and black and streamed astern of her in the wind, fouling the whole south-eastern horizon. Tansy wrinkled his nose as he turned again to me. 'Yes . . . that was in 1890 that we shoved off for the Gold Coast. It was blessed awful out there, what with the heat and everything, and a lot of our blokes died from malaria and a lot more went home with it, too. Inshore, near the jungle, it was terrible with the mosquitoes. We used to look forward to going out to sea for some breeze and to get away from the damp heat. We sailed up and down the coast, all the way up to Freetown and down as far as Sao Tomé, because we were still doing anti-slavery patrols, see?'

'Anti-slavery?' The wind had shifted a point. I adjusted the wheel.

'Yes. You see slavery had been abolished in Brazil only two

years before, although the importation of slaves into Brazil had been illegal for a long time. The Portuguese and the West Africans – it was mostly the West Africans, though, from Fernando Po and Sao Tomé – were still trying to smuggle cargoes of Negroes over the South Atlantic, and it was our job to stop them. It was strange, in many ways . . . there we were on the one hand doing our best to defeat the Africans in the Gold Coast, and on the other hand trying to stop them being sold into slavery. The Portuguese were supplying arms to the Ashantis too, even though they were supposed to be our allies. But eventually the Ashanti gave up, and their king, we called him Pompey, though I don't know his real name, was exiled to some ocean islands somewhere. I was out in the Gold Coast for six and a half years, and it's a wonder how I survived it. A good half of the men I went out there with didn't get home. The sickness rate was terrible. That's where I first found the Lord, out there . . .'

Tansy was silent for a while, his face serious, his eyes slitted as they gazed at the coast to the north. The wind now was backing a touch. He said, 'That there change of wind is very convenient – get us in nicely, that will.' Then he fell silent again.

'Did you come home in the ship. Or were you sent home . . . I mean from the Gold Coast?' I asked. My liquorice stick was almost chewed to a frazzle.

Tansy grinned, 'Oh, we sailed her home all right, with our commissioning pennant streaming out from the maintruck as we were towed up the Medway to Chatham Dockyard, and they gave us two weeks leave, too. It felt good, I can tell you, to be on the train heading for London with twenty gold sovereigns in my kerchief and a bolt of woven silk for Nancy . . . she was only a bit older than you then, and it was some years before we got married . . . when I got back from the Boer war. We used to sail out of Durban, patrolling the coast of Mozambique, because the Germans up in Tanganyika and the Portuguese were smuggling arms down to the Boers, and our job was to prevent it. I came home in a trooper from there, because my twelve year man's time in the *Andrew* was up, see? I can't say I was sorry, either. It was quite some time before Nancy and I had enough money put by to get married properly and set ourselves up in a home. I worked on river craft and then on schooners and boomies as mate for seven years. Then, when I had enough of my wages put by, we bought a little place in Sandwich . . . but I stayed on at sea, because by then I had my first captain's appointment.'

'What about the Great War, Tansy?'

'Oh, we had some fun and games, I can tell you. The Germans were sinking our coasters like bowling over skittles. At first the submarines weren't too bad. Some of their skippers even let our captains take a few of their belongings with them when they were ordered into the jolly-boat before the ship was sunk. They didn't waste torpedoes on a coaster; they usually sank them by placing charges on board, or by shelling them. On a couple of occasions, at the start of the War, the U-boat commanders even let our captains dismount their compasses and take them into the jolly-boat, too. But as the War went on it got worse and worse. By that time I was back in the Navy, in the Reserve on armed trawlers. We rescued quite a few coaster crews and we knew all about what was happening. The worst of the younger U-boat captains were machine-gunning the crews as they took to the water. In a few cases they took the jerseys and oilskins from the crewmen, even in winter-time and quite a few of our chaps died from exposure. But the worst of the enemy were the surface raiders. They opened fire without any warning at all, and did not wait around to see if the survivors were all right or not. They just left them to drown. By that time the Jerries were using armed vessels disguised as peaceable craft – some of them were auxiliary sailing ships. Then the Admiralty decided to give Jerry a dose of his own medicine. They mounted four inch guns on strengthened sailing coasters, but the guns were hidden behind raised bulwarks and hatch-coamings. "Q-ships" we called them.'

'Yes, I've heard of them.' I spat out the last strands of liquorice over the leeward side.

'Well, I was on one of the first "Q-ships". We had a merry old time, I can tell you, patrolling between Scotland and Norway. The weather was mostly blessed awful. We stayed out for weeks. We never challenged any craft. We always waited to be challenged or attacked ourselves. That was the tricky bit. If she was an enemy craft, as soon as she showed her colours or surfaced our bulwarks dropped down, the hatch-coamings after them. The four-incher, with the gun crew already ranged and ready, opened up, and we sank or captured the blighter.'

'Did you pick up the crews from the sunken craft?'

'Only the officers, and not all of them, either. By that time we'd lost too many chums . . . That was the U-boats. There were never more than a couple of survivors from them, if any. But the crews of the surface ships, we did our best to collect them. Too often, though, the weather was too bad, and in many cases the surface raiders were shadowed by a U-boat, so we had always to be wary that any compassion didn't put us in jeopardy.'

Tansy reflected for a moment or two, then he said, 'War is a terrible thing . . . no young people ought ever be sent to war. It should be fought, if it has to be, by people over the age of sixty.' He thought for a moment longer, and added, 'and the admirals and generals should all be under the age of eighteen; then instead of the stupid directing the inexperienced, we'd have the inexperienced directing the stupid. No – but seriously, Nipper, there'd be much more humanity, I think, shown at sea or on the battlefields. When you're my age, you're too conscious of your own mortality not to respect that of other people, see? You know, when you're old, that once something irreplaceable is lost, it can never be brought back, and besides, when you are a lot older you realize that nothing that the average . . . landsman . . . believes is worth dying for really *is*. That would be the thing! Start them all off as admirals at sixteen and let them work their way down to ordinary seamen at sixty! Then you'd see all the nonsense about the honour and glory of war exactly where it should be – over the side!'

'Do you think there's going to be a war, Tansy?' The Munich pact which sold Czechoslovakia down the river to the Nazis had been signed only the week before. Most of the bargees I had overheard discussing it thought that war had been avoided.

'Yes.' Tansy's voice was quiet, but he sounded quite sure.

'What should I do? Shall I join the Navy?' I didn't realize what I was asking; few boys of fourteen know the depths of their questions.

'Not until you're a bit older.' Tansy walked over to the starboard rail again. As he went he murmured, 'And trust in the Lord.' Then he turned and came to the wheel. Brightly he said, 'All right, Nipper, I'll take the rest of your watch. We'll be off Newhaven in a half hour and the tide's right. You nip off and make a nice cup of tea, eh?'

I surrendered the wheel to the captain. As I turned the corner he called to me. I stuck my head back to see him. He was gazing steadily ahead as the bowsprit rose and fell. Suddenly the wind dropped, and the ship slowed down. A rainy drizzle descended upon us from clouds as grey as gravestones. The sea was now as dismal as a copse of dripping willows. As the ship wallowed she cried; lurch, bang, lurch, bang, lurch. I steadied myself on deck.

Tansy slowly turned to me. 'Make it nice and sweet, Nipper,' he said, 'and don't fill the mugs more than three-fifths tide up!'

As I waited in the tiny galley for the kettle to boil I heard the sound of Bert mounting the ladder from his cabin. He greeted the captain.

'Evening, Bert,' I heard Tansy say. 'She's a bit sloppy, we just lost quite a fair drop of wind. Funny that, I'd just taken over from the nipper and the wind dropped just like that . . .'

'He's got the touch, that nipper,' I heard Bert say about me. 'He's either got the Devil or the angels looking over his shoulder.' There was silence for a minute or so, except for the hissing of the kettle and the creaking of the timbers and the slam, slam of the gaffs and booms. Then Bert added, as I listened with my ear cocked to the galley forward bulkhead. 'That little blighter must have been born with a caul over his head!'

'And probably upside down,' added Tansy.

Later, when we were turning in, I told Ted about what Bert and Tansy had said about me. 'Well, you are a lucky bugger, Nipper,' Ted said. 'Let's face it, you've got the luck of a pox-doctor's clerk. If you kicked over a pile of cowshit you'd find a bloody gold watch underneath!'

'But I wouldn't kick it over unless I was looking for a gold watch, Ted.'

'Clever sod,' replied Ted, as he turned over and went to sleep.

I dreamed that night a half-nightmare, a half-romance. I was a small boy in a man o' war with her cannons booming and men dropping dead and wounded all around me, and blood running down the scuppers. Then I was in a train with a red kerchief full of gold sovereigns. I was mounted in the shrouds of a Revenue brig, waiting, cutlass in hand, to board a transgressor. I was off a shore of bright sand, with deep-green palm trees waving and gleaming in the sun. I was floundering in cold water . . . I woke with a start. There were a thousand sacks of old rags and fifty tons of scrap metal to load in the morning. I went back to sleep.

16

Christmas in Wales

The most unusual cargoes we carried were live horses and
ponies. We did this three times; once from Harwich and twice
from Gravesend. The animals were all either too old to work,
or disabled in some way. We took them to Boulogne, in
France, on their way to the knacker's yard to be slaughtered as
meat for human consumption. We rigged three heavy lengths
of anchor-chain fore and aft in the hold, very taut, and to
these the livestock were tethered. I'm not sure, but I think
they all came from Ireland. By the time they were driven out
of the railway cattle-trucks, the animals always looked
exhausted, hungry, and dejected. It was as if they knew where
they were going. When they arrived they were fed with fodder
on the jetty. The animals stayed over-night, in the rain and
cold, in a temporary paddock. After that they were not
supposed to be fed until they were landed, because of the
amount of dung and urine they might deposit in the hold. But
Ted and I generally managed to sneak them a piece of sugar
and a handful of hay in the morning, and a few gulps of water
out of a bucket.

It was obvious that Tansy didn't like this kind of freight.
He was edgy and short with us when the animals were loaded
on board, one at a time in a net, kicking and neighing and
scared to death. Ted, too, was much affected when he
received each struggling creature, desperate with fear, as the
net landed with a bump on the hold-bottom. I held its tether.
Ted patted its nose and he usually gave it a lump of sugar and
a name, all the time murmuring into its twitching ears. 'Come
on, me old son, whoops . . .' A pony had nipped Ted's hand as
it nibbled away for the sugar he had offered '. . . steady on,

me old cock. *Sprucer*, that's what we'll call you, mate, because
you're too bloody eager . . .' All the while I tended the
animal's tether, keeping well clear of its hind legs. To me it
was heartbreaking, and I often felt torn between doing the job
I was supposed to do and sinking the ship. The agony of the
animals as the ship worked in a seaway was painful to see. All
the horses had worked for their living – harness marks about
them told the tale – and some of them were very old as horses
go. The thought of them having worked hard all their lives
only to end up in a knacker's yard was too much for me.

The only times I ever wept on board *Second Apprentice*
were when animals were involved; once when an old carthorse
collapsed in the hold while we were in mid-Channel, and
couldn't raise himself again. He lay there panting and
moaning until he was lifted out of the hold by French
stevedores, who passed three ropes under and around him,
heaved him up with their derrick and dumped him on to the
jetty where he lay, whinnying and kicking for a couple of
hours. All the while many of the French laughed at him and
prodded him with their boots and sticks until Ted threatened
to fight any of them. Then the French police arrived and a
gendarme shot the old horse. Because his body would take up
too much room in a cattle-wagon, they lowered him into the
harbour with balks of timber lashed around him, and a fishing
boat towed the dead horse off somewhere, probably to be
hacked up on a beach.

That was the first time I ever cried in my first ship, and the
only time I ever retched on board her was in dead flat water,
on the last occasion we freighted worn-out and 'useless'
animals. Some of them, when we went alongside, got into
such a panic, their eyes bloodshot and crying, that their
jerking and pulling was too much for the pelican-hook, which
secured the anchor chain to the forward bulkhead in the hold,
and it parted just as we moored in Boulogne. The animals had
been unsettled and in fear all the way across the Channel – it

was quite a rough day. It must have been the bump as the ship ground up to the jetty which caused a sudden extra spasm of terror among the horses. A whole line of them – about fifteen animals – while still tethered to the parted chain, milled and frothed, kicked and whinnied, struggled and heaved. Topsides, as we stared horrified at the pandemonium below, we could do nothing. The racket was excruciating. The dumb terror of the beasts was tangible. Then someone – I think it was Bert – got the bright idea of capturing the eye on the pelican-hook with the derrick hook and hauling it up, so that the chain could once more be tightened. This took a few minutes. It is not easy to fish down into a hold full of fear-stricken animals, a third of them loose and stampeding. Eventually the pelican eye was hooked and the derrick whip was hauled up taut, bringing the loose end of the chain with it. Then the whip was transferred to a big capstan on the quay. The French dockers heaved away at the capstan bars until they could heave no more. Now the chain below rose up at an angle of about forty-five degrees, which meant that the beasts at the high end of the chain were lifted off their front hooves by the pull of the chain. Below was a scene of utter terror as the horses struggled to free themselves. Three of them broke their necks and one broke its hind leg. From then on, until French police rifle marksmen arrived, nothing could be done and the hold was like a scene from the inferno. The gendarmes, grinning and evidently joking among themselves and with the dockers, shot all twenty horses on the broken chain. Eventually, when the rest calmed down somewhat, the corpses were unloaded, dumped into a dumb barge alongside, and towed away. It took another couple of hours for the live beasts remaining to settle down sufficiently for us to be able to unload them gently. All the while Ted cursed the French police in particular and all police anywhere and everywhere. 'Bloody frog-faced fuck-pigs! Bleedin' rozzers!'

'But they were only doing the only thing they could do,' I

told him.

'Well, the bastards didn't have to *enjoy* it, did they?' was Ted's reply.

Later, when the stinking hold was empty and we were cleaning out excrement, urine, blood, and straw, we found several bullet holes in the ship's side and floors, but the ship was built so solidly that only one of them had passed right through the stout timbers. Bert made wooden tree-nails and plugged up eight or nine holes.

It was night by the time we had finished work. We all – the captain, the mate, Ted and I – went about our business without a word. I prepared supper; I remember clearly what it was: shepherd's pie made from salt beef and potatoes. Down in the lobby, when I served the meal, everyone was glum. Only Ted ate anything, and even he left more than half his meal on his plate. That was the only time I can recall that Ted didn't lick his plate clean. As I cleared up the plates and the men drank their pints of tea, Tansy shook his head. Then he said quietly, 'We don't carry any more livestock.'

There was a silence pregnant with eager agreement for a moment, then Ted said, 'Thank God for that.'

Tansy glared at Ted. The captain's beard bristled, his green eyes were afire. His fist hit the table. 'Watch your blasphemy,' he said very quietly.

'Sorry, Tansy,' muttered Ted.

'All right,' replied the skipper. 'Too much risk involved, what with bullets flying around the hold. They could have scuttled the ship . . . I'll write to the agents tomorrow. Only dead stock from now on. It paid well, but the damage risk is too much . . .'

'What's the cargo from here?' asked Ted.

Bert broke in, 'Ballast.'

'Pity it ain't a few of those bloo . . . blooming froggie coppers. We could have landed them in Chatham. Them Navy blokes would give them a run for their money . . .' Ted saw Tansy's warning look and piped down.

For my first year on board *Second Apprentice* Tansy never once let me go ashore in France, Belgium or Germany unless I was either with him or with Bert on some errand or other. In England, on rare occasions, I was allowed to wander off alone. In Holland, on even rarer occasions, I was allowed to go ashore either alone or with Bert, but not in those other countries. Tansy had a very strict, typically Victorian idea on what was right and wrong. 'It's for your own good, Nipper,' he once said to me in Cherbourg after I had asked him if I could go ashore. He shook his head. I struggled to hold back tears of disappointment. He repeated, 'It's for your own good, Nipper. Some of these here foreigners are . . .' he searched for a word he might use to a fourteen-year-old '. . . a bit much. Can't trust . . . never know where you are with some of them . . .'

'How do you mean, Tansy?' It was a fine winter's day. The sun was shining on the grey dock walls and my voice was choking.

'Well . . . some of the blokes . . .' Tansy furrowed his brow and wrinkled his nose. He puffed at his pipe quickly. The smoke curled up into the windless blue sky over his bowler hat. The sunlight caught the edges of his suit so that it shone a paler shade of green than his eyes. He frowned and looked me straight in the eye. 'Some of their blokes *wear scent and play football on Sundays*!'

Tansy said this as if the miscreants were doomed to certain hell. For a moment I imagined the whole of Western Europe, except for Holland, crowded with millions of fancy-Dans all kicking soccer-balls over each other's frontiers. Then the captain added, 'And as for some of the fairer sex . . . they're . . . a *bit much* . . . but the less said about them . . . the better . . .'

Just before Christmas of 1938 *Second Apprentice* settled

down, as the tide left her, on barge-beds. These were long rows of old ship's spars, some two feet thick, which had been pegged to the river-bottom years before; some of them were said to have been there for over a hundred years and the timber was still sound. Their purpose was to seat the barges so that their bottoms could be scraped and cleaned, and painted with two coats of black varnish. This was a hard, wet, messy job and cold in winter. That first winter I was lucky. *Second Apprentice* took to the beds up the River Medway, near Rochester. Tansy hired another lad to take my place while the hull was cleaned and painted, and while I went home to Wales for Christmas.

Ted was to spend Christmas with Bert, though since his encounter with Mrs Bert he was not too cheerful about it. 'Might as well spend bloody Christmas in Battersea Dogs' Home,' was Ted's opinion on the prospect.

When the great day of my depature for Wales came along, I packed my sea-bag with enough clothes to see me through the week ahead. I also packed a cheap celluloid doll, but dressed up in fancy rig, for Angharad, some toffees for Caradoc, a carved model of *Second Apprentice* – not very expertly done – for Mam, and pictures of the ship, which I had painstakingly drawn and framed, for Dad and Cei Powell. For Branwen Powell, I took some pressed flowers from Holland. I had just my rail fare home and a shilling or so over, but I felt very grand as I stepped on deck in my shore-clothes all pressed under my mattress and clean and my sea-bag on my shoulder. Tansy was waiting at the gangway as I went to march over it on to the muddy bank, through the green meadow beyond and so on to the road to the town and the railway station. He, too, wore his best suit. I had shined his shore-going boots like mirrors that very morning. As I walked aft he gestured me over to him. His beard had been neatly trimmed. As I reached his side he held out an envelope. 'Here's a Christmas Box, Nipper.'

I took the envelope. It was sealed. I thanked him and stood before him, feeling somewhat embarrassed. I hadn't been able to give him or any of the others, except for Ted, a present. To Ted I had given a packet of five 'Woodbine' cigarettes and a few of my spare cigarette cards.

'Merry Christmas,' Tansy murmured. 'You can open it up.'

I tore open the envelope. Inside was a whole, crisp ten-shilling note!

'Gosh!' (I'd read quite a few of Ted's comics by now.) 'Thanks, Tansy!'

'Watch how you go, Nipper. Don't miss the train in London. A lot of people there . . . well . . . they're sometimes . . . a *bit much* . . .'

'Don't worry; I'll go straight across and catch the first train to Shrewsbury.'

'That's right, Nipper. Now off you go and don't forget to be back here on New Year's Eve!'

After shouted farewells and season's greetings to Bert and Ted as they scraped away, filthy and black, on the hull bottom below, up to their ankles in soft, slimy mud, I made my way across the bouncy plank, bound for Wales and Christmas.

I had excitedly sent a postcard to Mam two days before I went home, telling her that I was coming. For some reason or other it didn't arrive at Llangareth until after I did, so my turning up out of the blue was a complete surprise to everyone at home. I gave Mam six red roses I had bought on Shrewsbury station with two of my eleven shillings. Mam made a great fuss of me. Angharad was agog at the present I had brought her but would not show her until Christmas day, and Mam was pleased that I had grown an inch or so and filled out, but not too happy that my shore-clothes were a little too small for me, and my boots pinched. I was even more pleased, not only to be with them again, but also because Dad was coming home on Christmas Eve, the next day.

The only sad aspect was that Caradoc was sick and dying. But he knew me all right and cheered up when I fed him the toffee.

On the night of my arrival all the neighbours came to see me, and their change in attitude to me, when I recounted all the places I had seen, and the wonders in foreign lands, made me feel important and very grown up. I liked it when the old sailors came round and when I told them of Voorne and Rotterdam, Gravesend and Cherbourg, their eyes lit up as they listened to me. It was clear that they were reliving the days of their youth, because they laughed and smiled and sometimes frowned when they shouldn't have, and I knew that memories were flooding back to them.

The moment that Dad arrived and turned to me after embracing Mam it was clear that our relationship had changed drastically. He was more like a shipmate or a brother to me now, and instead of showing or explaining things to me, most of the time he asked me questions – about the ship, the voyages, and the crew.

On Christmas Day Angharad went into a transport of delight for a few minutes with her doll, and then sat quietly with it in a corner of the kitchen for most of the day, nursing it and murmuring as if it were a real baby. Mam, when I presented her with the ship-model, at first laughed as she hugged me. Then her eyes watered as she gently placed it in pride of place among all her other little ornaments – in the very centre of the mantelpiece in the drawing room. Dad thanked me gravely for the picture of *Second Apprentice*, and said that he would keep it in his kit, and show it to his shipmates on board his tug. Cei gave me a new jack-knife. His sister, Branwen, was very shy and quiet when I gave her the pressed flowers from Holland, but she promised to go to the pictures with me on Boxing-day. For my Christmas, Mam gave me a long, thick jersey she had knitted for me, and a bobble-cap. Dad gave me a real leather sailor's sheath, with an open seaman's knife and a marlin spike in it.

When Branwen turned up the next day, it was with her young sister, Lisbeth, but in the cinema I managed to wangle it so that I sat between them and could grope for Branwen's hand when the lights turned off. (Only the brave deserve the fair.) At first she seemed very nervous, and I don't think she said more than a dozen words during the outing but after a while she relaxed and there was an unspoken bond between us. When we returned to her home it was evening. She sent Lisbeth into the house first and let me kiss her on her cheek. She and her sister went off to visit relatives in Rhyl the next day, and I didn't see her again on that holiday. The only time that I was glad that Ted was not with me was when I was with Branwen.

It was good to be back in Llangareth and when I wasn't nursing Caradoc I walked out, sometimes with Dad, sometimes with Cei, but mostly I walked alone, even when it was raining and blowing. Then I turned my back to the sea's knowing and walked out into the hills. The heather was blown flat in the wind, as if in angry sorrow at the pending death of Caradoc. As I stood on the heights, leaning against the wind, gazing at the black peak of Cader Idris away in the distance, I reflected that I was as was our land and our air; I was as low or high as the sky about me, as was the breeze in my ears. They made me and they made what I did, the way I was and the way I learned about things and they shaped everything about me. Up on the heights I was sad and aching, happy and glorious, all at the same time; Caradoc was lying in his stable, slowly breathing his life away, and I was home in Wales, and bound again for sea, with all the world and my life ahead. I had no wish to escape the land, no longing to leave my people, no desire to abjure the blood and the spirit that Wales had given me. The hills whispered to me that I could never do that, no matter how I might try, no matter how far I might voyage.

The mountains thundered that I might try to do it, but only at the peril of my spiritual impoverishment; and that even so, in the end, the light, the fire of Wales within me, would triumph. But I must do what I must do.

Sometimes, when Cei was out walking with me in the wind, I looked at him. He showed little expression. I was gradually aware that he accepted everything about him. His conception of himself did not extend to the wild and beautiful Welsh landscape about us. It was as if, to him, Wales was asleep and he wished to live his life without waking it; as if the hills, the gorse, the heather, the sky and the wind were things not to be changed or antagonized. Cei unconsciously loved Wales, but he would never try to change it. He would never desecrate the land, and so it would be, for him too, in his soul forever.

When I walked in the hills alone with the wind and rain, I shook off my family, my home, my friends, the neighbours, the memories of my boyhood, and a young, violent spirit took over. I belonged then to no one but myself. I communed with no one but my own soul. I owned nothing, I wanted nothing but to be myself; I had no irreplaceable friends or deadly enemies; I had no road but my own, and that was the road to the sea and the land beyond the sea. Yet there is nothing I thought, this side of heaven to compare with walking the hills of Gwynedd on a blustery winter's day. Nothing ashore, that is, I reminded myself. It brought hope to my heart and glory to my feet, despite the pinch of my boots.

It was good walking with Cei, but I enjoyed it far more with Dad. At heart he was a poet, and we should only walk the hills with poets. When I was walking with Dad I knew that he was part of everything about him, even when he shivered on the ridges and puffed and scowled at the birds which made so light of rising high.

As we tramped along, Dad said that even if it was a cold morning if you greeted everyone you met with 'Fine day today!' then it would slowly become so (and it did). He said that when a person is content inside himself there is no such thing as bad weather, even at sea, even when the wind is howling its head off and the sky is as black as a widow's veil. He said that the prospect is enough to stir the blood in a healthy body. He said that anyone can enjoy a sunny day; it takes a poet to be uplifted in a storm. He also said that he was suspicious of people who talked too much about the weather. It made him wonder what they were really thinking and why they didn't come right out with it.

Dad wasn't impressed by most 'modern' British writers – he didn't think that they appreciated the romance of reality. 'They don't seem to know that the romance of reality is unparalleled. Reality has an ineffable beauty all of its own. No one can write a novel which is more kaleidoscopic than real life itself. But you have to draw a line somewhere, when you look at things as they really are, otherwise you might go insane; when you're older, that is. Now, you're lucky, Tristan. Only children and young people see things as they really are. If you can keep that ability, your life will be far richer. Most adults waste a terrible amount of time trying to see how things really are, when all the time they *aren't*, you see. Reality has the brute force of truth, and sometimes it can be ugly or filthy, but all the same, it's glorious, Tristan.' Dad stopped walking and looked at me. 'You'll never find much pleasure in reality, but you'll find a lot of joy. That's why many sailors seem, at least to landsmen or people who don't know us well, to be somewhat childish or innocent in their outlook; it's because, by the very nature of our profession we are *forced* to see things as they really are. That's supposed only to be a childish attribute. It's what makes children sanctified, no matter if they are little devils at times. Homer, Defoe, Cervantes, Melville, Conrad, London (though he was one of God's innocents anyway, even if he'd never gone to sea); even W. H. Davies; because they'd preserved the ability to see the nexus of everything that was about them . . .' Dad sat on a rock, his back turned from the wind, and gazed into the hilly distance, all green-tinged, blue and grey.

As I sat beside him, he said, 'But the only way to see true reality is in solitude. One of the tragedies of human existence is that reality cannot be shared. What's real to you may not be to someone else, you see? The writer's job is to try to break through the veil which exists between us all . . . and if he can do that once or twice in his lifetime, he has justified his existence.'

'What about bad realities, like cruelty or callousness?' I asked. I was thinking of the horses dying in the hold at Boulogne.

'They're still realities. The thing is not to rebel against them, or be complacent or comply with them. What you must do is figure out which bad realities are unalterable and which can be changed, and then try to change the alterable ones, no matter how unyielding they might seem.'

'What about realities like death, Dad?' A vision of Caradoc in his stall passed through my mind.

'Those realities which are unalterable you must learn to accept. That makes the difference between a wise man and a fool; knowing what is acceptable and what is not . . . and why.' Dad rose and started off back down the hill. I sat for a moment, thinking about what he had said, then I caught up with him, and stayed at his side until we were home again.

Now that I was grown up and yet seeing most things still as they actually were, the love that Mam and Dad had for each other was real. They had no fear of it, and no fear of showing it to each other. They were no longer young; they did not (except sometimes when Mam looked at Dad's unaware – or was it – face), gaze at each other very much. Somehow they always seemed to be looking together in the same direction. There was more an air of freedom about their feelings towards each other than there was of domination on either side. They were united, and yet they were separate, unified unto themselves. All the years of difficulties and hardship, separation, and struggle, had created a bond between them that not even death would break. They never were out of tune; even when they argued about some small domestic matter it was always with humour. What might start as a violent disagreement generally finished with everyone in fits of laughter. Whenever Dad did Mam some small courtesy, such as opening a door for her or drawing back a chair, it was more for his own satisfaction than it was to express any kind of superiority over her, and if she seemed pleased at these little actions, it was because Dad's face showed his pleasure.

It wasn't that Dad was more virtuous than other men, except to Mam. She had a great imagination. To love Dad only for his virtues she would have needed one. It would have been perfectly obvious to anyone with two eyes in his head that she loved him; for an independent-minded woman like her to wait on him as she did, it couldn't have been done otherwise. She must have had more good in her than Dad did. She had aged more, and that demands goodness, which is very wearing.

It took six months of absence from her for me to realize how much I loved my mother. Not in a sentimental way, not simply because I had by chance emerged from her body, but because she was who and what she was. Also because I realized now how much she loved me. That Christmas at home, I caught her watching me at odd moments, looking for signs of change, of perhaps improvements. She looked distressed when she noticed the callouses on my hands, but she said nothing.

I suppose that like all mother-love – as far as I have seen – hers had a reverse side to it, a mother-hate, but she was a wonder at hiding it. If it showed I never recognized it. I accepted her criticism just as I would accept anyone else's. It was neither more just nor more cruel because it came from her. I must have loved her very much, because whenever she did anything for me I never wondered how I might return the favour, as I did with anyone else who helped me.

I realized now that Mam was a wit, but never hard-humoured, as men often are. On my first day at home I stepped on Cesar's tail when I went outside. He yelped and howled. Mam stuck her head out of the kitchen door. Cesar, who was a great pet of hers, whined and moaned and gazed up at her pitifully. I stood, waiting to be chastized. Mam shook her finger at the dog and cried, 'You silly thing, I told you not to idle around in front of the door!'

Like all women, Mam was an aristocrat at heart and always made me feel that I was much better than I actually was. If I made an error in some way she generally dragged out the name of some long-gone ancestor from Dad's or her family closets and told me that 'Grand Uncle so-and-so would never have made such a stupid blunder. Where do you get it from?' She was no Darwinian.

It was obvious that Dad's absences were taking their toll of Mam. She seemed much thinner, and somehow smaller, than when I had first left home, and she fussed over Angharad more than she had ever done. But she put up a brave front, remarking, as if in passing, how much more freedom and ease she would have when Angharad, too, left home. Her relationship with Dad must have been one of intense union for short periods of time and abysmal loneliness for the rest. It was only her unconquerable love for him that kept her going while he was away. While I had been at home I had been a sort of surrogate father to Angharad, and, for Mam, a reflection of Dad which salved her pain, but now that I, too, was to be absent for months at a time, she dreaded my leaving. She fussed and coddled both Dad and me and gave us practically every moment of her attention, as if she was saving every word, every look, every smile, every gesture, to remember

when we were away. By the time our short visits were about to
end, she had darned every one of Dad's and my socks, washed
and ironed every shirt – even those that didn't need it – and
cleaned and brushed all our clothes.

When the morning of New Year's Eve rolled around (far
too quickly), all the neighbours came around to see me off.
Mam dashed around the house getting everything she could
think of together for me, while Dad blunted the end of the
jack-knife which Cei had presented to me for Christmas,
('much safer that way, my son') and shortened one of his own
belts so I could wear it. Angharad cried and snuffled to her
doll. Cei assured me that he would do all he could for
Caradoc. Blind Sioni felt my arm muscles and said that I was
stronger than he was at eighteen, and he'd won a gong-
hammering competition at a visiting fair then – took home
five shilling, he did, and five shilling was five shillings in those
days. After I shook his hand and drew away, Blind Sioni felt
for my hand and shook it again.

Before I took my leave, I went to the stable with Dad, but
he must have known that I wanted to be alone with Caradoc.
Dad waited at the door and I went in to bid my pony farewell.
He lay on his straw panting, with his tongue hanging out and
his eyes closed. I was so distressed that I could not stay for
long fondling Caradoc's nose. When I left him, I was crying
bitterly but silently.

'He's a gonner,' said Dad. 'Do you want me to put him
away?' I stared at Dad's eyes through my tears for a moment
or two. I remembered what he'd said about facing up to bad
realities and trying to change them, but I shook my head; I'd
seen enough of animal slaughter. But by Dad's silence I knew
that I meant 'Yes, but when I've gone away.'

Soon after I made ready to leave Llangareth. Mam had
made up a large parcel of food for me to take with me. Catrin
Powell came up the lane in her apron despite the cold, bearing
a meat pie in a brown clay dish with a blue and white

handkerchief tied around it. Cei gave me his most accurate catapult as a parting gift. 'Might see a rabbit on the North Sea,' he joked.

For one of the few times that I can remember Mam took hold of me and kissed me.

'*Yn iach fy mab*' (Goodbye my son') she sobbed.

'*Fe fydaff yn dda*' ('I'll be good') I assured her.

Cei shook my hand manfully. Dad walked with me in the light drizzle up the brew to the road wordlessly . We waited for the bus to trundle along and take me to the railway station. As we stood on the side of the road, we talked about how I was to try to get home for the next Christmas; how I was to try to write home to Mam more often and regularly, how I was to always hold on to something when the weather was rough and especially when I was aloft, and how I was to listen carefully to what Tansy told me. Then the bus rumbled up.

'*Hwyl fawr, 'nhad!*'

'*Ffarwel, bach!*'

I boarded and grinned at him as I took my seat at the back of the bus and stared through the rear window. I left him standing alone on the side of the road, gazing after the bus. Then he turned and walked slowly back down the brew, a lone figure moving through the rain to a little white cottage down a slope, fuzzy through the rain on the bus rear window.

I knew Dad was going to put Caradoc out of his misery.

It was the last time I saw my father.

PART THREE
The Crucible

Ar y ffordd wrth fynd i Lundain,
Hob-y-Deri Dando!
Gwelais hen wraig yn llyncu bricsen,
Can y gân eto!
Dwedais wrthi am beidio tagu,
Siân fwyn, Siân!
Fod y dwr yn agos ati,
Siân, fwyn, llawn o swyn,
Clyw y deryn yn y llwyn,
Siân fwyn; Siân, llawn o swyn,
Clyw y deryn yn y llwyn!

(To London along the road I was going,
Hob-y-Deri Dando!
I met an old lady who a brick was swallowing,
Sing this song again, boys!
I said to her you'll soon be choking,
Jane, sweet Jane!
But if you do the water's near you,
Sweet Jane, full of charm,
The birds are singing merrily,
Jane, sweet Jane, full of charm,
The birds are singing merrily!)

Hob-y-Deri Dando

From a Welsh sea-shanty of the middle nineteenth century.
It originated in Nefyn, near Portmadoc, and it was often
heard off Cape Horn.

The final verse was sung always in English:

> I'll sing bass and you'll sing solo,
> Hob-y-Deri Dando!
> All about the clipper *Marco Polo*
> Can y gân eto!
> See her rolling through the water,
> Siân fwyn, Siân,
> Wish I was in bed with the Old Man's daughter,
> Siân fwyn, llawn o swyn,
> The birds are singing merrily,
> Siân fwyn, Siân, llawn o swyn,
> The birds are singing merrily,
> Hob-y-Deri Dando, boys!

17
The Last Spring

When I rejoined *Second Apprentice* she was lying to anchor at Hoo, further downstream on the River Medway, just as Tansy had said she would be. All the way through Mid-Wales and England, I had been depressed at the thought of Caradoc's suffering and of leaving home again. That lasted as far as London. Once I left the train from Shrewsbury and boarded the bus to cross the city, though, it was as if I had started a new journey. I was no longer leaving, I was arriving, and so I felt better. Waterloo station had been crowded with soldiers and Royal Navy seamen making their way back from Christmas leave. On the train down from London to Chatham I had been one of the few civilians in a flood of navy-blue. They all carried little brown cases, and I felt out of place with my sea-bag. Quite a few of the sailors nodded or grinned at me. They must have thought I was a new recruit; some of them looked even younger than I did.

Tansy and Daisy were on board when I clambered over the side from another barge's jolly-boat. They had spent Christmas together, and Daisy had looked after the captain while Bert and Ted went to Greenwich. Daisy had decorated the skipper's lobby with coloured paper streamers, and she told me that they'd had many visitors over the holiday. Tansy grinned as he inspected me, and we talked about Dad and my family and Llangareth for a while. All the time Tansy's expressions changed, just as the old sailors' back home had done, and I knew that he was thinking of his visits to his own home long ago. I told Tansy about going with Branwen to the pictures. Daisy gave me a sudden look of surprise.

Bert and Ted arrived alongside just as I was walking forward to stow my gear in the fo'c's'le. They both looked refreshed, merry, and raring to do something. Ted told me, a little later, when we were in the fo'c's'le, that he and Bert had drunk three pints each on the station at Gravesend.

'How was your Christmas, Ted?' I asked him.

'All-blooming-right. Bert's old woman ain't too bad really, least-ways not once she gets used to you. She made us a bloody great turkey and Christmas pud, and me and Bert went down to the local every flipping day. She even came to the pub with us on Boxing day. They left the young 'un outside in her pram. She kept squalling her blooming head off, so I nipped out and slipped her a bottle of light ale.' Ted grinned broadly. 'That put her to sleep.'

'Meet any girls?' I wondered at Ted's 'cleaner' language.

'They got a pusher in to look after the kid while we went to the flicks. Real bit of all right, she was. That was on Boxing day, too, and I took her to the Pally. We didn't get back till flipping one o'clock . . . she works in a blooming grocer's – the Home and Colonial . . .'

'?' I shot a question at Ted. He knew what I meant. He grinned even wider and stuck one thumb in the air. 'She couldn't get enough.' Ted's voice deepened, 'She's going out with me whenever I get back, she said.'

'You'll be getting tied up, Ted.' I struggled into my new jersey.

'Wouldn't mind that,' he replied. 'Bert's right, you know, nothing like having someone to blinking go back to . . .'

We were soon back in the old routine. Our first cargo was bricks from somewhere near Rainham up to Grays Thurrock. We loaded them in the morning, sailed right away, and unloaded them that evening. That meant we handled one hundred thousand house-bricks (fifty thousand each time), inside thirty hours, because the passage took only about three hours. By the time that one and a half days were over our hands and backs had forgotten the ease they had known over Christmas.

Next we sailed round the North Foreland, into the English Channel, to Cowes, in the Isle of Wight, with treated leather from Germany bound for Parkhurst prison, where, so Bert told me, the convicts made boots, belts and harnesses for the government. It was a rough trip – one of the roughest we made while I was on board *Second Apprentice*. Once we rounded the South Foreland we got a southwester straight in the teeth, and it was slog, slog, slog all the way to Dungeness, beating this way and that. After a few hours crawling to windward against very steep seas, foot by foot, the wind and sea had risen into such a frenzy against us that Tansy handed all sail except the mizzen, lashed the helm alee, and called it a day. Bert stayed on deck and Tansy, Ted and I went down below for a spell of rest after I had prepared a meal of boiled codfish and strong tea. The contrast below when the ship hove to in the gale was a wonder. Topsides the noise and clatter of the sea and wind howling and crashing was deafening, and the movements of the ship, as she yanked, pulled, tugged, lurched, toiled, moiled, drudged, and grinded was enough to quell the boldest spirit. But when added on to that was the seemingly impossible task of bringing down and quelling a flogging jib, a mainsail weighing a couple of tons and a dozen wildly flaying halyards and sheets, along the decks, it was like a riot in hell. The only way for us lads to deal with it was to think of nothing else at all but the job in hand. For Bert and Tansy it was different. They had to keep alive to everything about the ship, and be ready for any eventuality all the while the bats of hell and damnation flew about their ears.

Down below it was like another world. In the glow of the small stove (with the fire guard in place to prevent live ash from falling) the skipper's lobby was like a haven for tortured souls. Beside the stove I ate my codfish straight out of the

cooking tray with salty, bleeding fingers and listened to Tansy
talk of tropical adventures, his quiet voice contrasting with
the storm over the deck-light. Ted tried to match Tansy's
tales with wild, incredible stories of the shrimp bawley in
wild, incredible seas. Above us the lobby lantern swung rapid
shadows across their faces. Tansy's old and craggy, Ted's
young and smooth, as I, the quiet listener, broke my silence
only to urge them on. Then it was Tansy's turn to go on deck.
Unhurried, he made his way up the companion ladder into
the wet darkness above, as always, murmuring a thanks to the
Lord for the meal. Minutes later Bert wetly descended, his
oilskin agleam in the lantern glow, and he and Ted reminisced
about a darts match in Bert's 'local' on Christmas Day. It
seemed that Ted had claimed too high a score while Bert was
at the pub-counter, getting in the beers. I rose and left them,
to join Tansy on the heaving deck.

We stayed hove-to all that night, but in the morning the
gods of the weather relented, and let *Second Apprentice* pass
against their subdued, still sulky anger, and go about her
lawful occasion. By midday the wind was back to a mild
breeze, every stitch of canvas aloft, and a sea that would make
a pea-sorter look like a sarcophagus-plinth. Dusk saw us east
of Bembridge in the lee of the Isle of Wight, sitting in an
apologetic sea and with no more wind than would blow out a
candle. We finished up sweeping the glassy sea with the hefty
oars up through Spithead. It was a clear night. A new moon
sailed a starry sky like a jubilant princess. As I pushed the
heavy sweep back and forth, back and forth, I could see the
low, black shores of Wight and Hampshire on either side and
streams of little twinkling lights and hazy glows in the sky
above them. The lights of Portsmouth, millions of them,
seemed to outnumber the stars above and to quell their light.
It is only when we look at a city at night from the sea after a
storm that we can realize fully how far man has come along
our road of destiny. The paradox is that upon arrival in port

after a storm at sea we also realize how far man has to go to ever start to catch up with the appalling forces, the unmeasurable strength of nature.

We discharged the leather in heavy batches with the electric crane at Pickford's wharf in Cowes and off it went in lorries, on its way to His Majesty's Prison, Parkhurst. The following day was a Sunday, and on the pretext of accompanying Tansy to chapel, Ted and I got ashore early. It was a foregone conclusion that when we emerged from the house of worship Tansy would let us stay ashore for a while. The captain returned to the ship, where Bert was preparing the midday meal, and Ted and I walked around the town. We had enough money to buy ourselves a decent meal in a cafe, then we strolled along the esplanade looking at the yachts moored in Cowes roads. Some of them were tiny and bobbed away at anchor yawing this way and that in the fresh breeze of the early afternoon. Many were about thirty to fifty feet long, and they were all obviously moored for the winter, with big tarpaulins stretched over their topsides. A few very big pleasure sailing craft rode to anchor, and some of those had uniformed crewmen on board, cleaning and scrubbing, even though it was a Sunday in mid-winter. As we strolled in a drizzle past a big yacht club, which seemed deserted, Ted waved at the crewmen of a big black schooner – I think she was called *Black Joke* – and one of the deckies waved back. Ted cupped his mouth in his hands and yelled 'Bloody flunkies!' I shushed him, but it was all right – the yacht was too far to windward for the crewmen to hear us. We carried on in the rain past the yacht club, along the otherwise deserted sea-front promenade. Ted shouted out to the waving crewmen, 'Bleeding gin-palace asshole creepers!' and 'Get me some Angostura, Jeeves!' and in an attempted refined voice, 'Don't forget to polish the Rolls, James, Master Montague's off for a drive to Ascot this afternoon!' I kept telling Ted to shut up, that someone might hear us, but Ted was enjoying himself, even though he thought no one else but I could hear him.

As we passed the end of the yacht club grounds a voice hailed us. 'I say, you there!'

We looked around, startled. A man was coming from the back of a boat-shed. He was beetle-browed, much bigger than either Ted or me, and dressed in expensive yellow oilskins and smart sea-boots. On his head he wore a black captain's cap with a gold badge, and a neatly trimmed goatee beard.

'Afternoon, mate,' said Ted. His voice quavered.

The big man ignored the greeting. 'Who are you bawling at?' he demanded. 'Where are you from?'

Ted said, 'We're . . . we're out for a walk . . . we're off *Secon* . . . we're from a ship in Cowes port.'

'What ship?' The man glowered at Ted and looked down at him.

'*Second . . . Apprentice*, sir,' replied Ted. 'Dandy ketch . . .'

'You too?' the man turned and glared at me. 'Well, boy, speak up!'

'Yes, sir.'

'Right, well buzz off! We know your type round here. If you want to make a racket like that go over to Portsmouth or somewhere.'

Ted and I turned and started walking back to the port. As we left we heard someone else come from around the boat-shed, and the big man say to the newcomer, 'Blasted barge-tykes . . . idling all damned day . . . never wash . . . ought to be bally-well locked up!'

We kept our backs to the yachtsmen and trudged on in the rain, hardly able to stop ourselves from spluttering with laughter. After that I was no longer 'Nipper' to Ted. He renamed me 'Tyke'. The first time that Bert and Tansy heard Ted's new name for me they mistook it. They thought he'd said 'Tiger', and that was what I was called from then on.

I was still the nipper of the ship, but I had a new name, and that name bred an air about me, as a name will with a lad. By the time they'd called me Tiger for a week or two I would (and could) take on any other boy of my own size in the frequent scraps which took place when we were in port, mostly with the local lads, but sometimes with youngsters from other ships, too. Once, in Poole, I came back on board all torn and bloody after a stand-up knock-down bout which ended up as a free-for-all. My adversary had made some remark, when he learned I was Welsh, about 'foreigners'; that was more often than not the cause of my fights. Tansy caught sight of me and my swollen eye as I sneaked over the side forward of the mainshrouds, and called me over. He looked me up and down and shook his head. Then he said, 'You know, Tiger, you're a funny little bloke. You've got your nose into Byron and Shakespeare one minute, then you're ashore getting seven bells knocked out of you the next . . . I can't . . .'

'He called me a foreigner, Tansy, and anyway, I beat *him*.'

'Oh . . . I see. Well, that's all right then. Now go forward and get cleaned up.' I started forward. I heard Tansy call me, 'Tiger!' I looked over my shoulder. 'Next time, keep your guard up more!'

Ted was a holy terror in a fight, and by the time that winter had passed and spring was on us, we had quite a reputation all around the south-east coast of England, and were more or less left alone. We even made good friends with some of our former taunters, and swapped cigarette cards with them, played them at soccer, and got to know their sisters.

During the winter-time we made quite a few passages, mainly up and down the English Channel. In late April 1939, we made our last cross-Channel voyage before the spring and summer passages with timber and foodstuffs up to the North country and coal back, or mineral water and scrap-iron to Germany or cheese from Holland. We took on a cargo of house-bricks from a lighter in Sheerness, bound for St Helier,

Jersey, down in the Channel Islands.

We had a fair run around the Forelands and down-Channel, with first a norther and then an easterly breeze. That made up to some small extent for the brick-loading, and by the time we were alongside in the small port of St Helier our hands were half-healed up. There was a mobile steam-crane on the jetty which could reach out over our hold and lower the brick pallets down to us. That meant that Bert did not have to work the gaff-derrick and so he could give Ted and me a hand with the bricks.

By the time we started loading the next cargo, of barrels of offal in brine and cow-hides to take to Greenwich we thought we were well off. There were perhaps fifty barrels of offal, which stank so rancid that we had to wear rags over our noses and mouths. There weren't too many hides – about a hundred or so. Everything was heavy, greasy and very smelly, but compared to the bricks it was a real pleasure to handle the new cargo, and we all knew that it was better than returning the two hundred-odd miles back to the Thames in ballast. Tansy said, as we warped out of St Helier to catch the swiftly running north-going tide, with the offal and hides below stinking to high heaven, 'Beggars can't be choosers. We're lucky to find this little lot.'

Running before the wind back up-Channel we were all happy; Ted and I sang (we weren't ever allowed to whistle – it was supposed to bring calms and other bad luck) but because of the appalling smell rising and blowing forward from the hold we stayed abaft the hatches, to windward, whenever we could. Ted and I took turns in sleeping in the galley, with our knees under our chins in that tiny space, because the whiff of the offal and hides down in the fo'c's'le was too much to bear for more than a few minutes at a time. The happiness that joined with the vile cargo in pervading the ship was because we all knew that this was the last of the hard winter Channel-passages, and that once the ship reached Hull and loaded scrap-iron for Emden, then the occasional summer cruises to Holland and up the Rhine would ease the monotony of the grinds up and down the East coast.

We departed from St Helier in the early morning, and by dawn the following day *Second Apprentice*, with a good steady breeze right on her stern, was bowling up past Beachy Head. By dusk we were at anchor off Whitstable, having found a fair north-easterly wind off the North Foreland. We weighed anchor the next dawn, and were soon moored off Greenwich a day before the hides were due to arrive. Tansy was so pleased with the fast passage that, in consideration of the unholy reek from the hold, he gave permission for Ted and me to go ashore with Bert to his home to sleep.

I was surprised at the change in Mrs Bert when she opened the front door before Bert could find his keys. She knew we were coming – the mate had hurried to the Post Office and sent her a telegram as soon as we stepped ashore. Her hair was tidied and she wore a clean frock, and she was all smiles.

'Oh, thanks for the telegram I knew you were coming and I've got tea ready and . . .' she blurted out even before Bert pecked her on the cheek. As he did so her wide-open eyes beamed at Ted over Bert's shoulder, then they fell to see me and glazed over. We all traipsed into the dark, boiled-cabbage-smelling hall. Mrs Bert took the lead, then Bert and Ted, and me taking up the rear-guard.

'Do make yourselves at home boys I've got some lovely ham sandwiches and jam tart and I know that Teddie loves jam tarts how are they feeding you on that blooming old boat Teddie? don't worry Bert dear throw your coat over a chair and what's that other one's name? where is he oh here you are . . .' Mrs Bert reached atip-toe and beamed at me over her husband's shoulder, then she flashed an even bigger smile at Ted. All the while we men said nothing. After being at sea for a while the insides of houses seem so small, such a small house as Bert's seemed even smaller, and yet, on the other hand there appeared to be so much more room for everything than there was in the living quarters of the ship. We passed through the passage to the kitchen, feeling bigger than we were, more awkward and lumbering.

'Now sit yourselves down boys Teddie you sit the other side from Bert and the other one can use the corner by you what's his name?' She addressed Ted with a coquettish glance.

'Tiger,' chimed in Bert; as he said it he winked at me.

'Tiger? oh I'm sure he is poor little mite looks like he should still be in school and what was the trip like dear and did you bring those shirts? the telegram must have cost an awful lot Mum's ill again I'm sure I don't know what I shall do if she has to go to the hospital it's those damn varicose veins again I'm going to see her and get supper ready at six o'clock now no pushing off to the pub again I'm sure you're a bad example you and Teddie for poor little what's his name? oh I forgot the teaspoons . . .'

'Tiger,' said Bert in a weary tone. Then he added, 'How's the baby?'

'Oh I wish you wouldn't call her that Hermione is two years old now she's already upstairs in her cot asleep and when do you think we can put the down payment on that wireless that blessed old gramophone I swear I spend hours every day winding it up and listening to those same old silly six records you bought when we went to Brighton for our honeymoon three days . . .' She was smiling at Ted now, 'we had in a real posh hotel but they didn't half look at Bert when he came back from the pub sloshed didn't they dear?'

Suddenly there was a shocking silence in the little kitchen. Bert was lifting another ham sandwich up to his face and studying the pattern on the linoleum table-cloth. Mrs Bert stood waiting, looking down at her husband.

'Bert!' she yelled.

Bert gave a start and looked up at her. 'Mmm?'

'Oh I never did he's always the same when he comes home never stops stuffing himself I'm sure Teddie won't get drunk on your honeymoon will you Teddie?'

Ted, surprised out of his concentration on the sandwich he was gobbling and his contemplation of the jam tart which took pride of place on the table, mumbled, 'What's that, Mrs Bert?'

'Oh Teddie I told you to call me Nora you know that this is your home from home oh I should have said ship silly old me whenever you want to come I said that you won't get drunk on your honeymoon Teddie will you?'

'No fear,' muttered Ted thickly as he munched away on yet one more sandwich.

'Not our Teddie no fear he knows how to appreciate a good girl don't you Teddie? and Rosie thinks the world of you and said what a good time she had at the Pally and I'll go round and tell her that you're here when I go round to Mum's . . .' Mrs Bert talked away as the gallant mate and crew of the dandy ketch *Second Apprentice* swiftly and silently reconnoitred, approached, attacked, seized, and demolished the small mountain of ham sandwiches and the two-feet round jam tart which the good lady had prepared for us, along with about a gallon of hot, sweet, milky tea.

When there was nothing but empty plates, a few crumbs and tea stains left on the table, Bert glanced up at the steamed kitchen window and murmured, 'Come on, lads, it's stopped raining. Let's take a stroll in the garden.' He spoke as if he was in Marlborough House.

'Not Teddie Teddie's got to wait here for Rosie haven't you Teddie? and don't come trailing in any dirt from the garden Bert last time what's his name?' Mrs Bert glared at me.

'Tiger,' repeated Bert.

'Was here you mucked up the kitchen floor something awful and it took me all the next day to clean it up and what about that new stair-carpet you promised Bert?'

As he stood up to go outside Bert stammered, but Mrs Bert didn't wait for him to continue. 'And. that there outside gutter-pipe has to be fixed too it just pours water down over the window every time it rains and this blooming weather I can't get any washing dry outside now you wait here Teddie and I'll go round and . . .' Her voice trailed off as she went through the front passage and Bert and I went out into the back garden. It was tiny – about sixty by forty feet square, surrounded by dirty brick walls except in one far corner, where stood a brick outhouse. 'That's the kaasy if you want it, Tiger,' said Bert quietly. Rain still dripped from an arthritic-looking tree which had exhausted itself in trying to escape over the garden wall for too long. Along another wall a small greenhouse with dirty windows, despite the rain, looked like it contained a leprechaun stoker's ash-pit.

Bert and I stood on the narrow concrete path outside the back door in the damp, blessed, grey silence for a moment or two, then he said, 'Come on, Tiger, we'll nip back in. She's upstairs getting her coat on.'

I wasn't too impressed with Rosie when she turned up. She reminded me of Lilly Lie-back, the saucy lass from Liverpool who worked in a cafe back in Barmouth, and whose moonlit escapades with the lads were legendary from Dolgellau to Aberdovey, and probably, by this time, to Cardiff. Rosie should have been about two inches shorter than my five feet six, but wore at one end lipstick and at the other three-inch heels which made her tower above me. Her dialect was even more difficult for me to understand than was Ted's at times. When she spoke she chewed on her words, as if they were made of some sticky substance. She completely ignored me, but she flashed Bert an old-fashioned look every so often, when she wasn't melting at Ted. I guessed her age at around Ted's, nineteen, but perhaps she was a bit older than him. She took delight in telling us how her parents told her 'noffink' and how she'd even forgotten that, too.

Most of the time Rosie was in the house, Ted stayed silent, flexing his arm muscles on the table-top. Soon Rosie had nothing more to say, so Ted jerked his head at the door and the pair of them went out. That left Bert and me to inspect the mate's war medals after we'd cleared the table and washed the dishes.

Later that night, when Ted came in all glowing and grinning, Mrs Bert gave him little Hermione's room, while I slept on the kitchen floor. 'I'd let you sleep in the front room what's your name? only I don't want you opening and shutting the door and letting air in and out it's very bad for the furniture you know but you'll be all right in here and don't be afraid if the cat jumps on you poor old Tibby's a bit nervous of strangers aren't you my pet and Teddie if you need anything don't be afraid to let us know eh Bert? you'll be all right in Hermione's room nice and warm in there because it gets the heat from the kitchen chimney bet you'd like to have Rosie up there with you eh? you saucy Teddie you she thinks the world of you I know she told me . . .' So it went on until Mrs Bert, followed by Bert, and shepherding 'Teddie', finally left the kitchen fire-light trembling in anticipation of her return downstairs next morning, and me dozing off on the rug before the fire, with Tibby the cat curled up by my side.

The next day we went back on board early. By mid forenoon *Second Apprentice* lay alongside an otherwise empty wharf. There we discharged our smelly cargo and loaded acetylene and oxygen cylinders for Hull. They were heavy, but at least they were reasonably clean. This took us all of that day. The next morning, when we shoved off downstream and round past Shoeburyness out into the North Sea, we found that our luck had changed. We were headed by an adamant northerly. After Orfordness was abeam we had to beat all the two hundred odd miles north around the coast of East Anglia and up to the River Humber. Two days later, when Spurn Head, at the mouth of the river, appeared low on the northern horizon, the fickle wind dropped. Once again we rowed the boat day and night for a full twenty-four hours before we were alongside near Goole. We felt cheerful about it, though. The weather was warming up, and the North Sea is generally a bit less rainy than the Channel, and it was now almost May and the sun came out more between the clouds.

I felt cheerful for more than that, however. It was almost my fifteenth birthday. Tansy had promised that if I did well he would raise my pay by a whole fifty per cent on the great day. That would give me one shilling and sixpence daily – just over ten bob a week. Then I could send Mam seven shillings and sixpence a week instead of only five shillings, and I would still have three shillings a week to myself. If I saved a shilling a week towards my fare home at Christmas, that meant two shillings a week in my pocket. Why, I would soon be able to buy myself a pocket watch, like Tansy's, at that rate.

We got infrequent and often inaccurate news of what was going on ashore, outside our own little world. We knew, from reading a few newspapers and from garbled accounts from other bargees or stevedores, that Hitler had marched into Prague and seized Memel in Lithuania. The former was a mysterious place far away in Central Europe, but to the sailors Memel was as well known as Dover or Calais. Many good sailors hailed from there. We knew that Franco had at last defeated the Government forces around Madrid, and that the Spanish Civil War was, to all intents and purposes, at an end. We also knew, and thought it was about time, that the British Government had at long, long last abandoned appeasement to Hitler and that he had been warned that if he took one step further – which meant against Poland – that we would stand by that country and fight him. But to most of the bargees and dockers, it all meant little. I can recall no one ever questioning our loading scrap-iron for Germany . . . It was all so far away, Poland and Prague, and anyway, the French were our allies. 'The French might be a poncey lot, but they've a big army, navy, and air force, haven't they, and they've been building those lines of block-houses (what's the name, the Maginot Line?) since the end of the last war ... Hitler would be a bloody fool to go against the Froggies, and our navy, too ...'

One quiet evening, it must have been at the beginning of May, I asked Tansy, 'Do you think Hitler will try anything against the Poles?'

'Of course he will. It's Russia he wants to really have a go at, and he can't do that until he takes Poland over. Anyway, like all bullies, he doesn't know his own limits.'

'When, Tansy?'

'Either this year or next.' The captain grinned as he looked at me and said, 'It had better be, otherwise I'll be too old to have a go, won't I?'

When, in the fo'c's'le, I later told Ted what Tansy had said, he snorted, 'What's the bloody difference? German government or ours, they're all bastards anyway. In any case, from what I've seen in Germany, the kids are well-fed and singing and everything, and them uniforms the government gives them free, I'm not so sure we wouldn't be better off with that silly sod Hitler in charge ... at least he couldn't make much worse of a cock-up than some of the silly old twits we've got at the top.'

'But, Ted, you don't want Jerry officers stamping around and ordering you about, do you?'

'Couldn't be worse than some of the masters in the bleedin' kids home I was in.'

'But you don't want Germans taking over and forcing everyone to work for them like slaves, Ted?'

'How many gas cylinders you loaded today, Tiger? The bloody Germans could hardly make you work harder, could they?'

'But ...' I was running out of arguments with Ted's logic. 'But you wouldn't want them marching and goose-stepping down Bert's street and taking everything over and raping all the women . . . even Rosie . . . would you, Ted? You wouldn't want . . .'

Ted didn't let me go on. 'Oh, for Christ's sake, Tiger, the old girls would just bloody-well love a bit of the old rape – and so would young Rosie, too!' Ted thought for a moment as I stared at him in shocked silence, then he added, 'As for Bert's street, any time the fucking German army wants it, or their poxy navy, or their bleedin' air-force, and that fat fucker Goering, they're bloody-well welcome to it. I'd even stow the whole sodding street on board and sail the bastard over to bleedin' Germany, and give it to them on a poxy plate if they want it so bad – bloody garden-railings and all!' He stomped up the scuttle ladder.

I found out from Ted the next day that Rosie had sent him a letter saying that she'd taken up with a soldier in the Royal Artillery barracks in Woolwich, and that she wouldn't be seeing him again.

18

A Cup of Tea

During the summer of 1939 *Second Apprentice* made several trips over the North Sea to Holland from East London or Hull with scrap-iron bound for Germany. We generally carried it to Dordrecht and there we transferred it into German or Swiss barges which took it up the Waal and the Rhine. One load we took up the Rhine ourselves into Germany, to Duisberg, a big industrial town. There were many more uniforms about, and we saw quite a few even on board the local barges. The tally clerk who came out in the lighter which moored alongside to accept our load of old boiler plate wore a brown uniform with a Sam Browne belt and a Nazi brassard on his arm. His jackboots were so shiny they looked like they were made of glass. After Ted had offered the clerk a 'Gold Flake' cigarette which that worthy had curtly refused, Ted said he looked like 'a bloody dog-track attendant'.

The last trip to Germany was in late August. That was to Brunsbuttel, near Hamburg, with scrap-copper from a ship-breaking yard in Inverkeithing, up in Scotland. There again the official who checked our cargo ashore was fully booted and brassarded, but he was an older man and quite friendly. The local stevedores seemed to get on very well with him. In Brunsbuttel I went ashore with Bert and Ted to buy a few fresh provisions and for the mate to send a cable to Hull, where our next cargo, of leather drive-belting for mill machinery, was bound. As we walked through the clean streets, there were Nazi flags everywhere. They hung from practically every window and draped every shop-front. In many of the shop windows there were pictures of the Nazi leaders, with Hitler taking pride of place. His picture was in every shop we called at, in the Post Office and on the walls at the agents and the harbour-master's office. On practically every wall was the legend, 'Ein Volk, Ein Reich, Ein Führer!' We called in at a stevedore's pub for beer. Most of the workers were friendly. Ted managed to talk to several dockers about soccer, while they told us where the girls' houses were, but with Bert a married man, and with the amount of cash Ted and I had between us they might just as well have directed us back to the ship. The German dockers invariably called us 'Tommy'.

There were only about fifty of the big leather driving belts, so when we sailed the ship was quite light in the water. There was very little wind. We thought we would have to row out to sea with the sweeps to maintain steerageway out of the River Elbe. Tansy had wanted to push off just before dawn, so we could take full advantage of the full ebb tide as well as the river current, but the harbour-master forbade it. We had to wait an hour or two, and leave with a flotilla of other non-German vessels – Dutch and Danish coasters, mainly – under the escort of a German Navy patrol craft. When the gaggle of craft got under way Ted and I started pushing and pulling with the sweeps, but of course we had no chance at all of keeping up with the other vessels, all of which had engines. When the escort craft saw our painfully slow progress she came over and without so much as a word to Tansy got right against our port side so fast that Ted was lucky she didn't smash his sweep. If the Kriegsmarine skipper said anything, or if anyone else did (we didn't), we couldn't hear it over the racket of the escort's engines. From the German craft a big man, by the look of him a Chief Petty Officer of some kind, gesticulated to Bert to throw him lines and make *Second Apprentice* fast to the escort. Bert had been rushing around placing fenders over the side and for a moment he seemed astonished almost out of his wits. Tansy was still at the helm, quietly studying the intruder. Bert turned and shot an unspoken question to Tansy. Our captain nodded his head, and only then did Bert obey the German. By the time I'd stowed my sweep, Ted had thrown his, too, down on deck, and we helped Bert tie up alongside the escort vessel, with German sailors helping on board their vessel.

We got under way, and the Kriegsmarine pushed *Second Apprentice* out to sea at about five knots with no effort at all from anyone on board except Tansy, who was still at the wheel. Ted, as much a clown as ever, climbed on to the cargo-hatch covers, stretched himself out, placed one hand under his head and the other on his waist and then pretended he was smoking from a cigarette-holder. Everyone laughed at his antic, the German sailors, too. Even the Kriegsmarine skipper was smirking over his bridge windshield.

It was a new experience, to be sliding over a calm sea with the wind of our headway blowing straight back from the bow and no sails up, and *Second Apprentice* actually keeping up with engined craft. The Germans' boat shoved us all forenoon, for about twenty miles, until we were well clear of Scharhörn and Neuwerk, the islands north-west of Cuxhaven. Then, without any kind of warning she slowed down, stopped, and the German sailors cast off our mooring lines and pulled away slowly from our ship's side. *Second Apprentice* kept way on for a minute or two and then she, too, stopped dead in the glassy water. As we collected in our mooring lines and stowed them away there was a sudden roar from the German craft. I looked up . . . there were all her sailors lined up on her deck at attention facing our almost black, tattered, drooping Red Ensign, with their chief at the salute. As the escort roared away her captain, too, turned and gave Tansy a brief salute. Our skipper, expressionless, touched one gnarled finger to his bowler hat. In a cataract of spray and a mighty roar, the gunboat settled her stern in the sea and shot off towards the clear, calm horizon, leaving *Second Apprentice* wallowing and shaking in her wake, juggling and jolting, like a jilted bride on the church steps. Ted and I shipped the long heavy sweeps once more into the irons. Ted said 'Blimey, that's the way to travel, eh?'

'They could have asked permission to come alongside,' observed Tansy in a piqued voice. 'Blessed – no manners . . . they could do with a year or two in the *Andrew*.'

'They must have good engines,' I commented to no one in particular, as I pulled away on my sweep.

'Yeah – they got fifty slaves down below, all peddling away like mad,' said Ted. After that there was silence on board, except for the groaning and swishing of the sweeps and the creaks of the rigging as we pushed *Second Apprentice* at a painfully slow rate westward over the sea as smooth and glassy as a fishmonger's slab.

That evening, as dusk fell and a slight north-westerly wind slowly roused itself, we could still see the low, grey, misty island of Heligoland over our starboard quarter, almost in the same spot where it had been when the gunboat left us. Even before the first zephyrs, Tansy was sniffing the wind and pulling a face. Before I felt any moving air, he turned to Bert who was on the wheel, and said, 'Muzzler, Bert, wester.'

We all knew what that meant. On our course direct to Hull the wind was just about directly against us, right slap-bang on the nose.

'Typical,' was all that Bert answered. Then he turned to me. 'All right, Tiger, stow your sweep and get supper ready. We might as well have it before it starts to blow . . .'

By the time supper was prepared all working sail was hoisted and the ship was driving north-west into an ever rising sea, close hauled on the port tack, so as to get plenty of sea-room. By the time supper was cleared away the wind had risen enough for us to hand the fore-jib and the staysail, and reef the main down a point. By midnight the wind hauled round to the north-west; we came about on to the starboard tack and it was time to hand the main topsail. In the overcast darkness all we could see was the occasional, faintly stabbing light of Heligoland on the port quarter and a liverish sea all around the ship. All night we ploughed into steep sea after steep sea, with the howling wind out-screaming the seas which crashed over the bow. By the middle of my trick on the wheel I could no longer control the helm. Bert ordered Ted to back me up. At about 3.00 A.M. out of a night as black as the Earl of Hell's riding boots, lightning blazed out everywhere, zigzagging across the solid black vault of sky and sea above, below, and all around us and seeming to stab through and through the ship. For about a quarter of an hour it was purgatory with the lid off. Then, with a mighty rumble, a hiss and a roar, down came the rain, and soon (in late August!) hailstones rattled down on to our decks and oilskins like gravel pouring down a hold-chute. In between surges of the sea over our bulwarks and topsides, the hail rolled along the decks inches thick, until it was swept away by yet another roaring watery boarder. So it went all night; wind, rain, hail, and frenzied seas desperately boarding the ship to escape their hellish parent's own anger. Bert, Ted, and I took turns on the bilge pump as the ship worked, pumping, pumping; up and down, up and down, slosh and creak, slosh and creak.

At 4.00 A.M. we lads handed the helm over to Bert and tried to get a few winks of sleep, but in the fo'c's'le it was impossible. The ship's head reared up and slammed down like an elevator gone wild. We sat by the bogey-stove for a few minutes, to warm ourselves up, and then we staggered our way over the roaring deck aft. I slept hunched up in the galley while Ted laid himself down in the skipper's lobby, under the table.

Just before dawn we were all back on deck. Bert had picked up the light on Borkum – the most westerly of the German Frisian Islands. He sent Ted below to let Tansy know. The captain took over the helm from Bert, after he had gazed into the storm ahead of us for a few minutes. Suddenly there was a blistering flash of lightning which showed me every wrinkle on Tansy's face, every hair in his beard. He was grinning to himself as he gave the wheel a turn and changed the course a point or so off the wind. There was another stab of blazing light from Hell's black forge. Every part of the sails and rigging stood out brilliantly for a second, despite the rain and spray. It was as if some celestial warlock had suddenly transformed the plunging, black, sky-sweeping rig and revealed to us a great three-dimensional display of water-streaming, silvery magic. Then it was gone and we were left in tormented darkness once again.

Dawn hid itself behind sheets of rain and spray as the ship repented the sins of all on board and again baptized us in unholy grey North Sea water. Above us the cloud, black-grey companions of the gale, mocked our labours at the pump as the bows sheered and dived, scurried, slid and smashed through and out of the unending seas ahead, always ahead. As the bows plunged into a trough, the force on the sails was eased momentarily, then as the forefoot rose there was a great strain on the shaking rain-dark canvas, then a pause as short as a shocked breath, then an almighty surge, then a seething of boiling whiteness along the lee bulwark and over the deck and a slamming over of more spray, and curses from Ted and Bert and silent prayers from me and no doubt from Tansy, as we were drenched again and again and again.

At one time, as I took a short breather from working the pump, I glanced forward. A momentary clear gap between the blankets of rain showed shoreline dead ahead of our hammering bowsprit. I wetly whipped around and shouted something to Tansy, but he merely held up one hand from the wheel and nodded his bowler hat in my direction. All the while the ship plunged on and on into solid, mocking rain and, as I thought, to our certain doom.

Suddenly – quite suddenly – as suddenly as when you walk out of a crowded, rowdy pub on to a night-quiet quayside, the ship was in calm water. The thick rain still sluiced down and the wind still screamed, but the sea was merely stippled, corrugated, grey with a yellowish tinge to it, the colour of an old man with jaundice. Now the ship still lay over to leeward, and plunged and soared, but not nearly as violently as before. I shook the water from my eyes and stared through the pouring rain. Bert and Ted, both holding on the windward shrouds, but with their backs to the gale, were grinning broadly. Tansy looked over at me, raised one eyebrow, then dropped it again.

Bert took over on the pump handle, saying cryptically as he did so, 'We're in the lee of Rotturmeroog now, in the Wadden Sea. We'll have a nice smooth passage from here on, until we get to Den Helder – that's about forty miles. We'll drop the hook there, and wait till this little tea-party blows its blooming-self out.'

We must have made an average of more than eight knots down the Wadden Sea in the lee of the Dutch Frisian Islands because we went to in the lee of Texel Island, north of Den Helder just after noon. I remember, as I made dinner, wondering to myself how many British boys of my age had ever even heard of the Wadden Sea. As Ted lumbered into the galley to drink his mid-morning tea, rain streaming from his black oilies, he mumbled, 'Wadden Sea – they ought to bleedin' call it sodden sea!'

The gale blew itself out by dusk the next day. We weighed anchor right after supper, and headed out into the North Sea again, still headed by a north-wester, but a lot more gentle. We were able to hoist our topsails and the breeze sang to us now to charm away the memories of the bells of hell ringing in our ears two nights before. We had a good fast passage across to the English shore and before dawn we sighted the welcome gleam of Orfordness light, on the coast of Suffolk. We went about and beat northward on the port tack all forenoon and afternoon, until dusk, when we returned to the starboard tack.

Off the East coast of England the North Sea plays up stink when any kind of a wind blows, except a westerly close inshore, and with all the tide rips and shallows offshore, navigation is anything but child's play. That evening our devilish old friend from three nights before decided we hadn't had enough. He came back for a return visit. We rucked again all but the main and stays'l. By midnight the rain and spray was slashing at us in a high wind again, the short frenzied seas were once more crashing on board. It was as if the Wadden Sea and our relatively smooth crossing to the English offing were but dreams. By one o'clock in the night lightning was again blasting like the cracks of doom and visibility otherwise was down to the ends of our cold, water-streaming noses. Once again both Ted and I were heaving and grunting at the helm, with Bert standing by. Once again we were warmly wrapped up in several layers of clothing under our oilies, and once again they were all sodden through and through with the water that had streamed up our sleeves and down our collars. Once again it was as much as both Ted and I could do to hold the ship on course against the kicking of the wheel, all the time watching the bucking compass in its dim binnacle-light, and trying to keep an eye on the mainsail, now reefed down to a quarter of its area and badly out of shape.

At about five o'clock in the morning all around the ship the obscurity was an unnatural and threatening light that showed up our slitted eyes and drawn faces. It was such an eerie light that to witness it only taxed our endurance even more. As the waves worked up, the horizon around us seemed to have closed itself into a narrow circle in which the seas furied at the ship, leaped on board and leaped out again. The spray and rain were like a flaying mist. Now and again a bigger, foaming sea came out of the mist and made for the ship with all its strength, looking like a maniacal, hulking, glassy-eyed murderer coming at us with a bludgeon. Then we hung on tight to the wheel or anything else which might be chained to the centre of Earth, stopped our breaths and held on in a welter of smashing coldness. The stern of the ship went down, down, and as the wave broke and scattered over the lee side the bows reared up, up, as if in supplication to the heavens, then down, down went the ship's head in the general direction of Australia as the mate, the deckhand and the ship's boy eased the helm all together, to meet the headlong pitch of the sea. Then another sea, a hill of grey glass topped with frothing foam towered close by and the ship, her sails flapping, rose to it like a ghostly pterodactyl rising into the sky. Ghastly gusts, roaring rollers, and toppling lurches, and down below the leather machinery belts broken loose and flaying around the hold like so many serpents gone insane.

I remember being jammed by a wall of water between the wheel and the binnacle. I was dimly aware that Bert had been bowled over by the same appalling force and was smashed over to the lee bulwark, and that Ted had spluttered curses as he went down to the deck still grimly grasping the wheel. I remember shouting to Bert, as the water-wall passed over the lee side, 'Good job we're sailing light!' and I remember his reply, in between curses, as he struggled up on to his feet from a cataract of swirling foam – 'She's much steadier when she's heavy!'

For the next few seconds it is all hazy. There was a sea which came on board, not as big as the previous one, but just as forceful, just as ruthless, just as careless. Ted somehow was back again on his feet and Bert had crawled back across the deck and was embracing the bottom of the binnacle, as the ship's bows flew up and smashed down. As *Second Apprentice* recovered herself from that blow and shook the sea from her yet again, there was an almighty CRASH! BANG! Then another . . . horrible *CRASH!*

To say that the shocks jarred every bone in my body would be an understatement – they shattered my soul. I am not aware of the next few moments. All I know is that I gripped on to the wheel with both hands and stared at the now darkened, now hardly shaking compass.

Tansy's voice was in my ear. He was shouting across me to Bert who was struggling to his feet on the strangely solid deck as it banged down, banged down, every few seconds on to something very hard indeed. 'The Hailsborough!' Tansy yelled. 'We've touched the Hailsborough Sands!'

One moment *Second Apprentice* had been plunging along, working and labouring as hard as a ship can against the sea, tossing ten tons of water from herself every few seconds, hammered and tortured, twisted and racked so that no landsman would ever believe that a collection of wood and metal could ever stand such punishment, but still in possession of her own soul; the next moment, with a bash, a crash that could, it seemed, have been heard in Llangareth, she had struck. In the mighty shock, the topmast had splintered and most of it had carried away and fallen on to the port bow and knocked the forward windlass right off its bed. In the slashing rain and spray coming from the dark night all around the ship it was a scene of utter chaos from the nethermost pit of hell. I was paralysed. I was deathly afraid. I could not move.

As soon as the topmast crashed down, Bert clambered on to his feet while Ted strived forward against the smashing walls of water which boarded the ship and let go of the sheets. In a blizzard of spray I stared as Ted let go of the staysail and main halyards. Still shocked rigid, I was aware of the clatter of the staysail as it shook itself down its staywire in the wind, and I was conscious that Bert was with Ted, grabbing the main-leach and somehow hauling the giant sail, flogging away and sounding like a machine gun, down over the main boom, heaving away with all their weight, grabbing the parrel rings and forcing them down the mast.

When the mainsail was almost mastered, Bert made his way aft. As he passed me he shouted in a thin voice, 'Give Ted a hand with the main, Nipper!' To me, still frozen to the helm, his voice was shouting at me as if I were somewhere far away, down the bottom of a deep, deep well. Then Bert was gone out of sight aft.

I still stared at Ted struggling away with the huge mainsail as it weaved across the deck like some crazy animal. Plainly I heard him yell, 'Give us a bleeding hand, Tiger!' but I was incapable of any movement. I wanted to help Ted – I knew I ought to but my limbs simply refused to move. All the while the ship banged the sea bottom, very, very hard each time. The shocks almost knocked me off my feet, but still my hands were welded to the helm. Again I heard Ted yell, 'If you can't give me a bloody hand then get on the fucking pump!'

All I could do was stare at the wreckage of the topmast forward through the rain; at the shambles which had been, only a minute or two before, a sturdy emblem of natural pride, power, and grace. Now our topmast lay splintered and bouncing on the banging bow with frenzied, white seas crashing over it from an evil darkness. My mind wanted to command my fingers to let go of the wheel-spokes, but the message was simply not passing from my brain to my members. I was cold and wet. The only place I was warm and wet was inside my trousers. The stinging spray was flaying my oilskins and face. I knew I could find shelter behind 'Yarmouth Roads' (the big deck locker) but my body would not move. I was rigid with fright. I stared for an eternity of seconds at the deadly broken rigging wire-cables flailing over the deck and threatening to take our heads off any second; I gawped at the cold, wet hell of flogging wet canvas, and the death-dealing seas smashing over all, and I knew I was going to die.

'What are you doing, Nip . . . Tiger?' It was Tansy's voice as low and steady as a naval pension behind my leeward ear. Something snapped inside my head. I was crying. I couldn't see for a blessed moment. '*Rwyn llawn ofn!*' I forgot to speak English . . . 'I'm afraid!'

'What are you doing, Tiger?' the captain repeated again, his voice still low.

My English returned. 'We . . . Tansy . . . we're going to sink . . . she's going to be smashed to pieces . . . what . . . what . . . can we do?'

The low voice waited a moment then it rose and said, '*Do? . . . Do?*' As he shouted, I looked round at Tansy. He was braced against the deckhouse. In one hand he held a tree-felling axe, in the other, the spare hull-pump handle. Each one of them weighed about as much as I did. His voice rose even higher. '*Do?* Well, Tiger, I'll tell you what you can do . . . You can trust in the Lord and go and make a cup of tea! That's what you can do!'

'But . . . but we're sinking, Tansy . . . she's going to break up!'

'We'll cross that there bridge when we come to it! Now, you nip into the galley, like a good sailor, and make a cup of tea!'

'But she's . . .'

Tansy's voice rose to the level of a foghorn. He bawled in my ear, 'THEN MAKE TWO BLOODY CUPS! – THEY MIGHT BE YOUR BLOODY LAST! AND MAKE 'EM BLOODY STRONG!' He turned away and clambered forward over the wreckage of his ship's rigging, somehow avoiding the flogging cable-wires. Then he started chopping away at the topmast stays, so as to secure the spar safe on deck. All the while the ship's bottom banged, banged.

I watched him dumbfounded through the streaming rain and spray. It was the only time I ever heard Tansy curse. It shook me down to my toenails. I was still staring at Tansy's dim figure, through the beating rain, when Bert staggered from aft, carrying a sledge-hammer and a big cold chisel. He struggled forward past me, holding himself against the wind, the spray and the driving rain.

I watched the two of them, and Ted, as they struggled to free their ship of the dangerous junk on her deck. Suddenly I knew we were going to be all right. Tansy knows what he's doing, and so does Bert, I thought to myself as I freed my fingers from the wheel and was half-blown aft. I clawed my way towards the galley. I caught another glimpse of the captain, the mate, and the deck-hand as they chopped and hammered and pumped away to ease the ship's appalling pain.

Inside the galley was a scene from the ninth circle of Hell. The hull bottom was still banging on the hard sand below, but not as hard as at first (the tide was going down, although I didn't realize that). The breakers still crashed every second or two against the ship's side and the wind was howling even harder in the rigging. What was left of the rig was not giving way before the murderous assault. In the galley there was no light as the oil-lamp had been shot off its gimbals. On the deck the black water was ankle-deep and violently sloshing around as the hull battered itself on the bottom. Many of the galley fittings had broken loose and were bouncing around.

I set to making tea, my hands shook with my remaining fear and excitement. I was completely unaware that the galley stove fire had been dowsed by a sea breaking in through the door, even though the galley was on the semi-sheltered side of the ship. I groped for the big kettle in the darkness, placed it empty on the cold stove and tried to collect my thoughts. Then I realized that the kettle was empty and the stove was dead, and I laughed at myself for having been so stupid. I grovelled around and lit the small kerosene stove which was stowed in one of the upper cupboards.

Now my hands were steadier. I knew that the situation we

were in was no one's fault but our own, and it was up to ourselves to get ourselves out of it. No amount of fear or moaning, whining or complaining was going to alter anything for the better. Fate was trying to overcome us and we had to resist it. By not resisting, by not struggling against fate we would be going against nature itself – our own nature. Man's nature is to fight for survival. Man's will to survive is part of nature itself. It is as strong as any other natural force, but the scales are tipped to Man's advantage because he has intelligence on his side. In the depths of my mind, in the pale flickering light of the little stove, I somehow became aware that fear is merely nature trying to redress the balance against man; trying to tip the scales again back in its favour. The discarding of fear makes man invincible. The realization of this and the doing of it is courage. I somehow knew that what I'd learned from Tansy that night was courage.

As soon as this realization became clear to me I turned off the little stove and said to myself aloud, 'Bugger the tea!' I made for the deck and clambered and staggered, dodged and clawed my way forward, to where Tansy was busy lashing down splintered bits of the topmast and bundling up the now tamed rigging-wires. Ted and Bert were taking frantic turns on the bilge-pump, trying to keep down the level of the water in the hull. As I watched, in the streaming rain, Bert started to shift one cargo-hatch cover, so he could go below into the bouncing hold to secure the leather machinery belts.

Tansy suddenly glanced up at me. He looked much older. There was exhaustion in his eyes, but there was still a gleam of wild will to survive – to fight on. 'What's up, Tiger . . . tea ready?' he shouted.

'Give me . . . the axe, Tansy, and let me have a go at the topsail halyards before they . . .' My voice tailed off.

Tansy broke in, 'That's it, mate, you do that and I'll give Bert a hand.' The captain handed me his axe, which I could just about lift, and made his way over to where Bert was struggling in the now-easing wind.

It was the first time anyone had ever called me 'mate'. It was the first time I had ever met real courage and recognized it. I had become a man.

Of course we survived the night. *Second Apprentice* had been constructed for that very kind of thing. She was built like Windsor Castle. As the tide went down the storm abated, and we found ourselves, after four or five hours sitting high and dry, stranded on the sand, with a clearing sky and even some sunshine. By that time we had re-rigged the running stays and sorted out all the mess on deck. Then, as the tide rose again we slept uneasily for a while until the tide changed. Bert had already been out in the jolly-boat and dropped the bower anchor well out in deep water, and as soon as *Second Apprentice* was afloat, we pulled her off, using the lee-board windlasses to do it. After she was clear, in a mild breeze, right on the nose again, this time from the east, we worked our weary way for some hours into Lowestoft, where we dropped hook and turned in for the night.

Next day, when we warped alongside the quay, was a Saturday. As we landed all the damaged wires and spars on to the jetty, Tansy came up to me. 'Here you are, Tiger,' he said. He held out a hoary, hard fist. He dropped a coin into my hand. It was a sixpence. 'An extra tanner for you today, my son,' he said.

I was delighted. It was supposed to be my afternoon off. 'Blimey, Tansy, thanks a lot . . . What's that for – keeping cool the other night?'

Tansy looked at me sternly. 'Keeping cool be jiggered,' he exclaimed as Ted and Bert and several bystanders looked on. 'That's for working right through today and tomorrow, helping Bert and Ted to get that blooming topmast replaced. We have to be up in Hull by next Thursday, or we'll lose our cargo for Emden . . .' Tansy started to clamber back on board when one of the bystanders, a docker by the look of him hailed, 'Captain!'

Tansy turned and stared at the onlooker. 'Yes?'

'I think you've lost your cargo for Emden already,' said the docker.

'What do you mean . . . why's that?' asked Tansy, as we all looked on curiously.

'Haven't you heard the news?' asked another bystander.

Tansy frowned, 'No, why?'

The first docker said, 'The Jerries invaded Poland last night. It was on the wireless early this morning. My missus heard it and told me.'

'Thanks,' said Tansy. Without another word he climbed aboard and went below.

'That's torn it,' muttered Bert. 'Now the balloon'll go up!'

There was silence for a moment or two as the small crowd all looked seriously at one another, then Ted said, 'Right, now *I* can join the bloody Royal Artillery!'

Everyone was quiet as Ted straightened himself up, and in an aside to me added, 'Rosie wants a fucking gunner, she'll *have* a fucking gunner!'

I clutched my sixpence for a minute, then I stuck it in my pocket and carried on helping Bert to lash the pieces of shattered topmast ready for loading on to a borrowed hand-cart.

19
Off to War

Early the next morning, after breakfast, even though it was Sunday, Ted and I went ashore to a local boat-yard to collect the new topmast. The previous day Tansy had gone to the yard and chosen a length of spruce for the job. The boat builders had worked far into the night to cut the timber to shape and plane it down. When we arrived at the yard with our borrowed hand-cart the new topmast was already waiting for us. It looked exactly like the old one had, except that it was not festooned with metal fittings, not yet varnished.

On the way back to the ship, as we manoeuvred the forty foot long, eight inch to eighteen inch thick pole along the quiet waterfront, we saw a small knot of people standing by the pub door. In the distance we saw a church clock, its hands near eleven. 'The boozers are early today,' observed Ted but as we neared the group it was obvious that they were not all boozers – there were some women and a respectable looking elderly gentleman with a prayer book under his arm. They were listening to a wireless turned up loud. A man was speaking sadly. Ted and I stopped our mast-pushing out of curiosity and listened . . .

'. . . and that consequently this country is at war with Germany.'

'Who's that, mate?' Ted asked the respectable-looking gentleman, 'Who's that bloke talking?'

The respectable-looking gentleman turned watery eyes to Ted and said in a quavering voice, 'That was the Prime Minister, Mr Chamberlain.' The gentleman walked slowly away, his head bent.

'Oh,' replied Ted. He turned to me. 'Well, Tiger, we'd better get this lot on board before Tansy gets back from church. He'll have our guts for garters if he sees us around this pub. It'll take all bleeding day for the fucking varnish to dry . . . let's hope to Christ it don't rain . . .'

The next day it was quite tricky wangling the heel of the topmast into the gammon iron and into the trestle as it swung around suspended from a crane-hoist. We had spent all day Sunday and most of the evening fitting on the topmast-head iron-band with lugs and eyes, to which running blocks and tackle and the standing rigging wires were fixed; making the fid hole at the heel of the mast, as well as drilling tiny holes at different points of the mast and squirting linseed oil into them from a sewing machine oil can, plugging up the holes, and then applying two coats of varnish to all the mast.

When the new topmast was rigged in place the ship no longer looked hurt and bald. Tansy brought out from his cabin a brand new owner's pennant, which we rigged on the nine-foot-long headstick and sent aloft. When the job was finished we all four went on to the jetty to inspect the set of the topmast, to see that Bert had properly raked it forward. Tansy nodded silently.

Bert said, 'Bristol fashion – couldn't have done better myself.'

Ted exclaimed, 'I've seen that there ship before somewhere!'

As we went back over the gangway, before pushing off for Hull, Tansy went down below again. This time he brought up a brand new Red Ensign, folded up like a blood-soaked sail. He made his way aft and substituted the new flag for the old, tattered one, which was almost black. Then he turned and said, 'Well, seeing as we've got a war on our hands, we might as well show our colours . . .'

Our passage to Hull from Lowestoft was uneventful. The topmast performed as well as its predecessor, if not better. There were some raised eyebrows when the Customs man came on board to check the cargo and found that it was from Germany. He turned to Ted and said, 'You were lucky. If you'd been over there a week later you'd have been interned for the duration of the War . . .'

Ted replied, 'I wouldn't mind a few weeks bloody rest.'

We landed the leather belting and took on a cargo of coal for London power stations, to be transferred into lighters at Greenwich. This cargo was what we called 'all or nothing', because power-station coal was either fine dust or great lumps anything up to three hundred pounds in weight. It was the coal which could not be sold for domestic, railway, or ships' use. Next to bricks, and cattle-hides, it was the worst kind of cargo both to load and unload. When it slid down into the hold on a chute, fine black dust flew everywhere, so thick that it was impossible to see for a minute or two until the dust started to settle, which it never did properly. One chute would send down a couple of tons of dust, and the next sent down five or six great rocks of coal as big as railway engines – or so they seemed. Our job was to spread the cargo evenly, by shovel, or by brute force. By the time it was all stowed properly Bert, Ted and I were like three black rats, wild-eyed and scurrying still, because the coal came down so fast there was hardly time to breathe, even if we had been able to with our dust-clogged noses and throats. Discharging the 'all or nothing' was even worse than loading it, because every particle of dust, every massive lump, had to be loaded with shovels, or manhandled, on to a skip. It was no picnic, handling over two hundred tons of that stuff, and we were never as glad to be back at sea as when we had been humping power-station coal, no matter what the weather.

Ted and I were a bit disappointed as the ship traipsed up and down the East coast between Hull or Scarborough and the Thames during September. There was little sign that we were at war, except that there were a few more naval in-shore vessels and destroyers sighted, and more planes passing

overhead. The only other difference to peacetime was that the
authorities forbade us to be underway at night-time, and
arranged that the coasters should wherever it was possible,
sail in company. But it was time-wasting and cost money to
wait around for other ships to work out their cargoes, so
mainly *Second Apprentice* went on her way alone. For the
whole of September we carried on the 'all or nothing' trade
along with quite a number of other coasters. By the end of
September the coal-tips at half a dozen power-stations in
London must have been built up to small mountains. It was
obvious to us that emergency stocks were being hoarded.

The only break we had from bashing up and down from the
North Country to the Thames was when we sailed around
into the Channel to pick up a cargo of 'finished leather goods'
at Cowes. When a hundred or so crates were loaded on board
they were all marked 'Boots, left, infantry, Sizes . . .' and
were consigned from His Majesty's Prison, Parkhurst, to
Kettering Basic Training Camp, Yorkshire. When Bert saw
the markings on the crates, he burst out laughing. Ted joined
him, and Tansy made a wry face. It took some minutes for
Ted to explain to me that the boots were probably made from
the German leather which *Second Apprentice* had delivered to
Cowes the previous summer. I still couldn't see the joke, until
Ted pointed one finger shaking with merriment at the
markings. 'Can you imagine, if we get sunk with about fifty
thousand infantry left-boots on board, a whole bleeding
regiment limping to the front with only one boot on?' I
laughed too, but only until I thought of Ted's words, 'if we
get sunk'.

We landed the boots, at Grimsby I think, after I had spent
the whole voyage wondering where the right boots for the
infantry were coming from.

Our voyages were taking twice as long now, as we had to go
to anchor each dusk until dawn. Wartime coastal cargo-
hauling was much easier, from a point of view of getting sleep,

than ever it had been in peacetime. The cargo-rates were now higher, and this helped the owners to balance up the loss of time caused by not sailing at night.

As the first wartime weeks went by, it was obvious that sail-in-Trade was being revitalized. Old sailing-coasters which had been laid up for several years suddenly made their reappearances in the boat-yards to be refitted. Sail-makers and carpenters were almost instantly the kings of the coasts, and old men who had retired from the sea for years were eagerly sought out for their irreplaceable skills in those crafts. Old captains and crewmen started to turn up, too, and by mid-November, we saw some coasters which looked, at first glance, more like floating old-folks' homes, until we looked more closely and saw how clean the decks were, how tidily patched were the sails, how smartly belayed were the lines, and how ship-shape was everything on which the octogenarians had clapped their gnarled and hoary, experienced hands.

I don't recall hearing of any sinkings of sail-coasters in 1939. The sprittie *Ailsa*, along with some others, was blown up by magnetic mines, but that might have been early in 1940. *Ailsa* was a steel vessel, and we were never so glad to be in a wooden ship as we were in the first months of the War. The magnetic mine was a new devilish device, and at first there was no answer for it. The Germans were dropping them by night at a steady rate in the North Sea, especially off the Thames. We had seen the smoke palls of blown-up ships many times by the end of November.

Another reason why sailing coasters were suddenly in such great demand and cargo-rates shot up, was that many motor-driven barges were being converted to barrage-balloon craft, to be moored in the Thames Estuary. With her masts and spars, *Second Apprentice* would have been useless for that kind of duty. As the motor craft were filched from the Trade (and rightly so), so the sail-craft were worked the more, and soon we were working every day. I don't think that from the beginning of December until I left her, *Second Apprentice* spent one day without cargo in her hold. Even Tansy cut down his Sunday church visits to one a month and we worked cargo on Sunday, a thing never heard of on board the ship before the War.

Early in December, Ted left the ship to join the Army! He had been to the recruiting office in Gravesend, soon after war broke out. The recruiting petty officer did his utmost to persuade him to join the Royal Navy, but Ted would have none of it, and volunteered for the Royal Artillery. In due course, his calling-up papers arrived at Bert's house and Mrs Bert tearfully handed them over when she and Hermione, the latter still in a push-chair, visited us in the rain on the coal dock at Greenwich. Ted wasn't due to report to his training camp at Aldershot until two or three days later, but as soon as Mrs Bert handed him his brown envelope, he disappeared down into the fo'c's'le. After a few minutes, Ted showed up again wearing one of Bert's cast-off blue suits, which had been presented to him the previous Christmas. He'd worn it only once before, the day it was given to him. It was much too small, but as he said to me, 'Fuck it, it'll do. It's only till I get my bleeding uniform.' He did look strange in the suit, a bit like a ship's deck broom poked through an oil drum. Ted had no socks, so I gave him a pair of mine. They were much too small for him, but they did for the time being. When our ship left Greenwich we expected to be at sea for at least four days on our way up to Newcastle for more coal, so Ted bade us all farewell.

Tansy presented Ted with a small Bible and told him to keep it in his breast pocket. Bert gave him a jar of 'Brylcreem' and I gave him a packet of twenty cigarettes. Ted said he bet the Army only had right boots in Aldershot. We all shook hands with our erstwhile deckhand before he took off in the rain with Mrs Bert, pushing Hermione's push-chair through the layer of sodden coal slack on the jetty. At the last minute

Bert asked Tansy if he could buy Ted a pint. Tansy nodded and the mate hurried off after the sad procession out of the dock gates, into the grey town beyond.

As our eyes followed Mrs Bert and Ted, with the mate running behind, Tansy said to me, 'Well, that's that. Now there's only you forward until we get a new nipper. I'll go round to the Labour Exchange before we sail . . . see if there's any . . . then we can pick him up when we come back . . .'

I turned-to, somewhat downcast on Ted's departure, and started flaking out the wet sheets and halyards, ready for sailing. Our cargo on that trip was ammunition from Woolwich to Newcastle, although none of us could puzzle out why the shells and bullets were heading north, when the 'fighting front' was south of us, in France.

Now that Ted was gone my work was almost doubled, though both the mate and the captain helped a lot more with the deck-chores. The fo'c's'le was a much more lonely and gloomy place without Ted.

The first night's anchorage on our way north from Woolwich was off Southend (there was not a lot of wind that day). About midnight the air-raid sirens sounded in the town. Bert and I stayed on deck, watching the play of searchlights in the sky, but we didn't hear the dull throb which German bombers were supposed to make. It was quite an experience, sitting on top of two hundred odd tons of nitro-glycerine, waiting for a squadron of Nazi bombers to do their worst. An hour or two later the 'all clear' sounded, and I went back to sleep, leaving Bert his anchor-watch just as Tansy appeared on deck for his ablutions.

As Tansy went aft in the moonlight, he called to Bert, 'If you see any mines floating around, give me a shake, Bert.' As he said that he was so poker faced and his voice was so steady that I have never been able to figure out, to this day, whether or not he was serious, but he certainly gave me a sleepless night. I lay in my berth, eyes wide open, listening intently. About an hour after I turned in, I heard something bumping the bow gently. I jumped out of my berth, in a panic, in my shirt-tails only, and scampered up the scuttle-ladder in a cold sweat. Bert was down aft probably making himself a cup of cocoa in the galley. I rushed on to the foredeck and stared over into the darkness. As my eyes cleared, I almost died with relief. There was a small tree branch caught on the anchor chain and tapping the bow. I was walking aft, still in my shirt-tails and bare feet, thanking God and looking for the long boathook to push the tree-branch free, when Bert emerged from the galley. We were both so surprised that we both stopped in our tracks. Bert stared at me in my shirt-tails and bare feet. My knees were shaking with cold. Then, with a laugh, Bert said quietly and slowly, as he shook his head, 'Why should England tremble?'

I explained to him what had happened. He reached down for the boathook and, still laughing, sent me back to bed. 'I thought it might be a mine, Bert,' I chattered in the cold.

'Nonsense, Nipper,' he murmured. 'If it had been a mine you wouldn't have even heard it.'

Later we learned that twenty-seven big merchant ships and a destroyer were sunk by Nazi mines in the approaches to London during November 1939.

We reached Greenwich again after about a week with another hellish cargo of 'all or nothing' coal. As Bert and I warped alongside the dumb lighters which took the coal upstream on the Thames, we suddenly heard a thin, piping voice shouting at us from a landing stage. I saw a small boy in overalls standing on the stage in the rain. All the while we worked at mooring the ship and removing the heavy cargo-hatch covers, his voice hallooed us. When most of the covers were off I clambered up on top of the bulwarks by the starboard shrouds. The boy was still waiting, but silently. In one hand he clutched a small box. He looked very lost.

'You the new nipper?' I shouted. The boy nodded. 'He's the new nipper,' I called to Bert.

'Good, now we'll be all right,' Bert replied as he studied the tiny, thin figure through the drizzle. 'That's just what we need, a good hefty chap that can make a back-splice with one hand and steer with the other; just what we've been looking for. All right, Tiger, let's unship the jolly-boat and you nip over and collect Charles Atlas over there before the wind pipes up and blows him away.'

The new nipper looked very nervous as he sat down in the jolly-boat. The first thing he did was drop his cardboard box into the rainwater in the boat's bilge and stick out his hand. 'Wot cheer, mate,' he said, 'my name's William, but everybody calls me . . .'

'. . . calls me Billy,' I finished off for him. I shook his hand and told him my name, '. . . but everybody calls me Tiger.' We were then silent as I rowed Billy to the ship and he collected his water-soaked bits of clothing from the bilge. He was about five feet three inches short and had shoulders like a Guinness bottle. His wet hair was dirty, damp, dark-auburn. His face was covered, under a layer of coal-dust streaks in freckles. His eyes were a sad brown, and he reminded me of a half-drowned spaniel puppy Ted had once dragged out of the river at Hull. Billy's once-blue overalls were about two sizes too big for him and one of his boots had its sole adrift and dangling down so that it looked like his foot was laughing.

Bert helped Billy over the side. 'That's Bert – he's the mate,' I called up as the laughing foot preceded me over the bulwark. Billy stood in front of Bert, nervous, small and damp.

'My name's . . . Billy, pleased . . . to meet you . . . sir,' Billy greeted the mate.

'Now we'll have none of that high-faluting nonsense here, Nipper, don't "sir" me . . . my name's Bert, and I'm the mate on board this here ship. Where's your working gear . . .?'

I walked forward and untriced the bowsprit dolphin-striker, to get ready for sailing. Bert only needed an audience of one for such a well-rehearsed routine.

It must have been the thirteenth of December when Billy joined us, because I remember an excited bargee boarding his lighter and shouting up the news to us that the Nazi battleship *Graf Spee* had been sunk. This cheered us all a great deal. The news from the sea had been depressing. The liner *Athenia*, bound for America with hundreds of children on board had been sunk by a U-boat on the second day of the War. The aircraft-carrier *Courageous* was sunk soon after; the battleship *Royal Oak* had been sunk in October at anchor in Scapa Flow, and magnetic mines were taking a toll of ships around the British coasts. Even the lonely, gallant fight of the auxiliary armed merchant ship, *Rawalpindi*, which, with her little pop-guns had tackled the heavy Nazi battle-cruisers *Scharnhorst* and *Gneisenau* was little cause for celebration for we were told she was now up against the *Deutschland*. *Rawalpindi* had gone down quickly and only a few survivors had been picked up. Further out in the oceans the deadly U-boats had started to sink one victim after another, day in, day out.

Tansy called down to the stevedore, 'Where was *Graf Spee* sunk?'

'Somewhere in South America. She scuttled herself. She was clobbered by the cruisers, *Ajax*, *Achilles*, and *Exeter*.'

'How about the crews?'

'Nearly all all right. Even the Jerries. They've all been interned.'

Tansy closed his eyes for a second and said, 'Thank God for that.' I didn't know whether he gave thanks for the sinking of the battleship or for the safety of the crews.

In mid-December some officials came on board at Gravesend bearing two large boxes. 'What's that?' demanded Tansy.

'Radio transmitter and receiver – orders.' The official in charge showed Tansy some papers. Tansy frowned as he stared at the forms. He looked around him first at Bert, then at me, then at Billy, but finding no expressions among us but blank stares at the boxes, his brow creased in a deep frown. He turned back to the official . . . '?'.

'Where do you want it installed?' asked the official. 'We usually put the set in the master's cabin and the batteries . . .'

'Not in my cabin you don't,' broke in Tansy. He looked over at Bert. 'How about you, Bert? How about your cabin? It'll be all right there, I suppose, so long as you don't play it too loud . . .'

Eventually, after a muted argument between the chief official, the captain, and the mate, a compromise was reached. The wireless set was installed in the skipper's lobby, in brackets over the meal-table. From then on it was Bert's job to report any unusual sightings at sea. Tansy huffed at Bert as the men unshipped the wireless in its grey casing and started to fix it in place. He said in a sarcastic way, 'Now you can report a Frenchman with his topsail still hoisted in anything more than a light breeze . . . that's an unusual sighting, if there ever was one!'

A poster, showing the silhouettes of German and Allied planes was fixed on the lobby bulkhead so that we could learn to identify them.

That Christmas, with Ted gone to the Army, I could not go home. Tansy asked around for someone to relieve me, but most experienced deckhands had either joined up or were badly needed on their own craft, or were in well-paid jobs ashore. Through Bert's address, I received a letter from Mam at the beginning of November. Dad had already been home on leave before going out to South Africa to take command of a merchant ship whose captain had been German-born. Mam did not know the name of the ship which was taking him out, nor from where she was sailing, nor when. By the time I received the letter, owing to Mrs Bert's oversight in not delivering it to me as soon as she could, Dad was presumably already at sea. I would not, it seemed, hear from him until he reached South Africa. I wrote Mam saying that while I couldn't be home for Christmas, I hoped to be at Llangareth early in the spring, and not to worry, we were only sailing on the north-east coast most of the time, out of range of German aircraft. This was a lie, but it would prevent her worrying about any additional danger to me. From all accounts the news of the terrible depredations on shipping by the Nazi magnetic mines was being kept out of the newspapers and off the wireless. I comforted myself that that, too, would save Mam extra anxiety.

Taking on cargo and discharging was much more work for me now as 'Ginger' (as we had nicknamed Billy) was not very strong. He had been brought up, like Ted, in a boy's home. He had been employed, at the start of his working career three months earlier, as tea boy and general dogsbody on board a floating crane in London docks. Ginger was one of the shyest people I ever met. It took weeks before he volunteered a conversation. Then it was mostly about food. Ginger simply could never eat enough. It seemed that he had been deprived of anything like a good square meal throughout his childhood. On board the *Second Apprentice* he certainly made up for what he had missed in the past. A few days after he joined us, on his first trip, I caught Ginger stealing from the galley. It was only some bread and jam. I knew if I reported the matter to Bert there would be hell to pay, so instead I made Ginger sit on the coal-box and stuff himself with two full loaves of bread and a whole pot of jam. By the time Ginger finished that lot, he could hardly move and swore he would never steal food again. I reported the bread lost over the side through my own carelessness, and soon the whole thing was forgotten.

Christmas 1939, Bert, Ginger, and I spent under the dripping hull-bottom of *Second Apprentice* as she lay on the beds at Queenborough on the Isle of Sheppey in the Thames Estuary. It took us three days between tides to scrape off all the growth, barnacles and grass from the bottom and then to paint her with black varnish twice, using two-foot wide brushes with long handles. It was one of the most miserably. cold, wet, dirty periods in my time with the ship. After three days of sloshing around in slippery mud, climbing over the slimy bed-timbers under the ship's dripping, filthy bottom in the gloomy darkness, I was ready to try anything else.

It may have been the memory of those Christmas days, the most truly miserable I was to spend for years, that propelled me to the recruiting office in Greenwich in February 1940, when *Second Apprentice* warped in with yet another cargo of 'all or nothing' coal. It may have been that, or it may have been that I felt that I could do more, perhaps advance quicker in the Royal Navy, perhaps see more of the world. It was probably an amalgam of both those motives. Perhaps also, more than anything else, it was the news of the action of the destroyer HMS *Cossack* when she smashed alongside the Nazi armed merchant cruiser *Altmark*, boarded her and freed three hundred British merchant seamen prisoners, who were being taken to Germany after having had their ships sunk from under them. *Cossack*'s exploit fired the imagination of all the boys in the Trade. That was good old-fashioned 'Standby to board, boys, and at 'em!' stuff. The kind of thing at which our lads are superb. There was also the prospect of sending Mam a few shillings a week more than the ten she was then receiving.

Tansy reluctantly gave me time off to go to the recruiting office. The petty officer seemed happy to see me, until I told him my age. At first his face dropped, then he told me that he would, in any case, sign me in as a boy-seaman, regular, on a twelve-year engagement from the age of eighteen, and that I should report again to him, or to any recruiting office, as soon

as I liked after my sixteenth birthday. He made out the
recruitment form and I signed it. (Twelve years plus two
equals fourteen!)

Later that day, when I told Bert what had transpired at the
recruiting office, he pointed up at some of the dozens of
barrage balloons floating over the Thames Estuary and said,
'You might as well be in the Navy, Tiger, because when old
Hitler really starts we're going to cop it on the East coast, you
know. They haven't got that little lot floating around up there
for nothing . . .'

In the Thames Estuary, in mid January the destroyer HMS
Grenville passed us close by only two hours before she hit a
mine and sank with the loss of over 100 lives . . .

In early March we headed round into the English Channel,
with military textiles in crates which were off-loaded in
Southampton. The crates were then re-loaded on board and
Second Apprentice ploughed again with the 'textiles' around
the Straits of Dover back to Greenwich. The reason for this
round-trip with the same cargo was not clear to us, but when
we yet again off-loaded and reloaded the 'textiles', then
turned the ship round and headed once more back to
Southampton we had given up worrying about it. As Bert
said, 'Well, at least it's better than carrying live ammunition.'

In the next few weeks we made several cross-Channel runs
over to Le Havre in France, mostly with military stores. On
two voyages across the Channel we were loaded by crane in
Southampton with small khaki vans for the British Expedi-
tionary Forces in France. When the cars had been secured in
the hold, big drums of petrol were lashed on deck. Tansy and
Bert looked a bit glum as the drums were loaded and lashed,
but when we found that two Royal Navy motor patrol boats
were to escort us across Channel, they livened up. However
the weather was so contrary, with very slight breezes most of
the way over, that the heavily armed escort got tired of
waiting around and circling us like hunting dogs on leashes

After a discussion with Tansy, and an offer to take *Second Apprentice* in tow, the Navy craft shoved on without us. Bert, Ginger, and I finished up rowing the ship into Le Havre.

As soon as the escort roared away over the horizon, Tansy rubbed his brow with a knuckle and muttered, 'Thank goodness for that. I thought they'd never leave.'

'Why's that, Tansy?' I asked him.

'Well, I was worried in case they got into a fight, and us with all that blessed petrol on board . . . I was ready to order Bert to ditch it the moment anything happened!'

The activity in Le Havre was frenetic, with war vessels, French and British, and merchant ships of many nations, arriving and departing day and night. Whenever *Second Apprentice* arrived there, Tansy was supposed to go ashore to the harbour-master's office and report, but he always sent Bert round with an excuse. There was a fuss the first time this happened. The French harbour master and his British naval counterpart marched on board demanding to know where the captain was. When Bert showed them down to the captain's cabin, they found Tansy on his knees praying before his open Bible. They fell silent then and left him severely alone on subsequent visits. It was strange for Tansy to have been found like that, because moments before he heard voices coming on board, he had been sitting at the lobby table explaining to little Ginger how to make a crown-knot.

I never once, during many visits to France, ever saw Tansy step off the ship in that country. Once when I tackled Tansy about this, he said, 'I just don't want their company, Tiger. Any time we get mixed up with that lot we lose something; it's like we start sliding downhill. Some of them might be well-mannered on the surface but I'm positive they're not down below. They're supposed to be so civilized, so artistic, but you watch them closely, Tiger, and you'll see a herd of farmyard animals all scared to jump any real fences. They're supposed to be so charming, lively and witty, and everyone who doesn't know France seems to think of a beautiful lady when they talk about it, but you keep your eyes wide open, Tiger, and what you'll see is a painted old hag counting up her pennies. I never saw a Frenchman yet that could do anything without beating around the bush, and when a Frenchman does you down, he's not playing with you, Tiger. He's deadly serious, and when you really need him you'll never find him, or if you do he'll be making a deal with your competitor.'

In April, a bomb-shell dropped. Hitler invaded Denmark and Norway. To many landspeople this meant only that he had attacked yet two more almost defenceless little countries, but to the sailors it meant much more than that. If the Nazis controlled the coasts of Denmark and Norway, they also controlled the entrance to the Baltic, and Arctic access to Finland and Russia (if we ever might need it), and they controlled a good half of the North Sea and all the Norwegian Sea. From Norway their planes might even reach the North of England and Scotland. There was a good chance that soon the whole of Britain would be under air attack, and nowhere would it be safe to navigate. The Channel, the average sailor thought, was a lot safer than the North Sea. 'The French would always see to that.'

At first the news from Scandinavia was gloomy. The Germans seemed to be landing everywhere they wished with impunity. Then came cheering word of the sinking of the German cruiser *Königsberg* in Bergen harbour by the Royal Navy dive-bombers. (We didn't realize it at the time, but this was the first occasion when a major warship was sunk by planes – it completely changed naval surface warfare strategy.)

When Tansy heard the news about Norway he took it calmly. 'They'll put our coast in range of *them*,' he observed 'but they'll also put their Navy in range of *us*.' I little realized how history would bear Tansy out. When he heard the new about *Königsberg* Tansy was concerned about me. 'Try not to join any big ships, Tiger,' he advised me. 'They're the ones the German Air Force will be after. Get in the smallest ships you can find. They'll hardly bother to waste bombs on *them*.' How mistaken Tansy was!

In mid-April we ourselves came under air attack, although everyone afterwards agreed that it must have been more a matter of *Second Apprentice* accidently finding herself in the enemy's line of fire. We still could not believe that the *Luftwaffe* would waste its firepower on a little old sailing barge. We knew that other coasters and some trawlers had been strafed by Nazi planes, and that some had been sunk, but they had been power-vessels and we imagined that the German pilots might have mistaken them for armed patrol-vessels. Most of the other sinkings until then had been caused by mines, magnetic and otherwise.

We had taken a cargo of tomato baskets to Guernsey, then we had been in ballast to Poole. From there we took on a load of sawn timber for Greenwich. We had spent a night at anchor off Eastbourne, and set sail very early in the morning so as to be in the Thames Estuary that night. We had a fine north-westerly breeze and we were soon under all sail, on a broad reach. It was a brilliant morning and a lovely forenoon. There were a few clouds and the Channel seas played, as boisterous as ever; for the rest the day was a happy-looking harbinger of a good, warm spring.

Off Dungeness we were very slowly overtaken by a convoy of six fair-sized merchant ships under the escort of an armed trawler, which was slowly plodding its way up through the Straits of Dover. With our broad breeze we were almost able to keep up with them. On we all ploughed, past Folkestone, Dover and Deal, with the ships to seaward of us, like protecting policemen. As *Second Apprentice* passed the South Foreland we were no more than a mile from the coast. From the galley-door I gazed at the cliffs and the green downs and wondered what the very tall steel masts were (we knew nothing about radar, of course).

Bert was on watch at the helm; Tansy was asleep below, having kept the middle anchor-watch. I was in the galley preparing the midday meal. Now and again, to clear my head of smoke and fumes, I stuck it out of the galley door and watched the coast of Kent slide by, all green and grey and white and pale yellow. By late forenoon it was obvious that the convoy was pulling slowly ahead of us, but Bert thought that we would be within sight of the naval escort for at least until we reached the offing of the North Foreland. Then, when we headed westward into the Thames Estuary we would come under the protection of the forts which had been built on platforms between the coasts of Kent and Essex, and of the balloon-barrage. We were now right in the middle of what was later to be infamous as 'Hell-fire Corner'.

At first there was something unreal about the attack – it seemed to be more like a rehearsal than anything else. The first indication that I had that anything untoward was happening was a loud screech from the direction of the naval trawler, then a dull thump-thump-thump as her anti-aircraft guns opened up. As soon as I heard the screeching of the siren and the thumping I rushed out on deck still holding a soup-stirring spoon and a salt pot. I stared at the convoy ahead, straining the sea past the fluttering luffs of our headsails. The naval trawler was firing her guns all right. At first I couldn't make out in which direction she was firing, but then, in the direction of Walmer, I saw tiny gun puffs bursting in the blue sky. They weren't white, as I'd expected, but dirty brown and yellow. I turned to Bert, who was also staring at the shell-bursts. 'They might be practising,' I called.

'Practising be blowed, Tiger.' Bert turned the ship off the wind a little. 'This is the real thing! If I was you I'd get under cover, but give Tansy a holler first!'

As I turned to go to the companionway and rouse our

captain there was a loud banging noise from the direction of the shore-line. More gun-puffs, white this time, blossomed in the April sky, almost directly over the convoy. It was at that moment that I saw them; five tiny black specks flying from the north towards the ships. At first they hardly seemed to be moving. Suddenly there was an ugly-sounding rat-at-at-at-at . . . and all the while the trawler thump-thump-thumped away at the oncoming pests.

With my eyes still fixed on the far-off specks over the windward side I shouted down the companionway, 'Tansy!' The specks very rapidly turned into the same shape as the silhouettes of Dornier DO 217s on the recognition chart down in the skipper's lobby. I heard Tansy's muffled reply from what seemed like a million miles away, 'Be right up!'

I seemed to be two persons now – one watching the enemy planes as they strafed the ships, and one trying to rouse the captain below. 'Tansy! Air attack! The Jerries are . . .' But my throat went dry. I didn't feel in the least bit heroic, standing at the top of the companionway with a soup-spoon in one hand and a salt pot in the other.

'What's up, Tiger?' came Tansy's voice from his cabin. I didn't reply. The Dorniers were streaking over the convoy and I gazed stupefied as little black dots left the planes and splashed into the sea all around ships ahead. It took a second or two for me to realize that the black specks were bombs. The enemy formation split up as they left the convoy. Four of them turned east, but one headed directly for us. I was paralysed as I watched a line of machine-gun bullet splashes hit the sea, quickly nearing *Second Apprentice*. It was not the same kind of feeling that I'd had in the storm, when we'd gone aground on the Hailsborough Sands. I don't think there was much fear in me at all, if any. It was more surprise and curiosity, astonishment and indignation. How dare they do this to us . . . we're under sail and that's *Britain* over there! How dare they have the gall, the presumption to do this within sight of the cliffs of England! Very quickly the splashes in the sea got closer and closer and I remember thinking that whoever was in that plane couldn't, simply *couldn't* be firing at us. He must be mistaken. He must be attacking someone else . . . when suddenly, for no apparent reason at first, the Dornier sheered off, his guns still firing rat-at-at-at-at and banked right around and took off in the direction of where his comrades had disappeared into the clouds. There was a stunning silence for a moment or two, then from over the English shore came a dull humming, a roar, and a sudden noise of thunder. It was two squadrons of fighters, one of which passed almost directly overhead of *Second Apprentice* as we gawped up at them. Then Bert shouted 'Hurricanes!' and we both danced and waved at them, but they were gone, climbing as they shot off towards the direction of the enemy.

Tansy came on deck just as the last of the fighters disappeared into a cloud. There was still an air of unreality about the whole episode. It was now as though the attack had never taken place. The sky was clear; there was no noise of guns; England was bathed in warm sunlight; the seas frisked and the ships ahead plodded on past the North Foreland. It had all happened in the space of no more than three or four minutes, yet it had seemed, while naked violence rent the air, to be an aeon. Now that all the planes were gone, excitement and indignation, curiosity and pride, were all replaced with an intense feeling of relief.

'What happened?' asked Tansy, rubbing his neck.

'They were RAF Hurricanes! Cleared the blighters off!' shouted Bert, still excited.

Tansy turned to me, 'Did you see them, Tiger?'

Bert broke in, 'They shoved off quick. You should have seen them go when the Hurricanes came on. Them old Jerries must have been scared out of their wits . . . they took off like a dose of blooming salts. Went east they did, back to Germany you can bet your life.'

I was going to contradict Bert; the Royal Air Force fighters had been Boulton-Paul Defiants. I had plainly seen the mid-ships turrets on at least two of them. Instead I said, 'The Jerries were Dorniers, because they had bloody great . . .' Tansy glared at me. 'Sorry, Tansy . . . they had a big sort of glass-house all over their noses and two engines and six machine-guns. I could see the gun-flashes on the wings as clear as I can see your hat.'

'Any damage done?' asked Tansy. We all stared as the convoy, now wearing the North Foreland and heading into the Thames estuary.

'Don't look like it,' said Bert, 'and they never even got anywhere near us, even though one of the . . . bas . . . baskets tried it, but he saw them there Hurricanes and he was off. Those Hurricanes, they're so fast you can hardly see them coming. Did you see that RAF pilot wave back at us, Tiger?'

'No. They were much too high, Bert, and they weren't . . .' I got no further.

Tansy broke in and said, 'Well, even if old Jerry had put a few holes in us, we'd have been all right with that sawn timber . . . it floats.'

By late April I was half looking forward to my sixteenth birthday, half dreading it. *Second Apprentice* took a cargo of house-bricks(!) to Guernsey and brought back sacks of ormer (a kind of oyster) shells to Poole. There Tansy found a young man of twenty to replace me. Sebastian was hale and hearty, but had flat feet. He had volunteered for the Navy, but was judged by the doctors to be unfit for sea. He sailed with us around to Greenwich with a cargo of Portland stone for transfer to lighters. On the voyage, which was rough, he showed himself to be a strong, healthy and an expert deck-seaman who knew almost as many strange knots as Ted had. He had been at sea in sail-coasters from the West Country since he was fourteen. He had fingers like marlin spikes, hair

like caulking oakum, and swore like a trooper, much more
than even Ted had. Tansy, when he first heard the name
Sebastian, by mistake called him 'Sebastopol' (the name of a
dockside pub somewhere on the coast) and so he remained.

When the ship was in Harwich on the second week in May,
just after my birthday, I reported to the local recruiting office.
When I told the Army sergeant that I had first reported to
Greenwich recruiting office he firmly but kindly told me that
I should report back to Greenwich. I returned on board and
told Tansy what the sergeant had said, 'Well, Tiger,' he
observed, 'there's no hurry, is there? I expect the Navy can
wait for you for a few days . . . come on up to Yarmouth with
us. We're taking a load of fish-boxes up there, then up to
Tynemouth for coal, then back down to Greenwich, see?' I
accepted Tansy's offer.

Before the ship arrived in Yarmouth we heard the news
over the wireless that the Germans had invaded Holland and
Belgium and that their armies were driving into France.
'That's it,' observed Bert. 'That's it. Now the balloon has
really gone up!'

As the wireless in the skipper's lobby gave out grave reports
of one city after another falling to the Germans or being
pounded from the air, even Tansy listened, but expression-
lessly.

I had sent Mam the money I had saved for my cancelled
Christmas holiday rail fare, and I had only a shilling or two. I
borrowed my rail fare from Yarmouth to Greenwich from
Bert, and promised to write to Mam and ask her to repay the
money to his wife by mail. Bert agreed, and between them he
and Tansy gathered together the ten shillings or so I needed
for the fare and a couple of shillings more as a parting gift.

When I left *Second Apprentice* it was raining. Bert was
working the dolly-windlass, winching pallets of fish-boxes out
of the hold and on to the jetty. Ginger and Sebastopol were

down in the hold piling up more smelly, scaly boxes, and Tansy was standing in his bowler hat and oilskin by the gangway, puffing at his upside down clay pipe.

'Cheerio, Tiger,' called Bert, 'we'll call you on the wireless if we get any fun and games with old Adolf.' As I went to shake his calloused hand he added in a low tone, 'Now don't forget what I told you, you find yourself a nice little homebody like Nora and get yourself a nice home and a nice family to go home to. It's the best thing a man can do, believe me, I know.'

'Good-bye, Bert. I'll see what I can do.'

I shouted farewells down the hold and I walked over to Tansy. The captain held out a gnarled hand. Rain dripped on to my wrist from the brim of his bowler. I was always short of farewell words. I muttered something about hoping that he would have good cargoes and a lot of them.

Tansy replied, 'Oh, we'll be fine. We've got a good crew together.' His voice lowered, 'Not as good as you and Ted, of course, but we'll manage, and we've got all the cargoes we can handle. It's a good steady trade now . . .' He shook my hand again, and pressed a small Bible into it. 'God speed, Tiger, and trust in the Lord . . . give them blessed Jerries a few for me!'

'Good-bye, Tansy, I'll make the most . . .' I was going to say, 'the most of what I can of it,' but my voice failed. I turned and walked on to the slippery plank which served as a gangway. As I reached the other side, Tansy hailed me, 'Tiger!'

I turned in the rain and saw both the captain and the mate grinning at me. I looked Tansy straight in his green eyes. He looked impish. He shouted, 'AND MAKE 'EM BLOODY STRONG!'

I laughed, waved, turned away and walked towards the dock-gates. Before I reached the gates I looked back over my shoulder for a last sight of *Second Apprentice*. The sun shone for a few moments, even though it still rained. My ship's varnished masts caught the sun. The reflection of sunlight from her spars was so bright that my eyes watered. I turned and hitched my sea-bag more firmly on to my oilskin shoulder and marched straight through the gate, towards the railway station without once looking back. I was off to war . . .

20

Personal Effects

Blind Sioni was walking home in late 1939 and was knocked down by a motor bus. In her letter, Mam said that thank God the doctor said he didn't suffer. He is buried in the shadow of Cader Idris. His only memorial is the mountain.

Towards the end of July 1940, at the end of my basic training course, I went home on leave for a week. There Mam handed me a letter from Mrs Bert thanking her for the repayment of the twelve shillings I owed her husband. She also wrote about Ted. When he joined the Army he had appointed Mrs Bert as his 'next of kin'. When he had completed his training, the Army drafted him into an armoured regiment as a tank-gunner. Young Rosie had been so impressed with Ted when he came home on leave in March in his new uniform that she had agreed to become engaged to Ted and they were to have been married when he returned home on his first leave from France. On 21 June his battalion was part of a small force which attacked the Nazi Panzer divisions south of Arras, to take pressure off the Allied armies fighting their way to the beaches of Dunkirk. Ted was killed. His commanding officer had sent to Mrs Bert a 'very nice letter' and Ted's personal effects. They were a small Bible, badly mangled, a leather sheath containing a seaman's knife and marlin spike and a packet of cigarette cards, together with ten French francs and a British half-crown piece.

'Would I like the cigarette cards?' Mrs Bert asked in her letter.

In 1941 my ship, badly damaged and weather worn, hove

into Greenock in Scotland, for repairs. Among several letters from my family and friends was one scrawled on lined paper with a pencil. It was from Sebastopol, who had obtained Mam's address from Mrs Bert. In March 1941 *Second Apprentice* had departed from Tynemouth with coal for the Thames in the company of a sister ketch, *Martinet*. They had fair weather and a 'good fancy' westerly wind (when bargemen said that they meant it was rough). Suddenly out of the clouds five Heinkel bombers had appeared. Three of them left formation and attacked the two sailing barges, first with machine-gun fire and then with bombs. Both *Martinet* and *Second Apprentice* had been directly hit almost at the same time. Both ships had sunk within a matter of a minute or two. Sebastopol, Tansy, and little Ginger had been blown over the side by the blast of the bomb which struck the foredeck. Bert, who had been taking refuge from the machine-gun bullets behind the fore-hatch coaming, must have been blown to bits. Little Ginger struck his head on a floating plank when he hit the water, but Sebastopol and Tansy managed to keep the nipper afloat for two hours by lashing him to the plank with Tansy's belt. They were in the water for an hour or so before they and two crew from *Martinet* were picked up by the crew of a steam trawler out of Grimsby who had heard the attack from afar. Ginger was alive all right, but the doctors feared that he would never be able to hear or talk again.

Tansy was so angry about Ginger and Bert that he had gone ashore in Grimsby straight to the Navy recruiting office and tried to join up, but they had turned him down for regular sea-service. Somehow, however, he had managed to get into a naval armed trawler as mate, under the 'TI24X' scheme, which allowed men otherwise considered as 'odds and ends' to serve for non-specified periods of time. Now he was up on the coast of Scotland. Sebastopol supposed he was mine-sweeping. As for himself, Sebastopol was still looking for a coasting berth or if he couldn't get that, a river job; but considering all the bombing going on around the Thames Estuary he thought he'd be safer at sea. It was a pity he had his 'foot-trouble', or he would join the RAF and try to get on a bomber and 'give the buggers a taste of their own medicine'.

I wrote several letters to Mrs Bert, and called to see her twice on the rare occasions when I was ashore in the London area in 1941 and 1942. The first time she was taking Bert's loss badly, and it was as much as I could do to cheer her up. The second time I introduced her to a Leading Seaman close to her own age, whom she later married. Much later, in the late 1950s when I asked Tansy's daughter, Daisy, about Mrs Bert and Hermione, Daisy wasn't sure where Mrs Bert, her daughter or her husband were, but the house on the long street had been demolished by a buzz-bomb in late 1944 and has since been rebuilt.

The last time I heard from Cei Powell he was a successful businessman in Australia. What happened to my own family is part of another story . . .

Epilogue

And death shall have no dominion.
Dead men naked they shall be one
With the man in the wind and the west moon;
When their bones are picked clean and the clean bones
   gone,
They shall have stars at elbow and foot;
Though they go mad they shall be sane,
Though they sink through the sea they shall rise again;
Though lovers be lost love shall not;
And death shall have no dominion.

And death shall have no dominion.
Under the windings of the sea
They lying long shall not die windily;
Twisting on racks when sinews give way,
Strapped to a wheel, yet they shall not break;
Faith in their hands shall snap in two,
And the unicorn evils run them through;
Split all ends up they shan't crack;
And death shall have no dominion.

And death shall have no dominion.
No more may gulls cry at their ears
Or waves break loud on the seashores;
Where blew a flower may a flower no more
Lift its head to the blows of the rain;
Though they be mad and dead as nails,
Heads of the characters hammer through daisies;
Break in the sun till the sun breaks down,
And death shall have no dominion.

DYLAN THOMAS
'And Death Shall Have No Dominion'